The Sociology of Ethnicity

Siniša Malešević

July 2012

SAGE Publications

London • Thousand Oaks • New Delhi

First published 2004

SAGE Publications Ltd
6 Bonhill Street
London EC2A 4PU

SAGE Publications Inc
2455 Teller Road
Thousand Oaks, California 91320

SAGE Publications India Pvt Ltd
B-42, Panchsheel Enclave
Post Box 4109
New Delhi 100 017

British Library Cataloguing in Publication data

A catalogue record for this book is available from
the British Library

ISBN 0 7619 4041 3
ISBN 0 7619 4042 1(pbk)

Library of Congress Control Number available

Typeset by C&M Digitals (P) Ltd, Chennai, India
Printed and bound in Great Britain by Athenaeum Press, Gateshead

For Vesna

CONTENTS

ACKNOWLEDGEMENTS

I am indebted for perceptive and inspiring comments, suggestions and criticism to many colleagues who have read selected chapters or heard me presenting some of the ideas developed in this book: John A. Hall, John Rex, Richard Jenkins, Mark Haugaard, Ricca Edmondson, Pete Morriss, Michael Banton, Pierre van den Berghe and above all Syd Jeffers. Special thanks go to Kevin Ryan for his meticulous editing, as well as for his comments on the entire manuscript.

Chapter 7 is a revised and abridged version of the paper that was originally published in *Ethnic and Racial Studies*, 25 (4), 2002: 193–212 under the title 'Rational Choice Theory and the sociology of ethnic relations: a critique'. I am grateful to the publishers for permitting me to republish the article in the present form.

Chapter One

INTRODUCTION

The sociological understanding of ethnicity

Although the term 'ethnicity' has its roots in the Greek term *ethnos/ethnikos*, which was commonly used to describe pagans, that is non-Hellenic and, later, non-Jewish (Gentile) or non-Christian, second-class peoples, its academic and popular use is fairly modern. Sociologically speaking, the term was coined by D. Riesman in 1953 and it gained wider use only during the 1960s and 1970s (Glazer and Moynihan, 1975).[1] However, from its inception ethnicity has remained a 'hot potato' of sociology. Although the term was coined to make sense of a specific form of cultural difference, it acquired a rather different set of meanings. While the Anglo-American tradition adopted 'ethnicity' mostly as a substitute for minority groups within a larger society of the nation-state,[2] the European tradition regularly opted to use ethnicity as a synonym for nationhood defined historically by descent or territory. At the same time both traditions shared a joint aim to replace what had become a popular, but heavily compromised (due to the Nazi experiment), concept of 'race'. Nevertheless, popular discourses, in both Europe and North America, have 'racialized' the concept of ethnicity, that is 'race' was largely preserved (in its quasi-biological sense) and has only now been used interchangeably with 'ethnicity'.

Furthermore, the collapse of the colonial world in the 1950s and 1960s has brought even more confusion on questions of 'race', culture and ethnicity. The homelands of former European colonizers have become populated with new, post-colonial immigrants, who are visibly different. Following the consolidation of North American popular and legislative discourse these groups have also become defined as 'ethnic', thus simultaneously preserving old definitions of historical ethnicity by descent or territory (i.e., Welsh, Flamans, Walloons, etc.) while adding the new definition of ethnicity as an immigrant minority (i.e., Pakistani, West Indian, Sri Lankan, etc.).

The fall of communism and the break up of the Soviet-style federations along 'ethnic' lines and the emergence of 'ethnic cleansing' policies in the Balkans and Caucasus have further complicated these definitional issues.

With the wars on former Yugoslav soil, extensive and influential mass media coverage of 'ethnic conflict' has seen the term 'ethnic' degenerate into a synonym for tribal, primitive, barbaric and backward.

Finally, the ever-increasing influx of asylum seekers, refugees and economic migrants to Western Europe, North America and Australia, who do not necessarily express visible or significant physical, cultural or religious differences to their hosts, together with their uncertain legal status (i.e., waiting for a decision on asylum), has relegated the term 'ethnic' to a quasi-legislative domain. In this context, the term 'ethnicity' often refers again to non citizens who inhabit 'our land', just as it did in the days of ancient Greece and Judea; that is, to second-class peoples.

What is obvious from this brief history of the term is the fact that 'ethnicity' contains a multiplicity of meanings. Such a plasticity and ambiguity of the concept allows for deep misunderstandings as well as political misuses. While the concept was solely confined to the academic world this was not such a big problem. However, once it acquired legislative and institutional underpinnings through formulations such as 'ethnic minority' or 'ethnic group' it has had much more devastating effects. Institutionalized and bureaucratized definitions of the concept, such as imposing the idea that a particular individual legally belongs to an 'ethnic minority' or to one 'ethnic group', is not only the strongest possible source of reification of (always dynamic) group and individual relations, but it also becomes a form of oppression by caging individuals into involuntary associations. In such a situation cultural difference, which is by its nature changeable, flexible and fuzzy, is arrested and codified, thus preventing social change. Hence popular and legislative understandings of ethnicity are severely erroneous. This error comes from a profoundly unsociological view of cultural difference as something immobile and definite. To clarify all these historical, geographical and contemporary misuses and misunderstandings one has to explain who exactly is an 'ethnic', and what ethnicity stands for in contemporary sociology.

Since the classics of sociological thought, with the exception of Max Weber, did not operate with the term 'ethnic', sociologists had to turn to anthropology and, in particular, to the seminal work of Frederik Barth (1969) in order to explain the power of cultural difference, both historically and geographically. Before Barth, cultural difference was traditionally explained from the inside out – social groups possess different cultural characteristics which make them unique and distinct (common language, lifestyle, descent, religion, physical markers, history, eating habits, etc.). Culture was perceived as something relatively or firmly stable, persistent and exact. Cultural difference was understood in terms of a group's property (i.e., to be French is to be in possession of a distinct culture to that of the English). Barth's *Ethnic Groups and Boundaries* provided nothing short of a Copernican revolution in the study of ethnicity. Barth turned the traditional understanding of cultural difference on its head. He defined and explained ethnicity from the outside in: it is not the 'possession' of cultural characteristics that makes social groups distinct but rather it is the social interaction with other groups that makes that difference possible, visible and socially meaningful. In Barth's own words: 'the critical focus of investigation from this point of view becomes the ethnic boundary that defines the group, not the cultural stuff that it encloses' (1969: 15). The difference is created, developed and maintained only through interaction with others (i.e., Frenchness is created and becomes culturally and politically meaningful only through the encounter with Englishness, Germaness, Danishness, etc.). Hence, the focus in the study of ethnic difference has shifted from the study of its contents (i.e., the structure of the language, the form of the particular costumes, the nature of eating habits) to the study of cultural boundaries and social interaction. Ethnic boundaries are explained first and foremost as a product of social action. Cultural difference *per se* does not create ethnic collectivities: it is the social contact with others that leads to definition and categorization of an 'us' and a 'them'. 'Group identities must always be defined in relation to that which they are not – in other words, in relation to non-members of the group' (Eriksen, 1993: 10).

Furthermore, Barth's research established a foundation for understanding ethnicity in universalist rather than in particularist terms. Since culture and social groups emerge only through interaction with others, then ethnicity cannot be confined to minority groups only. As Jenkins (1997) and Isajiw (2000) rightly argue, we cannot study minority ethnic groups without at the same time studying the majority ethnicity. The dominant modernist paradigm of post-World War II sociology has traditionally viewed ethnicity as a parochial leftover from the past that will largely disappear with intensive industrialization, urbanization, universal national education systems and modernization. Ethnic difference was understood in rather narrow particularist terms. On the other hand, even the staunch critics of the modernization paradigm maintained this particularistic view of ethnicity. While trying to discredit the modernization thesis by drawing on the re-emergence of ethnicity in 1970s' and 80s' America, they have been equally responsible for confining ethnicity to minority groups. Their argument that the 'awakening of ethnicities' invalidates the melting pot thesis is equally flawed. Since this argument is purely historical it simply preserves a particularist comprehension of ethnicity. By stating that ethnic identities are more persistent than was envisaged by modernists, critics continue to operate with particularist, and also essentialist understandings of cultural difference. If ethnicity is understood in universalist terms as a question of social interaction, culture and boundary maintenance, it means that there is no culturally and politically aware social group which is able to create a believable narrative of common descent without drawing upon some conception of ethnicity. In other words, as long as there is a social action and cultural markers to draw upon (religion, language, descent, etc.), there will be ethnicity. And this is indeed where sociology enters the stage.

Ethnicity is not a thing or a collective asset of a particular group; it is a social relation in which social actors perceive themselves and are perceived by others as being culturally distinct collectivities. While Barth has made it clear that social contact is a precondition of ethnic group difference, mere contact is not enough to generate a sociologically meaningful sense of group membership. As Weber (1968) emphasized, it is the effectiveness of social action and, above all, a political aspect of group action that 'inspires belief in common ethnicity' and transforms group membership into a political community. Sociologically speaking, despite its obvious diversity, ethnicity is in the last instance a politicized culture.[3] As sociologists we do not study ethnic group behaviour simply to detect the variety of cultural difference that group relations can take. We become interested only when that cultural difference is mobilized for political purposes, when social actors through the process of social action (re)create the narratives of common descent to respond to a changing social environment. Cultural difference framed as ethnic difference is sociologically relevant only when it is active, mobilized and dynamic, and not a mere difference. However, the very fact that ethnicity, just as all other aspects of social relations, is for the most part a dynamic and mobile force, it makes the range of sociological inquiry much wider and more penetrating than it would otherwise be.

Although Barth has provided a groundwork for the elementary understanding of ethnicity, his approach fell short of accounting for these political and structural repercussions in the construction, organization and institutionalization of cultural difference. Why, when and how do individuals and groups maintain ethnic boundaries? In trying to give an answer to these questions post-Barthian sociology has moved in different directions. The main aim of this book is to set out clearly epistemological differences and similarities between these diverse sociological accounts of ethnic group reality, and to critically assess the explanatory potential of the leading sociological interpretations of ethnic relations. However, before I introduce these distinct sociological perspectives in the study of ethnicity, it is necessary to make some conceptual clarifications.

Ethnicity and the neighbouring concepts

In popular discourse, just as among some academics working in this field, there is a tendency to use terms such as 'ethnicity', 'race', 'nationality', 'religious group' or a specific regional, mostly continental, designation interchangeably.[4] Thus in the British context, a label such as 'Asian' often refers to an ethnic collectivity whose descent can be traced to some geographical location in the Indian subcontinent (Punjabi, Sindhi, Pashtun, Baloch, etc.). It can also, simultaneously, be a 'racial' description referring to an individual with markedly darker skin colour, brown eyes or glossy black hair. This label is also used for making reference to nationalities such as Pakistani or Bangladeshi. For the most part it also indicates a specific religious denomination, and it is regularly employed to denote Muslims. And finally the very name designates a particular, non-European continental location. Similarly, people from Northern Ireland are sometimes labelled as religious groups (Catholics or Protestants), sometimes in terms of their nationality, that is loyalty to a particular nation-state and the passport they hold (Irish or British), sometimes in terms of their geographical origin (Ulstermen or Northern Irish), and sometimes they are categorized in ethno-political terms as Republicans and Loyalists or Unionists and Nationalists.

The problem with these interchangeable uses is twofold. First it is obvious that although these labels, from the point of view of those who make a categorization, often refer to the same groups of individuals, they conflate very distinct forms of collective membership. Not only is it not the same thing to describe a particular collectivity in religious, geographic, cultural or racial terms but, more importantly, such an approach to categorization links together and naturalizes forms of collective membership that do not necessarily have anything in common. Such an attitude essentializes and reduces cultural, political and value diversity of an individual to a single clear-cut label such as 'Asian' or 'Irish'. This, in turn, works as a form of circular reasoning, where Asian = Muslim = Pakistani and vice versa. No group designation is clear cut and unproblematic, and terms such as 'Pakistani', 'Muslim' and 'Asian' are in themselves extremely broad and vague descriptions which involve numerous very diverse forms of sub-groupings and particular ways of being a Muslim, Pakistani and Asian, making this labelling strategy deeply flawed and potentially dangerous.

Secondly, not only is it that these terms often refer to different forms of collectivity; some of the concepts used are, from the sociological point of view, simply not viable. Defining groups in terms of race, religion and continental origin are examples of popular, native or folk concepts which are often constructed in an ad hoc manner by social actors who are themselves trying to make sense of their everyday reality. As such they have no sociological or explanatory grounding. Although there are clear genetic and physical variations between human beings such as skin colour, hair type, lip size and so on, as biologists emphasize there are no unambiguous criteria for classifying people along the lines of these characteristics. Any such classification would artificially create groups where in-group variation would be greater than their presumed out-group variation. In other words 'race' is a social construct where phenotypic attributes are popularly used to denote in-groups from out-groups. Since there is no sound biological or sociological foundation for its use in an analytical sense, one should treat 'race' as no more than a special case of ethnicity. Hence when the term 'race' is used in popular discourse it cannot refer to a 'sub-species of Homo sapiens' (van den Berghe, 1978: 406) but is applied only as a social attribute. It is viewed as a 'socially defined group which sees itself and is seen by others as being phenotypically different from other such groups' (van den Berghe, 1983: 222). As Collins (1999: 74) rightly argues,

> a sociological distinction between ethnicity and race is analytically pernicious because it obscures the social processes that determine the extent to which divisions are made along the continuum of somatotypical gradations. Race is a folk concept, a popular mythology that elevates particular ethnic distinctions into a sharp break. As sociologists, our analytical challenge is to show what causes placements along the continuum.

Similarly, the use of concepts such as a 'religious group' or a regional-continental designation to pinpoint cultural difference is often misleading. While continental descriptions such as 'Asians' or 'Afro-Caribbeans' in Britain, or 'Afro-Americans' or 'Amerasians' in the US, might be workable in a politically correct administrative sense, they are clearly too vague and too broad to be of any sociological use. These geographic labels are often no more than a convenient bureaucratic strategy which evades engaging with the hegemonic role of state civil servants in shaping particular group-centred discourses. In the same vein, when referring to groups other than those bound together by a strict set of religious beliefs or a group association based on a particular theological doctrine, the label 'religious group' is often used as no more than a euphemism for a particular form that ethnicity can take. Since ethnicity is a common name covering many diverse forms of political action which are defined in collective – cultural – terms, 'ethnicity' is able to accommodate all of these specific labels such as 'race', 'religious group' or 'regional-continental demarcation'. This is not to say that ethnicity is a more clear-cut concept than the other three. On the contrary, it is as untidy a concept as can possibly be. Its main and perhaps deciding advantage over the competitors is its ability simultaneously to allow for sociological generalization without affecting particular instances of it.[5] Unlike 'race', 'religious group' or 'continental designation', ethnicity has more of a universalist potential which, on the one hand, is decisive for the conduct of coherent social research practices and, on the other, is sensitive enough to appreciate and accommodate the variety of forms which cultural difference can take.

Finally, concepts such as nation, nationality and nationalism do occasionally overlap with those of ethnicity (as for example in the notion of ethno-nationalism), but for the most part they refer to ideologies and political movements associated with historical projects of political autonomy and territorial sovereignty, that is, with the macro processes of state making, building or breaking. In many ways the study of nations and nationalisms belongs to an historically specific period of transition from the feudal agrarian world of multilingual empires to modern industrial monoglot states, and to current debates on globalization and decline of the nation-state.[6] Since this book does not explicitly deal with any of these large-scale historical events it makes no more than a sporadic reference to concepts such as nation and nationalism, and when it does it is only when it is directly related to the processes of ethnic group action.

The structure of the book

The key objective of this book is systematically to survey and critically analyse leading sociological theories of ethnic relations. As any review of this kind it is bound to be incomplete, selective in its choice of theories as well as in the parameters used for the classification of diverse individual positions. The work of any individual sociologist is, as a rule, always richer, internally less coherent and often more contradictory than standard taxonomic categorizations tolerate. Any attempt to find the common denominators behind distinctly personal sociological accounts of social reality has to be somewhat reductionist, omitting a great deal of theoretical and empirical research material that makes these individual interpretations so unique. Although development of a sociological understanding of ethnicity is impossible without the people who formulate these theories, what matters *sub specie aeternitatis* are not the particular individuals but their creations – the ideas, concepts and theories themselves. To fully understand the forces of social action based on ethnicity one has to focus on conceptual and explanatory apparatuses developed within particular research traditions that are always spatially and temporally less limited and more multifaceted than any individual interpretation could be. In this book I have focused on the analysis of eight such research paradigms, which can be considered as the most influential contemporary sociological statements on ethnic relations: Neo-Marxism, Functionalism, Symbolic Interactionism, Socio-biology, Rational Choice Theory, Elite Theory, Neo-Weberianism and Anti-foundationalism.

The focal point of Chapter 2 is a survey of what the sociological classics – Marx, Durkheim, Simmel, Weber – have to say about ethnic relations. By critically reviewing their contribution it is argued, contrary to what is commonly believed, that there is such a thing as a classical sociological theory of ethnicity. Even though ethnic relations were on the margins of their interest, the sociological classics have not only developed coherent understandings of ethnic relations but their views have also established foundations for the contemporary interpretations of ethnic relations.

Chapter 3 examines neo-Marxist approaches to the study of ethnicity. It differentiates between two fairly distinct strands in contemporary Marxist research – one centred on the study of the political economy of ethnic group inequality, and the other focused on the State's role in reproducing and institutionalizing ethnically divisive conditions, as well as on the function of racist ideology in preventing working-class unity. While traditionally Marxists have analysed ethnicity as an ideological mask that only hides class antagonisms, and thus focus almost exclusively on capitalist modes of production, contemporary neo-Marxism is much more sensitive to the autonomy of the cultural sphere. Recognizing the limits of class analysis, contemporary Marxism attempts to widen its analysis of ethnicity by directing its attention to the new social movements and identities other than class. However, it is argued in this chapter that these are still couched in antagonistic, economist terms where ethnicity remains a second-order reality, a tool of exchange and coercion.

Chapter 4 reviews and scrutinizes functionalist interpretations of ethnic relations, which draw on the Durkheimian heritage that views ethnic diversity and modernization as being inversely proportional. The chapter distinguishes between structural-functionalism and plural society theory as two key functionalist positions on ethnicity. While structural-functionalism is predominantly concerned with the patterns of ethnic group solidarity and their relation to the dominant value system of the nation-state, pluralism searches for appropriate modes of incorporation regarding diverse ethnic communities within a common political structure. Although contemporary functionalist interpretations have moved significantly from the simple evolutionism of their predecessors and have shed important light on the intense impact that industrialization and urbanization have made in transforming traditional ways of life, I argue that these interpretations are still chained to the reductionist value-centred view which posits modernization as an irreversible force set to obliterate 'parochial' modes of belonging.

Chapter 5 discusses symbolic-interactionist interpretations of ethnic phenomena and their view that, since social action is often more symbolic than economic, the focus of analysis should be on the individual and collective subjective perceptions of reality. In this perspective ethnicity is analysed as a social process through which individuals and groups acquire, maintain, transform or change their 'definitions of the situation'. Ethnic groups are seen as operating through the 'collective definition of the situation', according to which they participate in the ongoing processes of interpretation and reinterpretation of their experiences. For interactionists, the objective and unequal distribution of economic rewards or political power between ethnic groups does not necessarily result in group conflict. It is, rather, the nature of their mutual symbolic interpretations and collective perceptions that determines inter- and intra-group relations. The chapter argues that even though symbolic interactionalism rightly emphasizes the variability of individual and group perceptions and the dynamic quality of ethnicity, its logic of argumentation is too idealist and too relativist to make room for the economic and political realities of ethnic relations.

The view that human beings are predominantly symbolic and cultural creatures, who create their own worlds of meanings, has been fiercely criticized by sociobiologists, whose contribution to the study of ethnicity is dissected in Chapter 6. Sociobiology starts from a simple and apparent fact that humans are made of flesh and blood; that they need to eat, drink, sleep and copulate, which are features shared with the rest of the animal kingdom. According to sociobiologists, humans are, just as other animals, genetically programmed to reproduce their genes. When direct reproduction is not possible one will reproduce indirectly – through kin selection. Sociobiologists have persistently argued that ethnicity is no more than an extension of kin selection. Ethnic groups are defined by common descent and are seen as being ascriptive, hereditary and generally endogamous. While sociobiological rehabilitation of the fact that human beings are also an integral part of the natural world is commended, sociobiologists' explanation of ethnic relations are seen as methodologically too weak to generate credible explanation, as they oscillate between biological and metaphorical interpretations of kin selection.

Chapter 7 looks at the rational choice theory of ethnicity. Viewing individuals as utility maximizers who struggle over limited resources, rational choice sociologists believe that ethnicity is no more than an advantage that can be used for individual gain. Speaking the same language, sharing religious tradition, myths of common descent or any other form of cultural similarity helps actors to unite and thereby makes the price of collective action less expensive. Rational choice theorists argue that ethnic groups maintain their inter-group solidarity in two principal ways: by providing benefits to their members, and/or by restricting and sanctioning their individual choices to prevent 'free riding'. Hence collective action on an ethnic group basis is most likely when an individual can benefit from it or when individuals fear sanctions from alternative behaviour. Although successful in emphasizing dynamic and manipulative features of ethnicity, this approach has been criticized for the circularity of its argument, for the disregard of culture and politics, and for underestimating the structural conditions under which individual choices are made.

In Chapter 8 the elite theory of ethnic relations is analysed. Unlike sociobiology, elite approaches argue that what is crucial for an understanding of ethnicity is a focus on human beings as political rather than biological animals. The two strands of elite theory are termed 'cultural' and 'instrumentalist'. Whereas the instrumentalist position is centred more on the manipulative strategies of power holders to sway mass support, culturalists study the use of political symbols as a resource in ethnic in-group/out-group mobilization. Their argument is that cultural markers are, most of the time, merely arbitrary, and what matters in ethnic relations is how, when and who can manipulate these symbols to mobilize social groups. This chapter also explores the apparent lack of a well-articulated contemporary elite theory in sociology more generally, which also reflects pronounced conceptual weaknesses in the elite accounts of ethnic relations. It is argued that a stronger connection with the conceptual and methodological apparatuses from classical elite theory would generate the development of a perspective with much stronger explanatory potential. Despite a certain realism presupposed by elite theory in terms of its relatively unique stress on a single group of social actors (elites), a focus which may be vital in mapping ethnic group action, this position has been criticized for treating the 'masses' in a passive, conformist and submissive way, and for neglecting the study of motives and values behind ethnic mobilization.

Chapter 9 examines leading neo-Weberian approaches to the study of ethnic relations. The chapter emphasizes the relevance and freshness of Weber's original ideas – such as his non-essentialist view of collectivity, where ethnicity is understood as a potential social attribute and not as an actual group characteristic, and the links he provides between status and ethnic membership and the notion of monopolistic social closure. Two distinct neo-Weberian positions are discussed: the economistic reading of Weber's concept of social closure, and the more macro political studies that pinpoint the role of geopolitics, military and state prestige. While each perspective represents an original and creative extension of Weberian ideas, and as such successfully contributes to our understanding of the complexity of ethnic relations, the very fact that these perspectives are conceptually fragmented and epistemologically purist indicates certain degrees of departure from the theoretical accord of classical Weberianism. It is argued in this chapter that all the main shortcomings in the neo-Weberian accounts of ethnicity come from their diluted and one-sided reading of Weber's general theory of social action and their preoccupation with a single layer of social reality.

Chapter 10 critically assesses contributions of anti-foundationalist approaches. It deals in particular with post-modernist, post-structuralist, post-Marxist, reflexive feminist and socio-psychoanalytical understandings of ethnic group relations. Unlike most 'conventional' sociology, anti-foundationalism does not aim to explain or interpret ethnicity, but moves instead to deconstruct all group as well as individual centric identity claims. Since anti-foundationalism's view is that there are no ultimately privileged agents or interpretations of social reality, all identities are temporary, provisional and subject to hegemonic re-interpretation and discursive control. Psychoanalytical and feminist accounts aim to deconstruct nominally neutral but (for most part) phallocentric narratives of ethnic group reality. The chapter concludes with the view that sees deconstruction as a valuable research strategy and anti-foundationalism as a powerful social critique, but it finds this perspective epistemologically destructive in its unbridled and uncompromising relativism while bearing disguised cultural determinism.

The final chapter compares and contrasts all eight leading sociological theories of ethnicity by identifying the principal differences and their main points of dispute. Using the example of the Rwandan genocide of 1994, the chapter briefly assesses the explanatory strength of each perspective, demonstrating how all eight theories are able to provide a coherent but often mutually opposed interpretation of the Rwandan catastrophe. While recognizing the possibility of epistemological plurality in answering the question of how and why the Rwandan genocide was possible, the chapter aims to avoid relativist, absolutist or syntheticist pitfalls by articulating an alternative epistemological strategy. The assessment of explanatory building blocks of each of the eight theoretical frameworks along the line of dichotomies such as individualism–collectivism, materialism–idealism, primordialism–situationism and subjectivism–objectivism has indicated that a more comprehensive sociological interpretation of ethnic relations can be generated through a subtle integration and reformulation of existing neo-Weberian and elite positions. Although it is acknowledged that there is no master key or blue-print to deal with each and every case of inter-ethnic group relations, the development of an integrated Weberian elite position is seen as the best strategy in bridging epistemological and policy requirements. The fact that ethnicity is a diverse, illusive and fluid phenomenon that, just like the avatars of the Hindu gods, emerges in so many different forms should not prevent our attempts to devise sociological explanations and policy recommendations, regardless of how imperfect they will always be.

Notes

1   Although, as Bartlett (2001: 39–40) indicates, the term 'ethnicity' was in sporadic use long before the 1950s, it still referred only to 'paganism', as in the following

quote from 1782: 'From the curling spume of the celebrated Egean waves, fabulous ethnicity feigned Venus their idolatress conceived.'

2   For example R.A. Schermerhorn (1970) defines an ethnic group as 'a *collectivity within a larger society* having real or putative common ancestry, memories of a shared historical past, and a cultural focus on one or more symbolic elements defined as the epitome of their peoplehood'. Most American editions of social science encyclopaedia apply an identical approach. So, the *International Encyclopaedia of the Social Sciences* (p. 167) defines an ethnic group as 'a distinct category of the population *in a larger society* whose culture is usually different from its own'. While in the *Dictionary of Concepts in Cultural Anthropology* the following definition is given (Winthrop, 1991: 94): 'Ethnicity. The existence of culturally distinctive groups *within a society* each asserting a unique identity on the basis of a shared tradition and distinguishing social markers such as a common language, religion, or economic specialisation.' (All italics mine.)

3   The term 'politicized' is used here in wide terms – it does not necessarily include effective mass mobilization but it can also take more tacit, banal forms, as argued in Billig (1995, 2002).

4   Connor (1978, 1994) provides illustrative academic examples of misunderstandings in distinguishing between some of these concepts.

5   As Collins (1999: 78) makes clear, 'Ethnicity is an intrinsically messy topic because the historical processes that produce it are intrinsically messy. Our analytical problems stem from the fact that ethnicity is always a distorted concept, an attempt to impose a pure category on a social reality that is not at all pure.'

6   As most macro sociologists and historians (Gellner, 1983; Hobsbawm, 1990; Anderson, 1991; J.A. Hall, 1993; Mann, 1995; Breuilly, 2001) now agree, nationalism is relatively novel as a mass event, that is, as a sociologically interesting phenomenon, while ethnic group relations in general are perhaps as old as the human species.

Chapter Two

CLASSICAL SOCIOLOGICAL THEORY AND ETHNICITY

Introduction

Commentators made it apparent on so many occasions that there was no place, patience or understanding for the study of ethnic relations in classical sociological theory (Stone, 1977, 1995; Zubaida, 1978; Berlin, 1992; Guibernau, 1996). It has been constantly and persistently argued that the classics of sociology had very little to say about ethnicity and that even when they made some comments, these were regarded as sporadic and largely irrelevant to their general theories of society. Although ethnic relations were not the primary focus of their analyses all four founding fathers of sociology − Marx, Durkheim, Simmel and Weber − developed coherent and, within their respective theoretical positions, consonant and well articulated theories of ethnicity. For if this were not the case contemporary sociological theories of ethnicity would not have a basis to build upon. Considering that most influential contemporary theories of ethnicity have deep roots in classical sociological theory and even bear names such as 'Neo-Marxist' or 'Neo-Weberian', it would seem paradoxical that they have developed out of a research tradition that does not exist.

This general misinterpretation is grounded in two main problems, one of nominal and the other of historical nature. First, 'ethnicity' in its full sociological meaning is a very recent term which was not in general use in the nineteenth and early twentieth centuries and, with the clear exception of Weber, no other classical sociologist employed this term in their works. However, having a new term does not necessarily imply a new social phenomenon: questions of cultural and physical group difference as well as social action, which is the basis of such a presumed difference, are certainly not that new, and so the classics had to engage with them. And they have done so under a variety of names: the national question, culturally distinct peoples, nationality, race, culture, and so on. Thus, to pinpoint their respective theories of ethnicity one has to dig deeper into the meaning and relationships between all of these different concepts and to look especially at links between these concepts and the general theories of society in the works of the classics.

Secondly, since sociology was largely conceived at the dawn of modernity as an analytical attempt to explain dramatic social changes which the onset of industrialization, urbanization and secularization have brought upon world societies, it was generally dismissive of any form of cultural specificity. Intensive ethnic attachments were commonly regarded as features of an homogenous and static *Gemeinschaft* that would in one way or another largely diminish with the inevitable arrival of heterogeneous and dynamic *Gesselschaft*. In this respect the classics of sociology did not have to devote much time to ethnicity: after all, this was seen as an old and disappearing phenomenon. However, a lack of extensive focus does not imply that one has no theory of such a phenomenon. In their different ways the classics of sociology had to explain why and how ethnicity was about to vanish or transform into something else. Marx found that answer in class struggle and capitalist development, Durkheim in the transition from mechanical to organic solidarity, Simmel in the nature of sociation and social differentiation, and Weber in changing status hierarchies and political mobilization. Hence, a concern with group cultural difference was at the heart of classical sociological theory.

Marx

Although Marx never wrote a separate monograph on ethnic relations, a closer reading of his opus indicates that he did develop a relatively coherent theory of ethnicity. The core of this theory can be found in his writings on the Jewish question (Marx, 1844 in Marx and Engels, 1977), in his and Engels' adoption of Hegel's distinction between historic and non historic peoples, his comments on the role of Irish immigrants in the UK, and his general remarks on the development of specific ethnic groups worldwide. There are three deeply interconnected thematic conceptions around which Marx's theory of ethnicity is developed:

1 the primacy of the economic base over the cultural and thus ethnic superstructure
2 ethnic particularity as an obstacle to the universal progress of humanity as a whole
3 the historical ascendancy of class over ethnic identity.

Let us briefly explore each of these themes.

The guiding principle of Marxist theory is class conflict. History is presented as a path of constant struggle between two leading classes, the position of each determined by their relations to the modes of production: from slaves and slave owners in the ancient world, to serfs and lords in feudalism, to proletariat and bourgeoisie in the era of modern capitalism. The economy is viewed to be the main basis of social change and social structure, while culture and ideas in general are seen as the 'superstructure', the existence of which is determined by the economic base. The position in the process of production, that is, the relations towards the 'material forces of production', establish relationships between individuals as well as between distinct classes: those who own the means of production exploit those who own nothing but their labour. Dominant capitalist relations of production, which are based on the principles of exploitation and inequality, lead to the alienation of human beings from their work, from other human beings and individual human beings from themselves, while the 'fetishism of commodities' leads to the situation where the alienated products of human labour overpower and dominate their creators (Marx, 1867 in Marx and Engels, 1977; Marx, 1985). In this view ethnicity belongs to the sphere of superstructure. The impact of group cultural difference has roots in the economic system and is determined by the nature of capitalist production. Ethnic hostilities in a capitalist society present an objective problem but only because of capitalism's alienating structure.

In *On the Jewish Question* (1844) and *Holy Family* (1845) (in Marx and Engels, 1977) Marx aims to explain how the emancipation of a particular ethnic group (Jews) can never be fully achieved within the existing (capitalist) political and economic formation, neither could such emancipation be undertaken for a single ethnic collective. For emancipation to be successful and complete it is not enough just to establish mechanisms for the protection of civic and political rights of a particular ethnic group, but rather it is necessary to create conditions for the full emancipation of all human beings. Marx makes a distinction between political and human emancipation and argues that while political emancipation, that is, formal political equality, can be achieved in the capitalist society, 'human emancipation, which signifies transcending alienation, necessarily presupposes the destruction of bourgeois society as the sphere of men's egotistic interests contrasted with universal human attributes' (Avineri, 1964: 445). For Marx the 'Jewish question' cannot just be framed as a purely religious or ethnic question, but rather it represents a symptom of the alienating structure of capitalist society which creates conditions where human beings are alienated from each other. As Marx (1844, in Marx and Engels, 1977: 15) argues

> Only when the real, individual man re-absorbs in himself the abstract citizen, and as an individual human being become a species-being in his everyday life,

in his practical work, and in his particular situation, only when man recognised and organised his 'own powers' as social powers, and consequently, no longer separates social power from himself in the shape of political power, only then will human emancipation have been accomplished.

Therefore ethnic relations are in the last instance determined by the human relations to the means of production and cannot change significantly until the economic basis of capitalist order changes. The economic base has a primacy over ethnic superstructure.

This argument ties in well with another theme present in Marx's theory of ethnicity – the view that ethnicity as a form of particularity for the most part presents an obstacle to history's universal march towards ultimate freedom. Marx shares Enlightenment's impatience with cultural specificity. His historical materialism envisaged that all societies pass through evolutionary stages, from prehistoric formation and slavery, over feudalism, to capitalism and, eventually, to communism. Focusing most extensively on the transition from feudalism to capitalism Marx believed that market-centred capitalism requires cultural uniformity. As Nimni (1991) rightly argues, Marx took the model of post-revolutionary France as a parameter for nation and state building, holding the view that 'state centralisation and national unification with the consequent assimilation of small national [ethnic] communities was the only viable path to social progress'. Marx was not opposed to the creation of new ethnically based nations and, in fact, viewed with suspicion the idea that nationalities will disappear in the near future (Marx, 1845, in Marx and Engels, 1977; Avineri, 1964).[1] On the contrary, the key element of his theory is, as we can read in the *Communist Manifesto* (1847, in Marx and Engels, 1977), the idea that 'the struggle of the proletariat with the bourgeoisie is at first a national struggle. The proletariat of each country must, of course, first of all settle matters with its own bourgeoisie.' However, what was most important here was the question of whether a particular ethnic group meets the condition of developing a sustainable polity which would contain 'a population large enough to allow for an internal division of labour which characterises a capitalist system with its competing classes' (Nimni, 1991: 18). This prerequisite was almost impossible to meet for most ethnic collectivities in and especially outside Europe. In this respect, Marx's theory of ethnicity was not only Eurocentric but, more precisely, West-Eurocentric. Following Hegel's crude and chauvinistic distinction between historic and non historic peoples (*Geschichtslosen Voelker*) Marx[2] argued that only some peoples are historic, that is, they possess a tradition of statehood or state building (e.g., Germans, English, French and Irish) while most others are considered to be non historic (e.g., Czechs, Serbs, Croats and Ukrainians). Marx believed that only historic ethnicities are capable of building sustainable and capitalist-friendly states, while the rest (i.e., the majority of ethnic groups) have to be assimilated into a larger nation-state. Regardless of how crude and prejudiced this argument is, it is fairly consistent with Marx's general theory of history: when ethnic differences can accommodate the universalistic project of class emancipation by helping to destroy the remains of feudal order they are welcome, but when they cannot they are 'ethnographic monuments' and 'residual fragments of peoples'[3] that are no more than an impediment to social progress.

This brings us to the final thematic section of Marx's theory of ethnicity – the historical supremacy of class over ethnicity. Although Marx recognized, being a witness of the 1848 revolutions in Europe, the strength of ethnic attachments, he ultimately believed that class solidarity will eventually prevail over ethnic bonds. His theory of class struggle incorporated a view that the development of class consciousness is determined by historical factors, and that in the long term workers will shift their loyalties from ethnicity to class. In this process the proletariat would be transformed from a mere category of people who share the same working and living conditions (class in itself), into a self-aware group who will act in accordance with their collective self-interests (class for itself) (Marx, 1895, in Marx and Engels, 1977). However, what prevents workers from achieving a high degree of class consciousness in capitalism is the fact that the bourgeoisie control not only 'the means of material production', but also 'the means of mental production', or, in the words of young Marx (Marx, in Marx and Engels, 1982a: 64), 'The ideas of the ruling class are in every epoch the ruling ideas: i.e. the class, which is the ruling material force of society, is at the same time its ruling intellectual force.' So the bourgeoisie does not only control factories, land and raw materials but also the mass media, schools and churches. Hence, capitalist rulers instrumentalize group cultural differences to benefit their own class position. As Marx illustrates on the example of ethnic animosity between English and Irish workers:

> Every industrial and commercial centre in England now possesses a working class divided into two hostile camps, English proletarians and Irish proletarians. The ordinary English worker hates the Irish worker as a competitor who lowers his standards of life. In relation to the Irish worker he feels himself a member of the ruling nation and so turns himself into a tool of the aristocrats and capitalists of his country against Ireland, thus strengthening their domination over himself ...

> This antagonism is artificially kept alive and intensified by the press, the pulpit, the comic papers, in short, by all means at the disposal of the ruling classes. This antagonism is the secret of the impotence of the English working class, despite its organisation. It is the secret by which the capitalist class maintains its power. And that class is fully aware of it. (Marx, in Marx and Engels, 1982b: 222)

Thus, in reality ethnic conflict is no more than a hidden class conflict, and by overcoming class inequalities ethnicity will diminish as a factor of social antagonism. The source of ethnic enmity is not in the cultural differences of groups but in the nature of capitalist modes of production and the inherent inequalities that it produces. For Marx class consciousness remains a real potent force of social change while ethnic identities are no more than an epiphenomenon, a second order reality, which will be transcended once a genuine communist society is established.

Durkheim

Just as for Marx, ethnicity was not a main focal point of Durkheim's work and he never explicitly dealt with this topic. However, the strength of collective cultural ties and the nature of ethnic solidarity are at the heart of Durkheim's theory. Analysing his major works, especially *The Division of Labour in Society* (1997 [1892]), *Suicide* (1996 [1897]) and *Elementary Forms of Religious Life* (1995 [1912]), as well as his comments on anti-semitism and patriotism in relation to the Dreyfus affair, one can identify a fairly consistent theory of ethnicity. The main premises of this theory are sometimes explicitly stated and analysed, but for the most part they are built into his wide-ranging theory of society. Durkheim's theory of ethnic relations is focused mostly on three interrelated sets of topics: the decline of ethnicity with the arrival of modernity; the nature of (ethnic) group solidarity; and the perception of an ethnic group as a form of moral community.

Durkheim shared with Marx an evolutionary vision of social development. He also saw societies as moving along the evolutionary ladder from primitive to more advanced. However, unlike Marx the central explanatory factor for Durkheim was not the social conflict resulting from class inequalities, but rather the opposite – different patterns of social integration were seen to be crucial for the development of any given society. As Poggi (2000: 39) rightly argues, Durkheim's key dichotomy here revolves around the question: 'How are societies put together?' Focusing on the morphology of social orders, Durkheim views societies as being composed of different components that have a distinct relationship to each other: while in the traditional, simple societies constituent parts are very much alike with very little mutual interaction, modern, complex societies are composed of very diverse, highly autonomous but also deeply interdependent entities. Not only is it that these two forms of societies differ in their internal organization (small culturally and socially homogeneous segments versus large heterogeneous and self-sustaining units), but their internal composition also affects the way these societies function externally. Because of their size, complexity and variation modern societies are structurally, functionally and organizationally superior to those with less differentiation and mobility, and in the long run all societies are destined to move from simple entities to the complex orders with an extensive division of labour.

When applied to the concept of ethnicity this argument reads as: whereas ethnically compact communities might differ in content (different customs, languages, eating habits, etc.) they are very similar in form (almost identical organizational structure, low levels of interaction between various ethnic communities, etc.). With the advent of modernization the bonds of ethnic communities gradually decline and they evolve into complex and culturally heterogeneous societies. However, this cultural diversity is built upon the common universal goals and values of the society as a whole ('collective conscience'), meaning that ethnic loyalties are first transformed into a devotion to the nation ('patriotism') and then into a devotion to entire humanity ('world patriotism').[4] In Durkheim's words: 'as we advance in evolution, we see the ideals men pursue breaking free of the local or ethnic conditions obtaining in a certain region of the world or a certain human group, and rising above all that is particular and so approaching the universal' (Durkheim, 1986: 202). Nevertheless, what is crucial in Durkheim's argument is the view that the evolution of societies does not lead to cosmopolitan individualism, or that with modernization ethnic bonds disintegrate into atomistic selfishness. On the contrary, modernity creates a morally superior community/society, since 'man is a moral being only because he lives within established societies' (Durkheim, 1986: 203). So what 'differentiates [modern] societies from ethnic groups is rather their unequal degree of civilisation' (Durkheim, 1996: 86).

This view is even more pronounced when Durkheim discusses the nature of group solidarity in these two types of social orders. According to Durkheim, traditional and modern society do not differ only in terms of their internal structures and external functions but they are also characterized by different types of group solidarity. While traditional society is held together by mechanical solidarity of group similarity, modern society is integrated through organic solidarity of autonomous (but mutually dependent) individuals. In the traditional social order, individuals are members of a particular group solely on the basis of collective resemblance and extended family ties, while in modern society people feel attached to others on the grounds of shared reliance on each other. As Durkheim explains, organic solidarity is the more powerful force because it is based on the shared dependency of individual actions and progress is possible only when there is a strict division of labour in accordance with skills and professional expertise. Hence ethnic solidarity grounded in kinship ties is a much weaker force than national or supranational solidarity built around the principles of mutual dependency. In the modern nation-state individuals 'are grouped no longer on the basis of kinship relations, but on the basis of the distinctive nature of the social activity to which they are devoted. Their natural and necessary context is no longer the context of birth, but the professional context' (Durkheim, 1997: 132). Following from the evolutionary argument above, organic solidarity replaces mechanic solidarity as (cultural) differentiation increases, and ethnicity is not immune to this force. When making direct reference to ethnic bonds Durkheim sees 'heredity' as loosing ground 'in the course of human evolution' (Durkheim, 1996) and he argues that 'Jews are losing their ethnic character with an extreme rapidity. In two generations the process will be complete' (Durkheim, in Fenton, 1980: 153). When faced with cases of ethnic hostility in an apparently modern society (such as anti-semitism during the Dreyfus affair in France), Durkheim explains this as a 'consequence and the superficial symptom of a state of social malaise'. Such a situation arises in the period of transition from mechanical to organic solidarity when the state of anomie prevails and when old forms of group morality are disintegrating and new ones are not yet in place. Poggi (2000: 80) captures this argument well: 'Anomie entails an inability to set enforceable boundaries to the individual's pursuits, a sense that nothing much matters, everything is possible; it destroys those normative frameworks that could at the same time bind and sustain individual existence, and thus threatens it with meaninglessness.'

Although ethnicity was largely seen by Durkheim as a relic of the past, it is none the less a significant force of group integration and morality. For Durkheim the merely mechanical solidarity of traditional social order still provides more social integration than the state of anomie. Analysing religious beliefs and practices as a force of moral integration, he argues that religion is a deeply 'collective thing' through which society worships itself. Durkheim finds in totemism the simplest form of religious practice, whose principles apply to any religion regardless of how complex it might be. These principles can be formulated simply as god = society. If the totem is, as Durkheim puts it, 'at the same time, the symbol of the god and of the society, could it not be the case that god and society are one and the same thing? ... The god of the clan, the totemic principle, cannot then be other than the clan itself' (1995: 208). Religion is a form of collective consciousness in which society celebrates its own image and power. Being primarily a social force that holds society together, religion is seen as a universal and omnipotent power fulfilling a similar role in the 'primitive' and 'modern' world: 'There can be no society that does not sense the need to entertain and reaffirm at regular intervals, the collective sentiments and ideas which constitute its unity and its identity' (Durkheim, 1995: 429). In this respect ethnic group solidarity is also maintained and reinforced through the reaffirmation of common 'collective sentiments and ideas', that is, through the existence of a collective consciousness. The primary function of ethnic community is its normative strength: group membership sets the parameters of social and hence moral behaviour. 'Ethnic group' stands for a moral unity which is achieved through the active participation in the group rituals. In the words of Durkheim, 'It is by virtue of screaming the same cry, pronouncing the same word, performing the same gesture concerning the same object that they achieve and experience an accord ... It is the homogeneity of these movements which imparts to the group the sense of identity and consequently makes it be'(1995: 232). Thus, for ethnicity to survive it is necessary that ethnic symbols are periodically and regularly reaffirmed. In this respect there is no substantial difference between explicitly religious symbols and rituals and those of a nominally secular character: commemorating the death of heroes fallen in an ethnic conflict is equivalent to Jews commemorating the exodus from Egypt or Christians commemorating the crucifixion of Christ. If not reiterated in a ritualistic way, collective (ethnic) identity disintegrates and with it crumbles the moral order of a particular community.

Simmel

Since Georg Simmel's theories are much more micro sociological than those of Marx and Durkheim, one would expect a more explicit engagement with ethnicity and ethnic group relationships in his work. However, although Simmel does indeed provide a more comprehensive theory of ethnicity, the main propositions of this theory are, as with Marx and Durkheim, seldom directly spelled out and are, rather, ingrained in his general theories of social interaction. It is only in his classic 'Stranger' and, to a lesser extent, in 'The Web of Group Affiliations' and 'On Social Differentiation' that Simmel specifically discusses the nature of individual and group cultural difference. Simmel's theory of ethnic relations is focused on three thematic blocks

1   ethnicity as a form of sociation
2   the nature of social (and thus ethnic) interaction
3   the decline of ethnicity through social differentiation.

Most of Simmel's work concentrates on the analysis of the societal micro cosmos, and he sees sociology as a study of the forms of sociation. Sociation is defined as 'the form (realised in innumerably different ways) in which individuals grow together into a unity and within which their interests are realised' (Simmel, 1971: 24). Simmel makes a distinction between form and content, where content refers to concrete individual psychological or biological qualities which require and eventually lead to social action, while form is a generalized pattern of interaction, in the course of which individuals truly become social beings. Thus sociation is a dialectical and open-ended process through which individual interests or drives are transformed into integrated and socially meaningful collective entities and actions. A form is a general configuration of social interaction abstracted from a number of particular contents. Following this distinction ethnicity would thus be a form of sociation induced from the more particular contents of individual cultural difference. Ethnicity is a general name for a multiplicity of specific modes of individual and group interaction on the basis of a cultural varia-tion. Ethnic relations not only always involve a degree of ambiguity and individual and group 'nervousness',[5] but they are actually built around these dialectical and wavering poles of interaction.

In Simmel's analysis of the 'stranger' one can observe these contradictory processes at play. The stranger is both near and far in the group but never a full member of it; he is a 'person who comes today and stays tomorrow', somebody who is defined by his potential mobility, his freedom to be detached from the group's destiny. He is a 'potential wanderer' but what really determines his position is 'the fact that he has not belonged to it [the group] from the beginning' and that 'He imports qualities into it [the group], which do not and cannot stem from the group itself' (Simmel, 1996: 37–8). The stranger has no organic or kinship connection to the group; he is not an 'owner of soil' and, as such, his presence is crucial to determine who 'we' in the group are. The presence of the stranger and the cultural difference that he represents sets the boundaries of the group's norms and values. In other words, ethnicity acquires its full sociological meaning only when directly confronted with the alternative forms of cultural organization of social life. In this respect 'the other' is perceived in much more abstract and generalized terms than any individual member of 'our' ethnic community: 'with the stranger one has only certain *more general* qualities in common, whereas the relation to more organically connected persons is based on the commonness of specific differences from merely general features' (Simmel, 1996: 39–40). The stranger is never really an individual, he always represents a particular (ethnic) group.

Ethnicity is not only a specific form of sociation, but it also encompasses different layers of social interaction. To understand society on Simmel's terms one has to focus on the variety of forms of individual and group interaction, since society is no more than a 'synthesis or the general term for the totality of these specific interactions' (1978: 175). The intensity and scale of social interaction is determined by a number of factors such as the group size, spatial configuration and social distance. For Simmel the size of the group has a deep impact on its internal cohesion: group 'solidarity decreases in measure in which numerical increase involves the admission of hetero-geneous individual elements' while 'a smaller minimum of norms can ...

hold together a large group more easily than a small one' (Simmel, 1950: 95, 397). Hence, the size of the ethnic group influences its internal cohesiveness – immigrant and diasporic communities (e.g., Jews in nineteenth-century Europe) exhibit a greater degree of solidarity *per se* than huge ethno-national entities (e.g., French or English in the twentieth century). This also implies that the ethnic bond and its corresponding ideology of ethnicism[6] are built around tighter normative parameters than those of the nation–state and nationalism. Furthermore, the interplay of space and social distance shapes individual and group behaviour. Groups often identify with the specific territory: a society 'possesses a sharply demarcated existential space such that the extensiveness of space collides with the intensity of social relationships' (Frisby, 1984: 127). Long before Frederik Barth (1969), Simmel was aware of the importance of boundary maintenance in developing and sustaining group identities. Spatial boundaries are strong social forces in a sense that 'the boundary is not a spatial fact with sociological consequences but a sociological fact that is formed spatially' (Simmel in Frisby, 1984: 127). Boundaries also designate the character of group interaction and distance since they are really socially meaningful to those who are near or not very far from 'us'. As Simmel nicely illustrates, 'the inhabitants of Sirius are not really strangers to us, at least not in a sociologically relevant sense: they do not exist for us at all; they are beyond far and near' (1996: 37).

Conflict is also an important form of social interaction in Simmel's theory. Unlike common views that see conflict as a destructive force, Simmel argues that conflict is a form of sociation that is largely positive, and, as such, crucial for group unity. First, conflict (including ethnic conflict) is a social activity – a lone individual cannot be in conflict and therefore cannot experience social interaction. (Ethnic) conflict involves actual group contact and so it brings individuals and groups together. Secondly, unlike indifference, which 'whether it implies the rejection or the termination of sociation' is 'purely negative', conflict is an active and positive interaction. It is motivated by the wish to 'resolve divergent dualism; it is a way of achieving some kind of unity'. Ethnic conflict is not aimed at the negation of unity but rather at the creation of a new form of unity. Finally, conflict is a source of change and development. Unity presupposes social conflict since a conflict-less, harmonious society is not sociologically realistic, and any abstract call to harmony might be no more than a device of political manipulation. Ethnic animosities are (as are other forms of animosities) an integral part of social life, which can be legislated against but can never be socially resolved.

The last thematic block in Simmel's theory of ethnicity deals with the idea of social differentiation. In this more macro sociological analysis Simmel echoes the central theme of Durkheim's sociology – the nature of group integration – but his conclusions are fairly different to those of Durkheim. Simmel starts with the assumption that there are different degrees of social differentiation in 'primitive' and complex societies. He follows an evolutionary scheme in arguing that complex societies exhibit a greater level of differentiation, whereas in 'the primitive collectivity the principle of heredity operates in favour of the similarity of individuals' (Frisby, 1984: 79). Small primitive communities are seen as having a strong organic connection and a greater degree of solidarity, while modern complex societies are characterized by loose group ties and diffuse individuality. For Simmel an individual in a small (ethnic) community is merged with the group and when conflict arises it is never seen as a relationship between individuals but rather as a property of a 'hostile' group. In other words, an individual action is regularly interpreted in collective, ethnic terms. In Simmel's words: 'the circle of social interests lie concentrically around us: the tighter they enclose us the smaller they must be' (Frisby, 1984: 82). Strongly integrated (ethnic) groups tend to be more distinctive from the outside since their members are more alike while complex societies have a propensity of being less specific and colourful since its members display much greater levels of individuality. In this respect ethnic group bonds are seen as something that decline as social differentiation and societal complexity increases. The feeling and content of individuality grows with the enlargement of the group. 'A strong development of individuality and a strong positive evaluation of individuality often goes together with cosmopolitan convictions' whereas 'devotion to a narrowly bounded social [ethnic] group hinders both' (Simmel in Frisby, 1984: 82). In a modern, complex society the 'web of affiliations' develops exponentially. Individuals have many partial links with a number of different social groups, which leads to fragmented individual experiences and, in the last instance, to fragmented personalities. With modernity an individual becomes a blasé cosmopolitan – highly individualized and socially detached.

Weber

Weber is the only founding father of sociology who explicitly and extensively engaged with ethnic relations. Weber not only developed a highly original and systematic account of ethnicity but his theory still remains a potent explanatory framework in dealing with the sociology of ethnic relations. The skeleton key of this theory is present in his chapter on 'Ethnic groups' in *Economy and Society* (1968), but elements of his theory of ethnicity are also vivid in other writings (the various other sections in *Economy and Society*, *Ancient Judaism* (1967) and *Religion of India* (1992); and articles on W. E. B. Du Bois). Although Weber provides a deeply integrated and coherent model for explaining ethnic relations, one can identify four central tenets around which this theory is built:

1 ethnicity as a form of status group
2 ethnicity as a mechanism of monopolistic social closure
3 multiplicity of ethnic forms of social organization
4 ethnicity and political mobilization.

Weber defines ethnic groups as 'those human groups that entertain a subjective belief in their common descent because of similarities of physical type or of customs or both, or because of memories of colonisation and migration; conversely, it does not matter whether or not an objective blood relationship exists' (1968: 389). So what is crucial here, first, is that ethnicity exists only on the basis of a particular group belief – if there is no group shared belief there will be no ethnic group. Secondly, ethnicity is rooted in a single but omnipotent belief – the belief in common descent. And finally, although this belief in common ancestry is for most part fictional it is reinforced and reconfirmed on the grounds of cultural or physical similarity or on the basis of shared collective memory. However, regardless of how powerful this belief might be in itself, it is not sufficient to create ethnicity: ethnic group formation is dependent on a concrete social and political action. Although ethnicity is couched in terms of kin relationships 'it differs from the kinship group precisely by being a presumed identity' (ibid.). A mere membership can assist in group formation but it does not create an ethnic group as such. As Weber argues: 'it is primarily the political community, no matter how artificially organised, that inspires the belief in common ethnicity' (ibid.). An ethnic group is first and foremost created through social and political action. Once in action an ethnic group often functions as a type of status group.[7]

For Weber ethnicity, as in the case of any other status group, is amorphous, determined by a certain 'social estimation of honour', and created through specific upbringing, training or other means of socialization. It is expressed in a particular lifestyle and it is often able to successfully claim 'a special social esteem' and 'status monopolies'. Status group membership provides individuals with a 'sense of dignity',[8] which is ingrained in the prestige and social honour of their ethnic group. As in other status groups, ethnicity tends towards endogamy, but an ethnic group's relatively unique emphasis on sharing common descent makes it, unlike some others, an 'hereditary status group'. This hereditary status group expresses itself through what Weber calls 'ethnic honour', which is defined 'as the conviction of the excellence of one's own customs and the inferiority of alien ones' and is a 'specific honour of the masses, for it is accessible to anybody who belongs to the subjectively believed community of descent' (1968: 391). In this respect ethnic honour is a form of a zero-sum vertical status differentiation: the social prestige of 'poor whites' depends on the subordination of 'blacks'. Corresponding to this but in a more 'egalitarian' sense for Weber is the horizontal notion of 'chosen people'. Unlike the discriminatory nature of ethnic honour demarcation which rests on the humiliation of other groups, any ethnic group can stake a claim in being the chosen one.

The restricted character of status membership provides a possibility for closing ranks around ethnic group membership, which leads us to the second tenet of Weber's theory of ethnicity – ethnicity as a device of monopolistic social closure. Weber (1968: 43) distinguishes between open and closed social relationships: open being those that allow voluntary participation of the 'outsiders', and closed being those 'closed against outsiders so far as, according to its subjective meaning and its binding rules, participation of certain persons is excluded, limited, or subjected to conditions'. Status groups often operate on the basis of social closure where their monopolistic position is regularly used to prevent non-group members from acquiring symbolic or material benefits. This was seen as a powerful mechanism for maintaining out-group political, economic and symbolic dominance as well as in-group solidarity and homogeneity. Social closure is most visible in situations where individuals or groups have to compete for scarce resources. Under these circumstances, 'any cultural trait, no matter how superficial, can serve as a starting point for the familiar tendency to monopolistic closure' (Weber, 1968: 388). One social group is then in a position to amplify the importance of some identifiable social or cultural attribute that competing social groups lack: a religion, language, ethnic descent, physical features, etc. These emphasized markers of cultural difference can, in the long term, be intensified and institutionalized to preserve group benefits. However, what is essential here is that the monopolization of social closure which provides instrumental opportunities for potential economic or political exploitation of the 'out-group', rests on the group monopolization of social honour and prestige. As Jackson (1982/83) rightly points out, once humiliation and social degradation of the out-group takes place and groups are symbolically subordinated, political domination and economic exploitation are open and easy options.

Arguing that any cultural marker can be used as a potential starting device for social closure, Weber emphasized the dynamic quality of ethnic relations. In Weber's theory ethnicity, having an amorphous and fuzzy structure, can take different forms of social organization. Although for the most part they operate as status groups, ethnic groups can take the shape of class, caste or estate (Rex, 1986a: 14). However, what was most interesting for Weber was the phenomenon of ethnic caste. Under certain conditions and after long periods of monopolistic social closure, status groups are likely to transform into a caste system. Unlike status groups, caste distinctions are much more rigid and closed social groups. They are separated from each other on the basis of conventions, laws and rituals; they develop distinct and often mutually opposing value systems (including different religious practices, eating habits, etc.), exclude social or even physical contact with other castes, and practise exclusive endogamy. But most of all, their group boundaries are fixed by walls of 'ritualistic impurity'. As Weber (1948: 189) explains:

> A 'status' segregation grown into a 'caste' differs in its structure from a mere 'ethnic' segregation: the caste structure transforms the horizontal and unconnected coexistences of ethnically segregated groups into a vertical social system of super- and subordination … a comprehensive societalization integrates the ethnically divided communities into specific political and communal action … ethnic coexistences condition a mutual repulsion and disdain but allow each ethnic community to consider its own honour as the highest one.

These sharply divergent degrees of social honour among different ethnic castes are often functionally related to their group's role within a given polity (i.e., the structural importance of warriors, rulers, priests, etc.). When ethnic groups acquire the caste structure they express deep and rigid status inequalities with hierarchical ordering of ethnic groups in terms of social honour and prestige. Unlike the dominant ethnic castes who 'live for the present by exploiting their great past', ethnic groups placed at the bottom of this hierarchy tend to develop ethnic ideologies (or, in Weber's terms, 'sense of dignity') which are oriented towards the future or an after-life. This brings us back to the concept of 'chosen people', which is often tied with the belief of a low ranked ethnic caste in their 'specific honour before God' or a special 'providential mission'. According to Weber (1967) this belief is particularly characteristic of what he termed 'pariah peoples' who often live in segregated communes and are associated with specific occupations (i.e., merchant minorities such as Jews in nineteenth-century Europe). They preserve a strong sense of dignity and social honour but primarily as 'chosen people' believing that 'in the beyond "the last will be the first" or that a Messiah will appear to bring forth into the light of the world which has cast them out the hidden honour of the pariah people' (Weber, 1948: 190).

The final segment of Weber's theory of ethnic relations deals with the political aspects of ethnic group mobilization. As already mentioned, Weber defined ethnicity in terms of dynamic political activity: the existence of a political community is a precondition for ethnic group action. Analysing ancient and contemporary ethnic communities, Weber argued that their political organization was almost regularly decisive for the formation and crystallization of ethnic group sentiments: group consciousness 'was primarily formed by common political experience and not by common descent' (Weber, 1968: 354). In this respect pre-Hellenic tribes were either 'identical with the corresponding political groups which were subsequently associated into a *polis'* or, if politically unorganized, were living from the memories (real or fictional) that they 'once engaged in joint political action'. It is similar with the contemporary cases – German speaking Alsatians feel attached to the French essentially because they share common political memories and experiences. Furthermore the popular use of concepts such as 'people' (*Volk*) and 'nationality' (*Nationalitaet*) which are perceived as entailing ethnic or kin connection, have much more to do with the group's political experience: 'using such terms one usually implies either the existence of a contemporary political community, no matter how loosely organised, or memories of an extinct political community' (Weber, 1948: 177–9). Hence, even though ethnicity is dependent on a belief in common descent, that belief can only be created and sustained through joint political action. There is nothing sociologically unique in ethnic sentiments, 'almost any association' can create 'an overarching communal consciousness' which would take 'the form of a brotherhood on the basis of the belief in common ethnicity' (Weber, 1968: 389). In other words, the sense of ethnic attachment developed in the ethnic ideologies and myths of common ethnic origin comes into play or becomes sociologically relevant only after or during group political mobilization. While political leaders and intellectuals regularly claim primordiality of 'their' ethnic group, invoking the sentiments and beliefs of common descent, these beliefs become meaningful and popular only when the group (as a group) undergoes the process of politically enthused social action. In Weber's words: 'all history shows how easily political action can give rise to the belief in blood relationship, unless gross differences of anthropological type impede it' (1968: 393).

Conclusion

Not only have the classics of sociology developed coherent theories of ethnic relations, well integrated with their general theories of society, but their diverse interpretations of ethnicity have set the tone and direction for contemporary debates. The classics have planted the seeds from which all existing sociological theories of ethnicity have grown. As we shall see in the following chapters neo-Marxism, with its focus on class, culture and capitalism owes a great deal to Marx's theory of ethnicity; functionalism, with its emphasis on group solidarity and disfunctionality of ethnic ties in modernity, is deeply grounded in Durkheim's view of ethnic bonds; symbolic interactionism's stress on the social construction of ethnic reality and the collective definition of ethnic situation are rooted in Simmel's perspective on ethnic relations, and Weber's notions of ethnicity as status group, monopolistic social closure and the political mobilization of ethnic membership are at the core of contemporary neo-Weberianism.

Even approaches that do not directly claim their roots in classical sociological thought build a great deal on the works of the classics. Rational choice theory borrows its economic determinism from Marx and its methodological individualism from Weber to explain ethnicity in terms of individual maximization of collective similarity. Elite theory draws from Weber and Durkheim its emphasis on the importance of symbols in ethnic relations, and from Marx and Weber its insights on the power of rulers to politically mobilize ethnic markers through ideological manipulation. Anti-foundationalist approaches are also in debt to Simmel's view on a fragmented reality of modern social ties and to Weber's multiplicity of ethnic formations of social organization, in their attempt to deconstruct ethnicity and in their relativization of group identities. And finally, even the socio-biological account of ethnicity as extended kinship, based on a belief in common descent, has clear links with similar notions employed by both Durkheim and Weber, whereas its evolutionary theory of societal development is shared also by Marx and Simmel. Let us now explore in greater detail the explanatory consequences of this classical legacy for the contemporary sociology of ethnic relations.

Notes

1   Although, as Nimni (1991: 25) rightly acknowledges, Marx expected that nations would disappear in the long term – in communist society nations would eventually wither away as the State withers away.
2   To be fair, it was Engels who most frequently used this distinction, but Marx never objected to this use, incorporating it into their joint works and making extensive use of these terms in his correspondence with Engels and others.
3   These are some of the more polite descriptions used by Engels, in Marx and Engels, 1977. He also writes about 'reactionary peoples', 'a bloody revenge of the Slav barbarians', the need to annihilate 'all these small pig-headed peoples even to their very names' and so on.
4   On Durkheim's theory of patriotism see Guibernau, 1996: 28–31.
5   According to Simmel (1950: 35) 'masses that are together in physical proximity' show signs of 'collective nervousness – a sensitivity, a passion, an eccentricity that will hardly ever be found in anyone of their members in isolation'.
6   On ethnicism as an ideology of ethnic identification see Jenkins, 1997: 85–8.
7   As Rex (1986a: 14) argues, although ethnic groups often function as status groups not all ethnic groups are status groups and vice versa. Most status groups are not hereditary and their members cannot successfully claim common descent, whereas the relationships between ethnic groups, unlike those of status groups, do not have to be of a hierarchical nature.

8   Weber (1948: 189–90) defines 'sense of dignity' as 'the precipitation in individuals of social honor and of conventional demands which a positively privileged status group raises for the deportment of its members. The sense of dignity that characterizes positively privileged status groups is naturally related to their "being" which does not transcend itself, that is to their "beauty and excellence".'

Chapter Three

NEO-MARXISM:
CAPITALISM, CLASS AND CULTURE

Introduction

One of the pressing aims for post-nineteenth-century Marxist theory was providing a successful answer to the question: Why have ethnicity and 'race' become much more potent sources of group solidarity in the contemporary world than class as predicted by the classics of Marxism? The response came in two forms, leading to the development of two quite different strands of neo-Marxism, one more focused on the political economy of ethnic group inequality and the other interested in the links between ideology, cultural difference and class divisions. These two traditions of research also differ in terms of methods and aims of analysis, wherein the political economy perspective attempts to provide a scientific explanation of social exclusion and ethnic group inequality, while the cultural perspective is more concerned with the strategies and tactics of class and ethnic struggle. Neo-Marxist sociology sees itself as extending analyses put forward by the classics of Marxism in ways that critically engage with and go beyond the main postulates of the classics. Neo-Marxist theories of ethnic relations attempt to overcome the class reductionism of classical Marxism and its apparent failure to predict the strength of ethnic attachments, by attributing a certain level of autonomy to culture in general and ethnic relations in particular. They also look for additional sources of ethnic group antagonism in the contemporary world. However, both traditions of neo-Marxist analysis remain heavily indebted to the arguments and analyses made originally by Marx and his direct followers, by giving primacy to the study of capitalism and the analysis of economic factors of social structure and social action.

Capitalism and ethnic division of labour: political economy of inequality

Drawing on some of the central propositions of Marx, Oliver Cox was one of the first sociologists who developed a coherent and well articulated

Marxist account of ethnicity. His analysis is rooted in a classical Marxist argument that 'race relations can be studied as a form of class exploitation' (Cox, 1945: 360). Focusing primarily on ethnic relations in the US, Cox maintained the view that ethnic group antagonisms are not universal but rather historically specific, that is, they are tied to the origins and needs of capitalist political economy.[1] According to Cox (1948) capitalist-driven expansion required a substantial increase in cheap labour, which was acquired through colonialism and the transportation of slaves to the New World. The cultural and physical differences between African labour and domestic white workers helped capitalists and big business to keep the working class divided along ethnic lines. Capitalism, being rooted in the economic exploitation of one class over another, was described as a social system that is heavily dependent on ethnic group animosity and violence: 'Racial antagonism is part and parcel of this class struggle ... The interest behind racial antagonism is an exploitative interest – the peculiar type of economic exploitation characteristic of capitalist society ... We can under-stand the Negro problem only in so far as we understand their position as workers' (Cox, 1948: xxx–xxxviii). In other words, ethnic group differences are politically meaningful only as an aspect of class relations, and ethnicity is sociologically relevant only as a segment of class politics: 'race relations ... are labour-capital-profits relationships; therefore, race relations are proletarian-bourgeois relationships and hence political-class relations' (1948: 336). Ethnic conflict is no more than hidden class conflict. Cox's theory of ethnicity is firmly embedded in classical Marxism which privileges class over ethnicity, gives primacy to the economic base over the cultural super-structure, and sees 'racial' and ethnic identity claims as something that hinders the development of proletarian consciousness in its long march forward to universal progress.

While Cox's arguments seemed highly persuasive among early post-World War II Marxists, the intensity, frequency and diversity of ethnic conflicts throughout the Cold War world indicated that classical Marxist accounts of ethnicity were unable to explain the variety of forms that ethnic relations can take. Edna Bonacich has tried to respond to shortcomings in Cox's theory by developing a more potent neo-Marxist interpretation of ethnic phenomena. Operating with Marx's and Cox's concepts of 'class' and 'division of labour', Bonacich has developed a much more subtle theory of ethnic relations that puts an interesting twist on classical Marxism – a split labour-market theory. Whereas orthodox Marxists interpreted ethnic antagonisms as an artifically generated 'tool' of the ruling classes to maintain the status quo and existing social conditions by keeping workers separate, Bonacich (1972, 1976) argues that the situation is, in fact, quite the opposite. Unlike Cox or Lecourt (1980), who maintained the view that workers have the same interests and the only obstacle to them uniting was the capitalist-manipulated ethnic and racial ideology, Bonacich believes that the ruling classes in multi-ethnic societies support an open market ideology which allows all workers to compete under similar conditions. Focusing on the examples from South Africa, she demonstrates the complexity of social relations among the labour force and the entrepreneurs. In addition to ordinary workers there is an 'ethnic labour aristocracy' that constantly attempts to keep a monopoly over the better paid and more privileged jobs. Thus, the labour market is, in Bonacich's view, split between three different interest groups: those who control and own enterprises ('the business class'), those who are better paid (and/or are already employed under certain 'ethnic' conditions), and those who are less well-paid (or are seeking employment) because of their ethnic/racial standing.

While the 'business class' has interests in employing a 'cheap labour force', and ethnically underprivileged groups have interests in becoming employed, the better paid 'labour aristocracy' is in danger of losing their position. According to Bonacich (1972), their reaction can be understood as 'pressing for the exclusion of the cheaper class from the territory or resorting to caste arrangements which restrict the cheaper group to a particular set of jobs paid at lower rates'. Correspondingly, the main source of ethic antagonism is the 'differential labour price'. Ethnic conflict does not have to be connected with the position of the dominant group: it is a class conflict between two differently paid labour groups.

While Bonacich's argument seems compelling when applied to two distinct ethnic labour camps, it acquires great difficulties when there are a multiplicity of ethnic collectivities which involve more complex relationships. Neo-Marxism had to go one step further to deal with this problem. The early works of Michael Hechter address the issue of the division of labour more comprehensively. Hechter sees the split labour-market theory as inadequate in accounting for a lack of class solidarity among different ethnic groups who find themselves in the same labour-market position: 'American Blacks and Hispanics are disproportionately represented in the secondary labour market, but neither group seems willing to relinquish its separate identity, and efforts to unite them into "rainbow coalitions" have proven notoriously unsuccessful' (Hechter, 1978: 296). To tackle this problem Hechter has developed a theory of internal colonialism[2] or the reactive-ethnicity model (Hechter, 1974, 1975), which aims to explain ethnic antagonisms, as well as ethnic group solidarity, as a reaction of the 'culturally distinct periphery' against exploitation by the economically and politically dominant centre. Hechter argues that cultural differences attain political importance when uneven economic development in general, and uneven industrialization in particular, generate a spatial division of the population between economically superior and inferior groups. When these structural inequalities overlap with objective cultural differences this is more likely to lead towards ethnic homogenization and group polarization. Echoing Marx and Bonacich, Hechter defines this situation as a 'cultural division of labour'. He argues (1976a: 216) that 'the establishment of a cultural division of labour is inherent to states in the modern world-system, and especially so since the advent of industrialisation. The basic reason for this is that certain types of industrial enterprises need to recruit unskilled labour at minimal cost.' A cultural division of labour is apparent when there is sharply defined group stratification around issues such as inequalities in the educational structure of ethnic groups, structurally imposed differences in the professional mobility of particular ethnic communities, differential access to religious or military institutions, monopolization of political recourses in the hands of a single ethnic group, and so on. Thus, ethnic solidarity is mainly a reaction of the periphery/minority ethnic group to the discrimination and oppression of the centre/dominant ethnic group. Ethnic conflict is more likely when cultural boundaries correspond with socio-economic boundaries: the closer they are, the more likely it is that ethnic conflict will occur. To sum up, economic inequalities increase intra-ethnic group solidarity and inter-ethnic group animosity.

However, this argument fails to explain cases of intensive ethnic group homogeneity among groups that are not economically disadvantaged, such as, for example, American Jews or Chinese in Malaysia and Indonesia. Hechter and Levi (1985) contend with this problem by accepting that the cultural division of labour can have two forms: hierarchical and segmental. While on the segmental level ethnic communities are 'occupationally specialised at any level of the structure', on the hierarchical level a range of ethnic groups is 'vertically distributed in the occupational structure'. This means that the degree of 'occupational specialisation' among some ethnic groups (i.e., identification of specific ethnic groups with particular professions) also has a decisive impact on group perceptions of ethnic group inequality. Hence, to deal with the ever-increasing plurality of ethnic group relations Hechter had to widen his explanatory apparatus in an ad hoc Weberian, albeit deeply materialist Weberian, direction. This solution was rather incomplete, temporary and only vaguely Marxist.

To overcome the problem of dealing with the multiplicity of 'ethnic situations' while remaining within a coherent Marxist theory – a problem that Cox, Bonacich and Hechter could not resolve – Robert Miles (1984, 1989) has developed a theory of the 'political economy of labour migration'. Miles argues that a consistent Marxist account of any group relations has to be formulated in reference to class and production relations. This means that concepts such as 'ethnicity and race' have to be rejected in favour of such terms as 'labour migration' or 'migrant workers'. For Miles 'ethnicity and race' do not describe the reality of group relations, since they are ideological products of an exploitative society: capitalism reifies ethnic group membership to hide real economic relationships. The cultural autonomy of social groups is largely an illusion: 'the "discovery" by "ethnic relations" research of culture constitutes an analytical trap if it is divorced, as it has been, from its historical and material context, that of the development of capitalist relations of production' (Miles, 1982: 70). In Miles' view this trap can be avoided by focusing instead on the capitalist state and its responsibility for the process of 'racialisation'[3] and the 'racialised fraction of the working class'. This can be achieved after identifying the structure of class relations in a particular society and then 'examining the means by which persons are allocated to specific positions within those relations' (Miles, 1984: 229). In his view (p. 230) 'the "black masses" are not a "race" which has to be related to class, but rather are persons whose forms of political struggle can be understood in terms of racialisation within a particular set of production (class) relations'. So, for Miles, race and ethnicity are epiphenomena that cannot be explained in their own right; they are deeply tied to the relations of production and the nature of the capitalist state. Cultural and physical group difference has meaning only in so far as it relates to the different class positions which people occupy in production relations. The so-called 'minority groups' are really migrant labourers (or children of migrant labourers) whose position is less determined by their cultural features and more by the irrationality of the capitalist economy. The migrant labour phenomenon is a product of the contradiction inherent in capitalism between 'on the one hand the need of the capitalist world economy for the mobility of human beings, and on the other, the drawing of territorial boundaries and the construction of citizenship as a legal category which sets boundaries for human mobility' (Miles, 1988: 438). The importance Miles attributes to the role of ideology in capitalism links his political economy perspective indirectly to the Gramscian tradition.

Culture, class and hegemony: the Gramscian legacy

The second and perhaps more influential neo-Marxist approach in the study of ethnic relations is built on the heritage of Marx's early works and especially on the contributions of Antonio Gramsci. The explanatory framework of this branch of Marxism is distinctively cultural, focusing predominantly on the role of ideology and cultural hegemony in a capitalist society.

Gramsci introduced the concept of hegemony in his analysis of the ideological power of capitalism. His main aim was to explain the apparent lack of support for proletarian revolution among the Western working classes. Classical Marxism, with its strong emphasis on political economy and modes of production, proved inadequate in dealing with this problem which, for Gramsci, was more cultural than economic. Echoing the early Marx, Gramsci argues that the capitalist state was successful in its prevention of radical dissent not only through its control of the means of material pro-duction but also (and more importantly) through cultural and ideological hegemony. Gramsci (1971: 328) characterizes hegemony as the potential of dominant social groups in society to ensure the 'spontaneous consent' of the dominated social groups by 'preserving the ideological unity of the entire social block which that ideology serves to cement and to unify'. Hegemony is an ideological terrain where the State and civil society meet and through which (contrived) cultural unity among distinct economic and political classes is achieved. For Gramsci, hegemony is not merely ideological mani-pulation or the brainwashing of one class by another, but rather, it is a form of subtle and partially negotiated cultural assimilation through which ideological consensus between the ruling and subordinate classes is estab-lished. As Gramsci argues, this is achieved in many different ways – through dominant forms of religion or philosophy, but also through hegemonic practices of everyday life in the form of prevailing conceptions of 'common sense', daily ritualism and folklore.

Although Gramsci was not explicitly concerned with ethnicity, his writings on the 'southern question' in Italy provide an insight into the relationship between culture, class and hegemony. For Gramsci the southern question was an ethnic, social and class question which could not be resolved along the principles of classical Marxism and its class dichotomy of proletariat ver-sus bourgeoisie. Gramsci developed a concept of 'national-popular' collec-tive to explain the lack of ethnic, cultural and political unity in Italy. The proletariat cannot become a dominant force and acquire a counter-hegemonic position unless it forges strategic alliances with other social groups, most of all multi-ethnic and predominantly peasant Southerners. Sardinian, Apulian or Sicilian peasants, together with Northern workers and organic intellectuals, have to form a 'national-popular historical block' that would emerge as a decisive agent of social change. As Gramsci (1978) points out, the proletariat can become a leading social group only when it 'succeeds in creating a system of alliances which allows it to mobilise the majority of the working population against capitalism and the bourgeois state ... [which] means to the extent it succeeds in gaining the consent of the broad [and multi-ethnic] peasant masses ... [since] only two forces are essentially national and bearers of the future: the proletariat and the peasants'. To achieve this 'national-popular' block one has to penetrate all pores of civil society by making an appeal to national unity through civic and religious rituals, folklore and 'common sense'. A 'national-popular' collectivity cuts across class and ethnic borders and is built around active popular consent, termed a 'collective will' by Gramsci: 'Any formation of a national-popular collective will is impossible unless the great mass of peasant farmers bursts simultaneously into political life ... All history from 1815 onwards shows the efforts of the traditional classes to prevent the formation of a collective will of this kind, and to maintain "economic corporate" power in an international system of passive equilibrium' (Gramsci, 1971: 132). So for Gramsci, unlike Marx, ethnicity has an autonomous strength which can be strategically utilized to obtain broader popular consent in the project of establishing a proletarian society.

Drawing on Gramsci's central ideas, a number of sociologists working at the Centre for Contemporary Cultural Studies in Birmingham in the 1970s and 1980s have developed original and influential accounts of ethnic relations. Hall, Gilroy, Solomos, Gabriel and Ben-Tovim became representatives of what is today known as the Birmingham school of cultural Marxism, whose main aim was to go beyond the narrow instrumentalism of class dichotomy and the economic determinism of classical Marxist positions. Starting originally from a similar and Gramscian-inspired position, representatives of the Birmingham school have developed fairly distinct approaches to the study of ethnicity.

Stuart Hall's work was the most influential and most strongly grounded in the Gramscian tradition. Hall follows Gramsci's argument that race and ethnicity have relative autonomy from other social relations. In his view rigid economistic analysis is unable to elucidate the subtlety of ethnic relations, which take a number of very distinct forms. In this respect he is critical of classical Marxism that sees ethnic conflict as no more than a hidden class conflict. For Hall (1980, 1986) ethnic antagonisms are historically specific: racism is not a universal characteristic of humankind, there are only particular and historically specific forms of racism. Uneven and differential historical developments of particular regions or societies determine that ethnic enmities have themselves an uneven impact within given populations. Because of these different and historically shaped conditions the relationship between class and ethnicity is often complex and contradictory. For Hall 'class subject' has a non-homogeneous character that allows for phenomena such as working-class racism: 'ethnic and racial difference can be constructed as a set of economic, political or ideological antagonisms, *within* a class which is subject to roughly similar forms of exploitation with respect to ownership of and expropriation from the "means of production"' (Hall, 1986: 25, italics in original.). Although ethnicity cannot be reduced to class it still is not possible to explain ethnic relations in abstraction from class relations. In Hall's view (1980) race and ethnicity have a decisive impact on class consciousness; they are reciprocal relationships, they affect each other and what is important is their articulation, not their separateness.

Articulation is a key concept in Hall's theoretical apparatus. It refers to an ambiguous, relative and often temporary link between different elements whose relationship is dynamic, open to change and to permanent re-articulation. It is a unity of elements that compose a complex structure, 'in which things are related, as much through their differences as through their similarities. This requires that the mechanisms which connect dissimilar features must be shown – since no "necessary correspondence" or expressive homology can be assumed as given' (Hall, 1980: 325). Hall emphasizes that the '"unity" which matters is a linkage between the articulated discourse and the social forces with which it can, under certain historical conditions, but need not necessarily, be connected' (1996a: 141). Articulation is shaped around the 'moments of arbitrary closure', which means that the dynamics of social processes are (artificially) impeded once one identifies a single element as an explanatory master key. Hence for Hall, ethnicity and class have a relative autonomy from each other but are deeply related to each other through this dynamic process of articulation. In the same way class and ethnicity have a relative autonomy from the State – unlike the classical Marxism that saw the State as an agent of the bourgeoisie, Hall, following Gramsci, argues that the State is not only a coercive force but, with its 'educative' and 'ideological' character, it is also an enabling force. In its dialectical relationship with civil society it provides potential for the construction of counter-hegemonic discourses and practices relating to the dynamics of ethnic group interaction.

John Gabriel and Gideon Ben-Tovim (1979) go even further in criticizing the classical Marxist assumptions of the reducibility of ethnicity to class. Their argument is that ethnic relations do not have merely relative autonomy from class relations but full autonomy. In their view the relative autonomy perspective is theoretically limiting since it represents no more than a sophisticated angle of class determinism, which is not only theoretically reductionist but it paralyses political action in the struggle against ethnic inequality and racism. While class can play a significant role in ethnic relations, the relationship between the two cannot be posed in such an *a priori* way. For Gabriel and Ben-Tovim (1979) ethnic and racial relations are the products of historical and contemporary struggles, where primary importance is attached to the ideological level, 'since it is only after the ideological production of racist [and ethnic] ideologies that they intervene at the level of the economy and of political practice' (Solomos, 1986: 96). The pair concur with Gramsci and Hall that the State is not simply an agent of the capitalist class but an arena of permanent struggles and compromises. However, they differ from Gramsci and Hall in their ambition to privilege agency over structure and to 'highlight the political and ideological context in which anti-racist struggles occur' (Solomos, 1986: 96). Theirs is a much more policy-driven approach, which aims to be closer 'to the spirit of Marxism', with the emphasis on the 'unity of theory and practice' or 'praxis' (Ben-Tovim et al., 1986: 151).

Paul Gilroy has pursued a different line of argument by engaging analytically with and borrowing from non-Marxist perspectives on ethnicity. Resonating some key ideas of symbolic interactionism (see Chapter 6), he sees race and ethnicity as essentially contested and open social constructions that, on the one hand, serve as potent symbols for and of group solidarity and political action and, on the other, operate as signifiers around which major political struggles are fought. In a Gramscian vein Gilroy (1987) sees concepts of 'race' and 'ethnicity' as powerful strategic images that can help to mobilize relatively coherent forces of opposition against the existing social order. While he recognizes that race and ethnicity are no more than just markers of group identities and that identities are always multiple, Gilroy still believes that these markers can be strategically employed to form pressure groups and social movements, which would bring about decisive social change. In this respect he advocates the fundamental revision of class-centred analysis, by suggesting that Marxism has to 'incorporate political movements that mobilise around forms of identity other than class' (Solomos, 1995: 413). He shifts the focus of his analysis from class to social movements, which are seen as having significant autonomy from class relations. Just like Gabriel and Ben-Tovim, Gilroy privileges the concept of class struggle over class structure, focusing in particular on the position of black workers as being 'racially structured'. In Gilroy's own words, 'The class character of black struggles is not a result of the fact that blacks are predominantly proletarian … [but of] the fact that their struggles for civil rights, freedom from state harassment, or as waged workers, are instances of the process by which the working class is constituted politically' (1982: 392). Gilroy is sceptical of the view that parliamentary democracy is an adequate setting for the realization of ethnic group equality, and sees organized social movements that include a plurality of marginalized groups as having much more potential in this struggle.

Is ethnicity class after all?

With all its explanatory diversity neo-Marxism remains occupied with the questions set within the parameters of classical Marxism: What is the relationship between ethnicity and class? In which way does capitalism influence ethnic conflicts? How do rulers justify their privileged economic and political position in ethnic terms? Where neo-Marxism starts to differ from its classical forefathers is in the answers given to these questions. While most strands of neo-Marxism remain firmly rooted in the legacy of the classics in explaining ethnic relations in economic and class terms, their answers to these questions tend to be much more subtle, analytic, empirically better grounded or theoretically refined. Neo-Marxism rightly emphasizes the link between ethnicity and class inequality. In the modern capitalist economies it is very often that one can identify formidable overlaps between class and ethnic group membership. Just travelling through North America, Australia and Western Europe one can easily observe the patterns of ethnic divisions of labour, wherein culturally distinct (first or second generation) immigrant groups occupy a disproportionately high percentage of unskilled or lower skilled professions. There is also very little doubt that such a situation benefits big businesses that thrive on the existence of a cheap labour force. It also seems plausible that when in a position to do so, powerful entrepreneurs would manipulate cultural differences in order to divide and more easily exploit workers. Neo-Marxists have been very successful in empirically documenting the cases of class-based ethnic inequality and in finding sources of this inequality in the discriminatory practices of the capitalist state. However, the problem with neo-Marxism is that its narrative is simply too wide historically, and too narrow geographically and epistemologically, to deal with the variety of forms that ethnicity takes. Neo-Marxism aims to explain too much with a single set of factors and it also attempts to universalize what often tend to be a set of particular social conditions. In other words, regardless of the much more refined theoretical and empirical tools used, neo-Marxism remains chained in the problematic logic of classical Marxism. I will focus here only on three main shortcomings of neo-Marxist accounts of ethnic relations: a) the tricky relationship between ethnicity and class; b) the economistic nature of neo-Marxist arguments; and c) the complex relationship between ethnicity and ideology.

While ethnicity can overlap with class the two are very distinct concepts. As Weber and Rex remind us (see Chapters 2 and 9) ethnicity can as easily overlap with status, caste or estate. Contemporary South Africa is a very good example of such ethnic group dynamics: whereas the apartheid era was characterized by the dominance of ethnic groups framed as castes, today they undergo restructuring along the lines of status and class groups, with the formation of a 'black aristocracy', 'multi racial middle class' and 'black underclass' (Sparks, 1995). Not only is ethnicity too dynamic an entity to be submerged under class, but the class relations themselves are equally hazy. In its search for a cheaper labour force and wider markets, a globalized capitalism (unintentionally?) fosters higher degrees of social mobility[4] than any other previous economic system, and in that way it breaks traditional class barriers with new lines of polarization between those with permanent and long-term employment, and those who are on short-term contracts or unemployed (Nash, 2000). Any reduction of ethnicity to class in the manner of Marx and Cox is guilty of this double error: class reductionism and class absolutism. While neo-Marxism does not reduce ethnicity to class, it still has to maintain the primacy of class and production relations in its explanation of ethnic group action. Attributing to ethnicity a degree of relative (as in Hall) or absolute (as in

Gabriel and Ben-Tovim) autonomy makes it more appealing to non-Marxists but, at the same time, it undermines its own explanatory potential. What is distinct and enlightening about the Marxist argument is its focus on the links between ethnicity and class. Once they recognize that this link is not so straightforward and is often rather provisional, the entire concept is at the verge of collapse. That is probably one of the main reasons why Hall and Gilroy have moved from neo-Marxism to anti-foundational post-Marxism in their more recent works (see Chapter 10).

Furthermore, focusing on ethnicity as an instrument of class exploitation only (as argued by Marxists who profess a political economy perspective) underestimates the significant power of ethnicity as a mobilizing, enabling force. In downgrading the potency of ethnic symbols and myths, such as a mighty myth of common ethnic origin, the political economy view is unable to explain non-instrumental aspects of ethnic group behaviour. As Smith (1983, 1998) and Connor (1994) rightly point out, economic exploitation in itself is not enough for the successful mobilization of ethnic group action. While economic inequality might help intensify a feeling of ethnic injustice, for the most part it plays only a 'catalytic role' in the process of ethnic group mobilization. So ethnicity does not have to be related to economic inequality at all, as we encounter cases of compelling ethnic group action among economically and politically superior as well as inferior groups, and in the context of economic decline just as in circumstances of economic boom. For example, it is evident that underdeveloped and economically disadvantaged regions such as Chechenia and Kosovo were able to generate as powerful ethno-political movements as economically advanced and privileged Catalonia and Estonia. On the other hand there are numerous historical and contemporary cases where one ethnic group persistently and systematically exploits another without any meaningful resistance on the part of the subordinated group (e.g., the subordination of Dalits in Southeast Asia, Buraku and Ainu in Japan, or Roma populations in Eastern Europe). Hence, although ethnicity can occasionally overlap with class, it possesses a decisive degree of autonomy from class and economic relations.

This brings us to the second criticism of the neo-Marxist theory of ethnicity. Both strands of neo-Marxism maintain a strong economistic line of argument where ethnicity is in one way or another perceived as an epiphenomenon – as a second order reality. Whereas the political economy perspective does this in a fairly explicit way, it is more implicit in the Gramscian tradition. Marxism sees ethnic group divisions as largely artificial products of the capitalist economy. Although entrepreneurs have interests in segmenting the working class along the principles of divide and rule, it is really the structural argument that is at the heart of this theory – the view that the structural features of capitalism determine group inequities. Capitalism is rooted in the process of production where the only real interest is accumulation of profit through appropriation of surplus value by the exploitation of the labour force and commodity exchange. According to the Marxist argument this process in itself creates mutually antagonistic classes. When subordinated groups are unaware of their disadvantaged position and the exploitative nature of the capitalist system, they are seen as lacking full class-consciousness within the environment of the hegemonic capitalist state. Even when it attempts to attribute some degree of autonomy to ethnicity, this model is so sturdily tied to economic structure that it cannot be refined, made more reflexive or reformulated without loosing its explanatory power. Not only is it that this model leaves very little room for individual action and free will, and pays scant or no attention to non class-based types of inequality (e.g., gender, sexual orientation, disability or age), more significantly, its crude economic materialism does not allow for the changing nature of in-group and out-group relationships.

Ruling out the genuine autonomy of culture, that is, allowing for the existence of non-materialist motives and sources of group action such as pride, status seeking, face saving, emotions, value-commitments, beliefs and so on, Marxism commits an error of which it (Miles in particular) accuses capitalism – it reifies group membership in seeing individuals essentially as little more than the bearers of particular class roles which are produced by the logic of the capitalist economy. Bonacich and Hechter's attempts to broaden and refine this model by introducing new actors (ethnic labour aristocracy) or by shifting the argument from agency to territory (ethnically distinct centre and periphery) cannot overcome this central problem of Marxist economism and its insensitivity to the dynamics of ethnic relations. More specifically, both accounts have been criticized for overextending their respective arguments and generalizing on the basis of very specific geographical or historical conditions (Burawoy, 1981; Kellas, 1991), thereby exhibiting factual shortcomings and conflating territorial regions with ethnic groups (Smith, 1998). Even though the Gramscian tradition is considerably more sensitive towards values, culture and ideology, which are the key concepts here, together with hegemony and articulation, it too remains tied to the logic of economic determinism. This is most apparent in its view of ethnicity as an ideology and a potential strategic device of social development.

The final point of criticism is the neo-Marxist conceptualization of ethnicity as a form of ideology. While Gramscianism has moved significantly from Marx's and Engels' description of ideology as a 'false consciousness' induced by the capitalist system to prevent development of proletarian unity, it still maintains a deeply instrumentalist view of culture and ideology. Ideology and cultural hegemony still have little power of their own and are coupled with the economic system of the capitalist state. Although Hall and Gilroy see the State in much more dynamic terms as a site of permanent ideological struggle between various civil society groups, hegemonic and counter-hegemonic practices are attributed not to self-reflexive individuals or changing and often amorphous collectivities, but to gritty large class blocks – workers, peasants or bourgeoisie. In this respect ethnicity appears as autonomous or semi-autonomous but never completely divorced from class politics or the capitalist system. In a Machiavellian vein the Gramscian tradition perceives ideology and hegemony most of all as a strategic device for acquiring the full support from 'racial and ethnic groups' in establishing a proletarian society. In this way Gramscianism stands firmly in the footsteps of classical Marxism, believing that regardless of its power of appeal ethnic group membership remains secondary to class identity. While 'hegemony' and 'articulation' appear to be useful categories in analysing subtle forms of achieving ethnic consensus between asymmetrically positioned in-group members, in Gramscianism they remain tied to the modes of production and the capitalist economy.

The general problem with this argument is that it is unable to account for ethnic antagonism in societies where industrialization and capitalism are minimal, such as in more remote parts of Africa, Asia and Latin America, or in societies where the economy is firmly in the hands of the all-powerful non-capitalist state, as it was in communist Eastern Europe or in Cuba. Unlike the political economy perspective, which flirts with positivist science, Gramscianism is much more prescriptive than descriptive or analytical. Following directly Gramsci's advice, Gabriel, Ben-Tovim and Gilroy explicitly state that the neo-Marxist position should focus on the mechanisms of class struggle (to arm ideologically disadvantaged ethnic groups and classes), instead of the 'mere scientific' analysis of class structure. This form of reasoning is clearly problematic since it is derived from the teleological neo-Hegelian theory of history that still believes that one can discover 'historical laws of social development', though in this particular case the laws of class struggle. As Banton (1987: 153) observes, since this Hegelian epistemology is grounded in the belief 'that future developments can be anticipated and inform present-day politics', it 'contend[s] that there is a moral obligation to direct research towards such issues'. This is a form of historical determinism that again leaves very little space for free-thinking agents or for genuine autonomy of culture, and only confirms that, despite its subtlety, sophistication and refinement, neo-Marxism cannot transcend the view that ethnicity is class after all.

Conclusion

Neo-Marxism originated as an attempt to overcome the pitfalls of the classical Marxist approach to ethnicity. Marx's emphasis on the primacy of the economic base over ethnic superstructure, and the historical ascendancy of class over ethnicity are softened with the introduction of new concepts and models such as 'internal colonialism', 'split labour-market', 'political economy of the migrant labour' or 'relative and absolute autonomy of ethnicity'. Neo-Marxism recognizes the social realities of the contemporary world, where ethnicity remains a much more salient and stubborn phenomenon than was originally envisaged. Contemporary neo-Marxist research is at its best when it empirically uncovers patterns of class-based ethnic group inequality and their links to discriminatory policies of the State in capitalism, and when it pinpoints the cases where the State functions as an arena for the reproduction of ethnically structured relations (e.g., the South African state and its role in institutionalizing the apartheid system). Nevertheless, neo-Marxism still shares a view with the Marxist classics that there is no problem of ethnic conflict or racism 'which can be thought of as separate from the structural features of capitalist society' (Solomos, 1986:107). While ethnic relations are now perceived as being historically specific and, as such, comparatively autonomous, they are still thought of as requiring an explanation which can only be provided through historical analysis that is concentrated on the rise and spread of capitalism and class inequalities. Despite the refinement of its theoretical and research tools, neo-Marxism remains deeply economistic and class centred and, as such, it is unable to produce a balanced and comprehensive theory of ethnic relations that can deal with the multiplicity of ethnic forms.

Notes

1   It is important to contextualize the development of Cox's theoretical position. As one of the first established 'black sociologists' in the US he was writing in an environment where the dominant views of the day where largely ahistorical, interpreting American 'race relations' as being nearly identical to the caste system in India.

2   The term 'internal colonialism' was borrowed from Lenin.

3   The origins of the concept of 'racialization' can be traced back to the work of Fanon (1967).

4   As the representatives of the anti-globalization movement argue, this might be predominantly downward mobility but that does not disqualify this argument.

Chapter Four

FUNCTIONALISM: ETHNICITY, MODERNIZATION AND SOCIAL INTEGRATION

Introduction

Just as in the case of contemporary Marxists, the Durkheimian tradition had to engage with the largely unexpected salience of ethnic attachments in the modern era. Durkheim's conviction that ethnic bonds will decline as industrialization, urbanization and a more complex division of labour take hold was as equally challenged by social reality as was Marx's belief that class will supersede ethnicity with the intensification and growth of capitalism. The neo-Durkheimian reaction to this unforeseen situation also came in two different but compatible functionalist forms: as a general theory of society formulated through principles of structural-functionalism, and as a specific theory of ethnic cleavages articulated as a plural society approach. However, the functionalist answer to the puzzle of ethnicity in modernity bears no similarity to neo-Marxist attempts to deal with this problem. On the contrary, unlike the Marxist emphasis on economy and strategies of class struggle, functionalism has developed a response that is completely focused on ethnicity as a peculiar form of group solidarity, and on modes of ethnic group incorporation into the larger framework of the functional nation-state. Moreover functionalism, in both of its forms, remains firmly loyal to the principles established by the early Durkheimian position, with its highlight on norms, values and ideas as being the main generators of social development. Although contemporary functionalists have developed more advanced and complex theoretical models and research tools for the study of social life, they are even more strictly grounded in preserving the legacy of Durkheim than neo-Marxism is with Marx. With the possible exception of Alexander's brand of neo-functionalism, functionalist approaches to ethnicity are stubbornly attached to their conviction that the process of modernization will, in the last instance, obliterate the existence of ethnicity. In this respect the structural-functionalist perception of ethnicity as a specific form of de-differentiation, and the pluralist's search for mechanisms of integration for 'ethnic units' remain, in explanatory and normative terms, chained by the logic of classical functionalism.

Modernization and ethnic group solidarity

Structural-functionalism was a dominant sociological perspective through-out the 1940s, 1950s and early 1960s and has experienced a revival as 'neo-functionalism' in the 1980s and 1990s. While this theoretical position is extremely rich and diverse, ethnicity has been an object of analysis only spo-radically. It is only in the works of Talcot Parsons and Jeffrey Alexander that one can detect a coherent and well articulated functionalist account of eth-nic relations. Although distinct, their interpretations of ethnicity are built around central tenets of structural-functionalism, such as:

- societies are social systems that share general value patterns
- social systems avoid conflict and aim towards the state of normality (equilibrium) analogous to the state of health in an organism
- parts of the system are generally interdependent and each performs a particular function that contributes to successful functioning and repro-duction of the system as a whole
- when the system is in crisis it searches for alternative ways by which its parts can be reorganized to attain a new state of equilibrium.

When analysing the role of ethnicity in the operation of the social systems, structural-functionalists resonate the three dominant topics of Durkheim's theory of ethnicity: the focus on ethnic group solidarity, the function of an ethnic group as a moral compass for individual behavi-our, and the view that modernization is a process that sweeps away ethnic identities.

All three of these themes are examined in Parsons' system theory. When dis-cussing ethnic relations Parsons predominantly focuses on the analysis of 'shared value systems'.[1] Parsons sees individual actors as normative creatures whose behaviour is largely determined by deeply internalized normative expectations, which are coincident with the process of socialization.[2] Social actors are directed by cultural traditions, that is 'shared symbolic systems which function in interaction' (Parsons, 1951: 11). Hence it is the general systems and not the individual actors that are at the forefront of his theory. Parsons (1951, 1966) identified four main prerequisites that every 'action' system has to fulfil to function properly: adaptation, goal attainment, inte-gration and latent pattern maintenance tension management. Adaptation relates to the system's ability to secure and distribute adequate resources from the environment. Goal attainment deals with the system's potential to mobilize those and other resources and to achieve the goals of a system through the creation of goal hierarchies. Integration involves regulation, adjustment and co-ordination of a variety of actors and units within a system with the view of keeping the system operational. And, finally, latent pattern maintenance relates to the system's ability to maintain common central values of the system as a whole, where social actors have to be motivated to manage tensions and preserve the dominant cultural patterns of the system.

According to Parsons (1966) 'action' systems also undergo social change. Focusing on the evolution of social systems he argues that societies evolve through the process of 'continually increasing differentiation', which involves an increase in the division of labour leading to the creation of new sub-systems. These new structures tend to be more specialized in their functions, and have to be more adaptive in a new and much more complex environment. Differentiation is a precondition for technological development, specialization, secularization and modernization. The dominance of 'kinship roles' decreases as more complex systems entail meritocracy. The system, in Parsons' own words: 'requires the inclusion in a status of full membership in the relevant general community system of previously excluded groups which have developed legitimate capacities to "contribute" to the functioning system' (1966: 22). Complex systems also stipulate 'value generalization', that is, a development of common value patterns shared by a great majority of the population, such as state patriotism instead of particular group attachments. However, systems can also experience a decrease in the division of labour when sub-systems assume more functions, leading to the process of 'de-differentiation'.

So where is the place for ethnicity in this scheme? Parsons defines ethnic groups as 'an aggregate of kinship units, the members of which either trace their origin in terms of descent from a common ancestor or in terms of descent from ancestors who all belonged to the same categorised ethnic group' (1951: 172). Ethnicity is seen by Parsons (1975: 56) as a 'diffusely defined group', with a unique sense of identity embedded in a 'distinctive sense of its history'. Building on Durkheim's emphasis on group solidarity Parsons argues that the main sociological feature of ethnic groups is their transgenerational group endurance. Although diffused, ethnicity is a specific form of group solidarity, composed of the two essential building blocks – 'transgenerational cultural tradition' and a voluntary adherence to the group (Parsons, 1975: 58). While voluntary commitment to group loyalty is a significant force it is really the impact of the cultural tradition, which includes components such as the maintenance of common language, common cultural history or the normative expectations for the continuation of a particular tradition, that remains decisive for the preservation of ethnic group solidarity.

In relation to Parsons' general systems theory, ethnicity belongs to the fiduciary system[3] (together with the educational system or the family), which is responsible for the transmission of dominant values, i.e., for the process of socialization and the internalization of group norms. However, ethnicity differs from 'collectivities with specific functions' because it represents a mixture of 'the community and kinship types'. Ethnic group solidarity directly entails that the ethnic group acts as a moral guardian of individual and group behaviour. The continuity of cultural tradition implies a symbolic link between what Edmund Burke (1968 [1790]) has referred to as a partnership between 'those who are living, those who are dead and those who are yet to be born'. The preservation of ethnic symbols such as language, religion, particular customs, eating habits or traditional clothing establishes a link between the past, present and future. Wearing a Sikh turban in New York or London is not only a symbol of the past but, more importantly, it is a statement about the future. It indicates a moral responsibility for passing on the ethnic group's traditions and, simultaneously, it is an indicator of the moral worth of a particular individual Sikh. In this context an ethnic group operates as a moral community in a true Durkheimian sense: the boundaries of an ethnic group set the limits of moral behaviour.

> Just as in the kinship context an individual is ascriptively the child of his parents, so in a societal community the citizen is ascriptively one of the heirs of his forebears in the societal community and will be one of the 'progenitors' of the future community so that many of the consequences of the actions of contemporaries cannot be escaped by future members in new generations. (Parsons, 1975: 61)

The final segment of Parsons' theory of ethnic relations deals with the impact of modernization on ethnicity. In line with his evolutionary theory of social development, he sees ethnic identities as a throwback to the past which will gradually dissipate in favour of national identities. A more complex division of labour, rationalization of social institutions, industrialization, the expansion of mass communication systems, the rapid increase in spatial and social mobility as well as urbanization have transformed the character of ethnic groups. With the arrival of modernization and the development of mass industrial societies, ethnic groups have lost their structural function and have become primarily cultural and symbolic groups. Parsons argues that ethnic groups undergo a process of 'de-socialization', which means that ethnicity persists only in form, while its content has changed to accommodate structural requirements of an industrial society: ethnic symbols are empty markers of group identity. The de-socialization of ethnicity is an aspect of broader historical change – the evolutionary differentiation of societies.

The revival of ethnicity during the 1960s and 1970s, however (something that Parsons himself experienced), indicated that ethnicity had not vanished as the theory predicted. Parsons sees this development as a form of social regression that can be explained with the help of his concept of de-differentiation. According to Parsons (1975: 69) 'the de-differentiating tendency is to select particular criteria and use these as identifying symbols for what the persons who constitute the group actually *are*'.[4] Echoing Durkheim, Parsons explains that the de-differentiation in this case arises as a result of dramatic and swift social changes, which lead to the state of anomie, individual alienation and 'intensification of groupism'. In the pluralized social structure of modern industrial society, individuals are forced to operate with multiple identities by having to perform multiple and often conflicting social roles. Intensification of a singe (ethnic) group identity provides a sense of security, serenity and stability. However, this model proved to be too narrow to accommodate unpredicted explosions of ethnic group sentiments from the 1960s onwards.

To deal with such a static and mostly anti-empirical research programme, Alexander has attempted to reformulate and revise some of the central principles of structural-functionalism. This new, more synthetic attempt, was termed 'neo-functionalism' (Alexander, 1985, 1998; Alexander and Colomy, 1990). Neo-functionalism strives for more empirical and historical analysis, a better-nuanced understanding of conflict and the incorporation of contingency and social change as well as more micro level analysis. Alexander also aims to widen Parsons' theory of ethnic relations to deal with the salience of ethnic group identities in the contemporary era.

Unlike Parsons, Alexander attributes a significant role to 'primordial attachments' in the retention of ethnic group identities,[5] and even defines ethnicity along these lines. 'We define ethnicity as the real or perceived primordial qualities that accrue to a group by virtue of shared race, religion, or national origin, including in the latter category linguistic and other cultural attributes associated with a common territorial ancestry' (Alexander, 1980: 10–11). He is critical of Enlightenment-inspired rationalism and classical structural-functionalism that saw, in a linear evolutionary model, ethnicities as relics of the past that will disappear under the wheels of uniform modernization. In his view, differentiation is a dynamic and uneven process dependent on the levels of social inclusion, that is, on the changes in 'solidarity status'. According to Alexander (1980) the levels and patterns of group solidarity determine the outlook of social inclusion in any given society.[6] Inclusion of ethnic groups is dependent on two key variables – the environmental (external) factor and the volitional (internal) factor. While the environmental factor includes 'the structure of society that surrounds the core group', the volitional factor 'refers to the relationship between the primordial qualities of core group and outgroup' (1980: 11) In other words, the external factor encompasses the social structure of a particular society (e.g., economic, political or religious system) whereas the internal factor relates to the cultural specifities of individual ethnic groups within a society. Alexander believes that the intensity of structural differentiation in accord with the environmental factor determines the level of social inclusion, while volition is shaped by the 'primordial complementarity' between the groups.

Alexander (1985), unlike Parsons, sees social integration not as a given fact but as a social possibility. He identifies three potential directions that ethnic mobilization and inclusion can take: assimilation, ethnically conscious inclusion, and ethnic secession. When the environmental factor advances intensive differentiation and the internal factor allows for the closure of the 'primordial gap', the ethnic out-group is in a position to identify with the 'primordial qualities of the core group', i.e., to become assimilated. In situations when there is a greater degree of 'primordial divergence' between the groups and a lack of vital structural differentiation, the ethnic groups are more likely to espouse group-centred social action and attempt equal or preferential access to state institutions. This is a case of ethnically conscious inclusion. In circumstances where there is a minimal or non-existent structural differentiation or extensive inflexibility in terms of 'primordial differences', and where there are favourable geo-political factors, strong ethnic consciousness is likely to lead to ethnic secession. In all three of these different 'incorporative strategies' the central role is attributed to solidarity since ethnic groups are seen as being 'founded by solidary core groups'. Uneven differentiation affects the levels of inter-group animosity but what is crucial for Alexander in the explanation of this antagonism is the concentration of the specific 'primordial qualities' of the particular ethnic groups. As he aptly sums it up: 'On the internal axis, inclusion varies according to the degree of primordial complementarity between core group and solidary outgroup. On the external axis, inclusion varies according to the degree of institutional differentiation in the host society' (Alexander, 1980: 24). At the heart of this position is a view that conflicts between ethnic groups have more to do with the dominant group values than with the individual or group material interests.

Plural society and the modes of ethnic incorporation

The theory of plural societies does not belong nominally to the corpus of conventional sociological approaches. As one of its influential proponents claims, plural society theory is 'neither a general theory of society, nor even a general theory of race and ethnic relations. It is a theory about a particular type of society, which seems somewhat unique and unpredictable, and which raises questions for orthodox sociological theory' (Kuper, 1980: 246). Plural society approach arose out of the need to explain the emergence of what was thought to be a new phenomenon inherited as a legacy of colonialism – internally divided societies under a single political roof. The inventor of the concept, J. S. Furnivall (1948), believed that this new situation could not be explained using standard sociological interpretations, and he argued that the specificity and particularity of ethnic divisions in the post-colonial world needed new theoretical and research tools. Following Furnivall, pluralism was conceived as a sole theory of ethnic relations, which would be able to engage with this new type of social phenomenon. It was argued that each post-colonial society is unique and demands a separate explanation. For pluralists no single factor, single general theory, or single set of general recommendations is possible. It was claimed that only the plural society theory is able to study ethnic cleavages as 'a phenomenon in its own right, a social force not reducible to other social forces' (Kuper, 1980: 240). However, as I demonstrate later, such a strong claim to explanatory uniqueness is not really justified. When placed under strict scrutiny most plural society positions exhibit features of functionalism: when analysing ethnic relations their arguments, just like their stated motives and recommendations, remain profoundly functionalist. Even the most influential functionalists such as Alexander find strong links between structural-functionalism and plural society theory.[7]

So what is a plural society? In a nutshell, a plural society is a culturally deeply divided society cohabiting under a single political and institutional system of authority. Furnivall (1948) distinguished between two main types of societies – those characterized by cultural homogeneity and based on 'normative consensus' and those strongly divided along ethnic lines and regulated by force, that is, plural societies. Kuper (1980) defines plural societies as political units under a single political authority that are based on the internal divisions of an ethnic, racial or religious nature, and which maintain distinctive ways of living. While the period of de-colonization has brought these societies into the focus of sociological analysis, ethnic antagonisms between distinct communities living under a single political authority are certainly not new. That is one of the key reasons why Furnivall's early emphasis on the post-colonial world has been widened by other pluralists to include all those societies that are characterized by deep cultural cleavages, and where ethnic groups experience institutional separation as well as differential and unequal incorporation.[8] While there is a general agreement between pluralists around the central principles of this approach there are also significant differences: Furnivall (1948) stresses the dominance of economic forces in the shaping and persistence of plural societies ('the groups are held together by the market place'); M. G. Smith (1965) emphasizes cultural and structural aspects of pluralism, and Kuper (1974) views plural societies as those that are largely determined by political factors.[9] Since Smith's account of plural society is generally considered to be the most influential and most representative of a pluralist position, let us focus more closely on his theory.

M. G. Smith writes about plural societies in terms of a 'unit[s] of disparate parts which owe[s] their existence to external factors, and lack[s] a common social will' (1965: vii). Different ethnic segments of a plural society are held together, according to Smith, only by the monopolization of one of the segments through political power. These 'ethnic units' function as independent entities that have very little mutual contact and almost no influence on each other. What is crucial for Smith is the point that these ethnic segments are 'differentially integrated' into a common society and as such they remain deeply unstable. These different forms of institutional integration establish the extent of internal normative cohesion in a particular society. As he argues:

> If the members of the society share a common system of institutions, then they will also share a common framework and pattern of social relations; and their internal differentiation by corporate and personal status will be governed by uniform criteria and principles. If the aggregate is institutionally heterogeneous in its base, then the system of institutionalised relations in which its society consists will be correspondingly heterogeneous in character and form. (Smith, 1971: 30)

In other words, it is the specific state/institutional framework that determines the nature of social integration: the existing type of structural incorporation influences decisively society's internal unity and operational functionality. There are three levels of pluralism in Smith's theory: cultural, social and structural (Smith, 1971). In his earlier work Smith was almost exclusively occupied with cultural pluralism, that is with 'objective' cultural differences between ethnic communities in a particular society. Cultural attributes such as language, religion or visible physical group differences were identified as a basis for institutionalizing cultural difference *de jure, de facto* or in both of these ways. However, in this stage culture is still largely free from politics; ethnic membership is not tied to citizenship and 'everyone has the same claim to societal resources and status regardless of ethnicity' (Simpson, 1995: 466). More complex is social pluralism, which is characterized by the simultaneous existence of institutional diversity and collective segregation: ethnic groups co-exist as separate but relatively equal entities. The most complex type of pluralism is a combination of cultural and social, that is, structural pluralism. In Smith's view structural pluralism is politically the highest form that pluralism can take and is expressed through different modes of group incorporation in a particular society. These modes of incorporation can be of three types: equivalent, differential (non-equivalent), and a combination of these two. Smith (1986: 197) describes those societies based on non-equivalent incorporation as hierarchical pluralities, those based on equivalent incorporation as segmental pluralities, and their combination as complex pluralities. The level of institutional differentiation also depends on the interplay between the public and private sphere: while many plural societies are formally and constitutionally defined as universalistic liberal systems and operate as such in a public domain, they nonetheless practise differential incorporation in the private sphere. Smith illustrates this with examples from the US and the apartheid era in South Africa, whereupon the US is a case of '*de facto* segmental organisation along ethnic lines within the private domain', while South Africa is an example of hierarchical plural society with *de jure* differential incorporation.

Upholding the central principles of the plural society approach, Smith argues that ethnicity in itself is a weak predictor of social conflict. Ethnic and racial relations are only explicable through analysis of the dominant structures of incorporation in a given society. The emphasis here is on the structural and institutional determinants of ethnic group behaviour. Ethnicity is not to be studied as a primordial certainty (as in sociobiology for example) or as a social condition resulting from group interaction (as in most conventional sociological approaches), but as a situation created, maintained and directed by modes of institutional incorporation. In Smith's words:

> the phenomenon of ethnicity depends for its social significance on its place in and under the prevailing structures of incorporation, directly or otherwise. It is easy to cite examples of structures that have fostered or created ethnic divisions where these were formerly absent, and ignored or eliminated them where formerly important … race and ethnic relations … are shaped by the place and sphere assigned to them by the structure of incorporation that prevails in each society. Identical ethnic or racial compositions may be regulated by different structures in different societies, while societies with differing compositions may have very similar structures. (1986: 198–9)

Hence, cultural difference alone is insufficient as a generator of social conflict. It is the difference in the modes of institutional incorporation that divides societies into those that are more prone to ethnic conflict and those where the structures of incorporation support normative consensus. Those states which are unable to separate public and private spheres from the ethnic and other communal bonds and interests are, to use Marx's phrase, their own gravediggers: by favouring one ethnic segment of their society over the rest they demolish the building blocks of the State's normative order. Analysing case studies in the post-colonial world, Smith has highlighted the central role of the State in fostering a common sense of belonging that would transcend ethnic and racial particularities (e.g., promoting nation-state-centred ideologies over specific ethnic-centred ones). Working with an evolutionary model of development he was concerned with the identification of general factors which could direct social transformation in the former colonies towards developing 'cohesive national units', which would enhance 'political integration on which modernisation directly depends'. Seeing societies as 'self-sufficient, self-perpetuating, and internally autonomous system[s] of social relations' (1971: 30), Smith has devoted a great deal of his attention to locating common patterns of social integration in post-colonial states.

To sum up, plural society theory sees differential institutional incorporation as a main source of group antagonisms. An intensive politicization of cultural difference is an indicator of whether a particular society is a plural, and, hence, deeply divided entity or whether it is governed by shared normative consensus. Ethnic relations cannot be explained by focusing on standard sociological concepts such as group mobilization, social action or individual or collective interaction, but by concentrating exclusively on divergent and dominant models and strategies of incorporation in a concrete plural society. The causes of ethnic group animosity can be most appropriately identified by directing our attention to whether a particular plural society is a case of hierarchical, segmental or complex plurality. The pluralist nature of a particular society can be gradually overcome as society moves from differential plurality towards social and cultural heterogeneity and normative homogeneity.[10]

Will ethnicity vanish with modernization?

Although structural-functionalism and plural society theory are traditionally presented as very distinct if not contrasting interpretations of ethnic group relations, the general logic of their argument is very similar. The approaches differ in their focus of analysis – one being occupied with deeply divided societies and the other with the societies with strong normative accord – but their general perception of the social world is almost identical. They both see normative consensus and cultural unity as key prerequisites for maintaining an efficient, conflict-free, sustainable society; they both believe that these prerequisites are also achievable and desirable goals for every modern/modernizing society; they both focus on the patterns of incorporation of 'dysfunctional' units into a larger functional whole governed by a single dominant value system; and they both perceive societies in a collectivist manner as autonomous systems of social relations. One might say that pluralism is just the other side of the same structural-functionalist coin: one is focused on internal dysfunctions and achieving internal equilibrium, whereas the other is concerned with emulating that blue-print externally – first by contrasting it sharply with plural societies, and secondly by modelling those plural societies on that blue-print. More specifically, when dealing with ethnicity functionalist accounts display the following three shortcomings:

1 Ethnic relations are tied too strongly to the one-way process of modernization.
2 This approach overemphasizes values and norms over interests and affectivity in its analysis of individual and ethnic group action.
3 The approach is unable to explain dramatic forms of social change such as ethnic conflict.

Both forms of functionalist thought are grounded in Durkheimian belief, where 'ethnicity is expected to decline as the "meritocratic" and individualist industrial society matures; ethnicity disappears as modern forms of association supplant such forms of identification and attachment' (Fenton, 1980:173). Despite the resurgence of ethnic politics in late modernity, functionalism remains couched in this view − that ethnicity is no more than a relic of the past. For Talcot Parsons, the salience of ethnic group identities is a temporary phenomenon, an aberration caused by de-differentiation tendencies inherent in dramatic social change. Once social change is completed, evolutionary processes will continue as social systems move towards more complex differentiation and a new form of organic solidarity. Alexander's model is perhaps more open and reflexive in this respect, accounting for uneven development and allowing a greater degree of 'incorporative strategies'. But he follows the same guiding principle in favouring assimilation and cultural integration as normative ideas of modernization. M. G. Smith is equally committed to this project of linking society's institutional structure to prevailing value systems. The problem with this link between ethnicity and modernization is that it looks only in one direction. As numerous empirical studies demonstrate (Olzak, 1983; Olzak and Nigel, 1986; Hodson et al., 1994), modernization is often manifest as ethnic competition. Intensive industrialization and urbanization often uproot individuals from different ethnic backgrounds and brings them to new urban and industrial areas to compete over scarce jobs, housing, education and other resources. As rational choice and other ethnic competition theories rightly point out (see Chapter 8) this situation creates environments where ethnic group membership is very likely to be used as a source of political mobilization. In this process modernization will not weaken ethnic group identities but, on the contrary, it will strengthen the salience of ethnic group membership as this membership becomes an important source of individual and group economic benefit or political power. In other words modernization does affect ethnic relations but they do not disappear. Rather, they transform from singular normative and moral universes of the pre-modern era into politically conscious interest groups able to manipulate their symbolic and cultural capital.

This also indicates that the functionalist perception of ethnic groups as primordial entities is deeply flawed, since the forms of group solidarity displayed in a modern context have very little to do with the original, pristine ethnic attachments: although modern ethnic groups regularly claim historical continuity with 'their' ancestors, sociologically speaking they belong to new forms of associations. So-called 'primordial attachments' are changeable: a number of distinct dialects can be integrated into a standardized language, groups may assimilate linguistically but remain 'ethnic' in other senses, religions can be secularized or transformed, and customs and symbols can be forgotten or selectively resurrected. To use Jenkins' terminology (1997: 72) the nominal ethnicity differs from virtual ethnicity: groups preserve the names of 'their' ancestors (nominal ethnic identity) but their experience (virtual ethnic identity) often sharply differs. Being Armenian in 400 BC during the Persian Empire, and being Armenian in present-day Toronto means something utterly different.

This stubborn and one-sided view of modernization is rooted in functionalist exaggeration of the role which norms, values and ideas play in the social world. Both structural-functionalism and plural society theory treat individuals first and foremost as products of their culture: it is 'cultural systems' and 'ethnic units' rather than free-thinking individuals or mobilized groups that are the carriers of social action; it is internalized cultural norms that govern their action and not economic or political interests or emotions. Even though ethnicity is a cultural phenomenon *par excellence*, it is not only a cultural phenomenon. Ethnic relations acquire their full sociological meaning only when they become politicized: we encounter cultural difference all the time but we become interested in ethnic relations primarily when there is a social dispute involved. Pluralism has more of an understanding of political variables as it identifies coercion as one of the key factors in the maintenance of plural societies. However pluralists are not concerned with the analysis of the interplay between culture and politics in ethnically segmented societies; they focus only on the mere description and categorization of such societies. As Jenkins (1986: 181) rightly points out, pluralism is theoretically vapid: it is 'profoundly descriptive, going no further than the extensive cataloguing of concrete situations by reference to a classificatory scheme of ideal-typical plural societies'.

Both positions set as their explicit or implicit goal the incorporation of different ethnic collectivities into a single dominant value system. Ethnic particularities are to be subsumed into the universal central-value system. The problem with this is twofold: on the one hand it blames the victim for unsuccessful assimilation and, on the other, it perceives societies as consisting of culturally integrated wholes. Assimilation is in political and status terms a deeply asymmetric process; it requires cultural accommodation if not also straightforward cultural submission of one ethnic group at the expense of another. In other words, functionalism overlooks how politically unequal the dominant and yet-to-be 'incorporated' ethnic groups are in a particular society. In this assimilationist tradition it is only minorities who are perceived as 'ethnic', while the majority is seen as the essence of the society: Afro-Americans and Native Americans are 'ethnic' whereas 'Wasps' are the Americans. Functionalism is equally blind to the stratified nature of social systems: ethnic groups are themselves segmented along the lines of class, gender, profession, status and so on. As Rex rightly points out in criticizing pluralism, segmented 'ethnic units' include individuals who are able to cross ethnic borders, such as in Malaysia after independence where, although Malays control the government and Chinese control the economy, 'some members of a group which performs an economic function actually enter the government, or members of the governing group engage in business' (Rex, 2002: 107). Different ethnic groups might also have a very different image of the society they inhabit, which is often determined by their political, economic or general social position.

Furthermore, functionalism makes little or no distinction between elite and mass culture or their corresponding ideologies within a particular ethnic tradition. As historical record demonstrates (Kedourie, 1960; Nair, 1977; A. Smith, 1981, 1991) the ethnic group movements often crystallize around specific sets of ideological doctrine promoted by, to use Gramsci's term, organic intellectuals and other elite groups.[11] However, to be widely acceptable these ethnic ideologies have to be articulated in a way that would make them appealing to an economically, politically and culturally diverse strata of people. The Greek myth of ethnic ancestry will be powerful only when it is able to accommodate equally well the identities of Greek nurses and Greek farmers as well as Greek judges and Greek schoolteachers. In addition, the dominant elite's ethnic ideology is open to constant challenge by counter-elite interpretations of what is an 'authentic' historical narrative for the particular ethnic group. As competing examples of Turkish, English or Roman myths of ethnic ancestry show, this is an ongoing process profoundly influenced by broader social and political changes.[12]

This lack of differentiation between elite and mass concepts of ethnicity is only a symptom of a general problem of functionalism. In treating social actors as passive and normative creatures, functionalist theory is incapable of explaining such dramatic social events and processes as ethnic conflicts and wars. Focusing predominantly on structures, social systems and their functionality, functionalism operates with a very static view of the social world. The obsession with group solidarity and system equilibrium leads functionalists to see social conflicts as dysfunctional products of de-differentiation. In other words, ethnic conflict is no more than a temporary anomaly caused by the system's momentary inability to progress towards continuous differentiation. This is problematic for at least two reasons: first social change and social conflict are an integral part of human life and, secondly, as we could learn from Simmel (Chapter 2), conflict is not only a destructive force but can equally function as a generator of social change. Ethnic conflicts and wars might be morally repugnant but as Joas (1999) rightly argues, large-scale social conflicts and wars were not only an integral part of modernity but they have 'shaped modernity as we know it in its innermost core' (p. 466). Ethnic conflicts and wars have been able to mobilize enormous human and natural resources and have provided powerful incentives for technological, administrative and scientific developments. As Hall (1985), Giddens (1985) and Mann (1988) document well, it was war and preparations for war that have constituted industrialization, urbanization and administrative professionalization and have, in the last instance, lead to the development of the modern nation-state and citizenship rights. Although ethnic conflict might be an extreme form of social action it nevertheless is a form of active social process that involves intensive group mobilization and individual commitment, and is a form of human sociability *par excellence*. The task of sociology is to understand and explain the sources of this ethnic animosity, not to treat it in a functionalist manner as an aberration that does not fit our grand meta-theoretical model. This criticism is especially relevant for Parsons, who unambiguously sees ethnicity as a form of anomaly that does not fit well with his model of fiduciary association.[13] To recap, far from stifling ethnic ties, modernization has actually accelerated ethnic group action. Instead of vanishing, ethnicity has ripened and proliferated with modernity.

Conclusion

Functionalism is a macro sociological perspective occupied with the general value patterns of social systems (as in structural-functionalism) or with the mere taxonomic ordering of such systems (as in plural society approaches). Adopting some tenets of evolutionary perspective, functionalists see societies as progressing from simple to complex and advanced ones through the process of differentiation, where old systems of operation become dysfunctional and are constantly replaced with new and more specialized and more adaptive sub-systems. To be fully functional new sub-systems have also to display value compatibility with the other sub-systems and with the general social system as a whole. In this schema there is not much space for ethnicity. Ethnic bonds are primarily seen as primordial attachments which, although potent and resilient, will eventually assimilate to the central value system. Ethnicity is no more than an unfortunate survival from the past. This is aptly summarized in the words of one of its exponents: 'The functionalist approach conceives race [and ethnic] relations as a problem of integration and assimilation or adaptation of minorities in a society that is fundamentally based on a widely-shared system of common values' (Berting, 1980: 183). Ethnic relations are not to be analysed and explained since 'we' are not ethnic; rather it is 'them', ethnic minorities, who are to be integrated and 'incorporated' through assimilation or acculturation.

While functionalist research has contributed enormously to our understanding of the tectonic social changes that modernity has brought upon traditional ways of living, and the profound impact modernization has had on the transformation of ethnic ties, functionalism, in both of its forms, remains one-sided in its analysis. Placing too much emphasis on the norms and values of social systems, it is unable to understand and explain motives for individual and group action, such as the typical example of ethnic group mobilization. While ethnicity, as functionalists rightly recognize, is a powerful source of group solidarity and moral integrity it is certainly much more than that. Functionalism fails to comprehend that because ethnicity is more than symbolic primordial solidarity, it is fully compatible with modernity. Intense social and spatial mobility, complex and ever-increasing division of labour and the fierce struggle for scarce resources make modernity an ideal arena for the articulation of individual and group political demands as cultural demands. Building on the structure that is already there makes much more sense than erecting a new one. Instead of constraining ethnic bonds, modernization intensifies them as politics is often (very successfully) orchestrated under the canopy of ethnicity.

Notes

1   Parsons (1971) analyses value systems as cultural systems that compose one segment of his general theory of action. This theory explains how societies develop through four systems – the cultural system (where the basic elements of analysis are values, symbols and meanings), the social system (where social roles and actor interactions are analysed), the personality system (where individual actor's motives, needs and attitudes are the focus of analysis) and the behavioural organism system (where the biological level – the nervous system and motor activity – of an actor's behavior is examined).

2   As Parsons (1951) explains, between the 'motivated actor' and his goal (defined by a cultural system) there are obstacles (conditions) that he has to overcome, the means (tools, facilities, etc.) to pursue his/her goals and normative standards that have to be followed.

3   Parsons (1975) has identified four sub-types of fiduciary association: the kinship association, the societal community, the religious association and the educational-cultural association. He makes frequent comparisons between ethnic groups and

kinship groups. Sometimes these analogies are only on the metaphorical level (how members of ethnic groups see themselves), and on other occasions (for example Parsons, 1951: 172) he uses these analogies as a form of explanation (the ethnic group 'can be regarded as an extension of kinship').

4   For example Parsons (1975) sees affirmative action policies as a symptom of de-differentiation.

5   A number of other structural-functionalist anthropologists and sociologists have emphasized the role of 'primordial bonds' in the development and persistence of ethnic groups. See for example Shils, 1957; Geertz, 1973 and Eisenstadt, 2002. However Alexander's account seems to be sociologically the most coherent.

6   Alexander (1980: 6) defines solidarity as 'subjective feelings of integration that individuals experience for members of their social groups'.

7   Alexander is very fond of the pluralist approach and is only critical of its neglect of the industrial Western world: 'the present essay may be viewed as primarily devoted to the causes and consequences of different degrees of pluralisation in the industrial West, a subject to which plural society theory has not yet devoted significant attention' (1980: 24).

8   As Simpson (1995) points out, M. G. Smith has expanded the use of the concept from Furnivall's initial application to post-colonial situations in Asia to the rest of the de-colonized and de-colonizing world, whereas Despres (1968), Kuper (1971) and van den Berghe (1971) have further expanded the concept to societies with little or no colonial experience.

9   As Banton (1983: 93) notes, Kuper's view on plural societies is very different from M. G. Smith's, because he speaks about plural societies mainly in terms of those that are built 'around conflicts of a kind other than class'.

10   Simpson (1995: 462) indicates that 'heterogeneity describes the existence of multiple societal components sharing one set of social institutions', whereas 'pluralism describes the situation of multiple cultural enclaves, each with its own set of social institutions'.

11   On the decisive role of organic intelligentsia in the articulation of ethno-national projects see Malešević, 2002d.

12   For more about competing myths of ethnic origin see Smith, 1998.

13   The following passage indicates the character of Parsons' ad hoc and provisional solution to the ethnic revival of the 1960s and 1970s: 'I think of the ethnic group as belonging by and large to this same category of fiduciary association ... It does not seem, however, to belong unequivocally to any one of the above four subtypes [kinship, religious association, societal community and educational-cultural association]. My inclination is to treat it as a kind of "fusion" of the community and kinship types' (1975: 62).

Chapter Five

SYMBOLIC INTERACTIONISM: THE SOCIAL CONSTRUCTION OF ETHNIC GROUP REALITY

Introduction

Although symbolic interactionism is historically and geographically a sole invention of American sociology, or more precisely of the two departments at the University of Chicago[1] it, just like other contemporary sociological approaches, owes a great deal to its European ancestors. While only occasionally acknowledged, the central principles of symbolic interactionalism are principally derived from the work of Georg Simmel. Simmel was the only classic writer of sociology who focused almost exclusively on the micro foundations of the social world. It was Simmel who formulated and articulated key interactionist concepts such as 'social interaction', 'social distance' or 'sociation', and it was Simmel who provided an epistemological groundwork for the theories of those who are the accredited forefathers of symbolic interactionism – George Herbert Mead, William. I. Thomas and Herbert Blumer. Nowhere is this more apparent than in the interactionist approach to the study of ethnicity. Simmel's perception of ethnic relations as a particular form of individual and group interaction, which is always encumbered with ambiguities and dependent on the changing dynamics of individual and group experiences, remains a key statement of symbolic interactionism. A focus on persistent and changing group interpretations and re-interpretations of theirs and others' social positions lies at the heart of Simmel's project, which is another crucial element that symbolic interactionists adopt in theorizing ethnic relations. Interactionist emphasis on the primacy of agency over structure, as well as of symbols and values over material interests and political motives in the everyday life of different ethnic groups is also part of Simmel's formalist legacy.

In saying all this it is not meant to downplay or disregard the originality and novelty of contemporary symbolic interactionist positions in the analysis of ethnicity. On the contrary, as this chapter will demonstrate Simmel's intellectual heritage has been creatively used and extensively developed to provide powerful and sophisticated accounts of ethnic relations. These initial reflections are intended only to emphasize that the link between Simmel's work and the contemporary symbolic interactionist interpretations of ethnic relations is much stronger than is usually acknowledged.

General principles of symbolic interactionism

While in nominal terms symbolic interactionism originated in the city of Chicago, it was created out of two quite distinct research traditions: one deeply empirical, prescriptive and reform oriented and the other profoundly theoretical, speculative and with less interest in everyday application. This difference was largely coincident with scholars working at the University of Chicago's departments of sociology and philosophy: whereas the Chicago sociologists were instrumental in developing an empirically grounded human ecology perspective, philosophers were responsible for the conceptual and epistemological backdrop of symbolic interactionism by re-articulating key concepts such as 'self', 'society', 'perception' and 'significant symbols'.

The Chicago school of sociology is represented in the works of R. Park, E. Burgess, W. I. Thomas, C. Cooley, L. Wirth and others, who borrowed initially from animal and plant ecology to establish a 'science of human ecology'. As Wirth (1945) explains, human ecology was concerned with developing research tools for an objective and systematic study of 'the spatial, temporal, physical, and technological bases of social life'. Human ecology was focused on identifying and analysing what is uniquely human: 'the capacity for symbolic communication, rationality, relatively great mobility, and formal organisation and control and the possession of a technology and culture' (1945: 483). Chicago sociologists were predominantly occupied with city life and the impact that intensive modernization, urbanization and industrialization had on everyday group relations. The city of Chicago was a readily available micro laboratory of modernity where ever-expanding immigration was constantly changing its social structure as well as its physical, spatial and ethnic make up. As Philpott (1978) shows, at the beginning of the twentieth century, first- and second-generation immigrants constituted around 80 per cent of the entire population of 1.7 million. Using what were at that time rather atypical qualitative research techniques such as participant observation, public documents, autobiographical sources (e.g., personal letters and diaries) and newspaper clippings, and focusing on the analysis of everyday life in slums and ghettos, the Chicago school sociologists were able to develop a distinct sociological research perspective. This approach took as its motto W. I. Thomas' (1969[1923]) guiding principle that 'if men define situations as real, they are real in their consequences'. Unlike the more dominant positivist positions of their day, the Chicago sociologists attempted to treat the objects of their research as free-thinking subjects capable of reaching rational decisions in their everyday conduct. Individuals were seen as conscious creatures shaped by the social and physical environment they lived in. In Cooley's (1964[1902]) view, a human being is a *looking-glass self* capable of, often involved in, and shaped by group consciousness, empathy and sympathetic introspection. Furthermore, influenced directly or indirectly by the work of Simmel the sociologists saw metropolitan city life as a dynamic environment that was decisive in changing social attitudes. Echoing Simmel's 'The Metropolis and Mental Life', Park argued that 'the great cities are now what the frontier and the wilderness once was, the refuge of the footloose, the disinherited, and all those possessed by that undefined *malaise* we call social unrest'(Park, 1950: 168). The metropolis was an epitome of restless modernity, which was not just a spatial, geographical or physical entity but also a 'mental state', a 'moral order' in the condition of flux and transformation. The Chicago sociologists were interested in how new social meanings were created in the everyday interaction of different groups and individuals, most of whom were uprooted migrants from Europe and the American South. They saw American cities as giant 'melting pots'; where all cultural difference would gradually be transformed into a singular American identity through processes of accommodation and assimilation.

While the Chicago sociologists were successful in devising research tools compatible with this new perspective, they were clearly lacking a stronger theoretical foundation for what was to become a symbolic interactionist approach. The Chicago philosophers, initially influenced by J. Dewey's and W. James' pragmatism, were responsible for the epistemological fundamentals of this approach, and among them it was G. H. Mead whose influence was pivotal in the creation of symbolic interactionism.

Mead's philosophy (1962[1934]) is action-centred, starting with 'the act' as an elementary unit of analysis. Drawing on behaviourism and pragmatism he identified impulse, perception, manipulation and consummation as four distinct and interrelated stages in the acts which are fundamental to human behaviour. These stages provide a setting for all possible relationships between an actor and his/her environment: impulse stimulates the actor's reaction; through perception an actor visualizes and thus creates an object as an object; manipulation helps an actor to conceptualize possibilities of his/her action, and finally consummation involves the actual process of acting (which is intended to fulfil the original impulse). However, in Mead's theory the emphasis is not on isolated action but on social action. Mead pinpoints the gesture as an essential building block of the social act. While most animals communicate through an exchange of gestures, it is only humans who are able to create and rely on a particular kind of gesture – termed by Mead a 'significant symbol'. Language is a prime example of significant symbols since, through the use of it, one is able to exchange a meticulous set of meanings. Significant symbols elicit similar, if not always the same, sets of images in speaker and in listener: by uttering a word 'horse' a listener and a speaker share an identical (if not perfect) mental representation of a four legged creature. Mead argues that without significant symbols human beings would not be capable of thinking and creating abstract concepts. Significant symbols help intensify and make complex social interaction between human beings possible.

With the capacity to think, human beings are able to choose from among different stimuli, that is, from among a variety of possible actions, and to resist the temporarily strongest stimulus in favour of the most beneficial course of action in the future. Or in Mead's (1962: 99) words: 'Delayed reaction is necessary to intelligent conduct.' However, this ability is much more socially than biologically generated. Meanings are created and located in social action. For Mead social action creates 'mind' and not vice versa. 'Mind' is no more than an individual's capacity to respond in an organized way to the wider society, while 'self' is an individual's aptitude to conceive of oneself as an object. In Mead's theory the self is truly a product of social activity: animals and infants have no selves. This requires the skill of empathy and role playing, where an individual can start thinking about how others can and do see him/her. The self can take the role of any other individual or group but individuals are most likely to centre on what Mead calls the 'generalized other'. The generalized other refers to the outlook of the communities one is a member of. For Mead the self can only be complete when an individual 'takes the attitudes of the organized social group to which he belongs towards the organized, co-operative social activity ... in which that group is engaged' (1962: 155). Even though society is decisive for who we are, since there are many generalized others around us, each self is unique and individuals are likely to develop as multiple selves. Differentiating between 'I' and 'me', Mead argues that self is a complex social process where 'me' stands for conventional conformist and routine behaviour of the self while 'I' stands for impulsive, unpredictable and creative action through which the self is fully realized as a unique individual. Social institutions such as the education system, family peer groups, or mass media help individual selves to internalize society's dominant values in a way such that 'me' often takes precedence over 'I'.

Although Mead provided a conceptual framework and the early Chicago sociologists supplied the research tools, it was only the creative synthesis of the two in the work of Herbert Blumer that truly gave birth to symbolic interactionism. Building on the research experience of Park, Thomas and others, Blumer adopted Mead's conceptual apparatus while moving it away from its behaviourist heritage and giving it a much stronger sociological underpinning. Just as for Mead, Blumer saw social action as being prior to thinking. Social interaction shapes our perception and through social interaction human beings create and exchange meanings. By acquiring a particular set of symbols and meanings humans are enabled with capacity for distinct individual and group interpretations of reality. Being rational and thinking creatures humans assess the outcomes for the potential courses of action and opt for, from the actor's point of view, the most logical. Following W. I. Thomas' dictum, Blumer operates with the key concept 'definition of the situation' which relativizes the nature of social reality: there is no single universal reality, it is rather that individuals and groups define what their particular social reality is. Here he differs significantly from Mead's universalism.

For Blumer actors often operate with different definitions of the same entity: 'a tree will be a different object to a botanist, a lumberman, a poet, and a home gardener' (1969: 11). Focusing much more strongly on collective action (or 'joint action' in his terms[2]) than Mead, Blumer, echoing Durkheim, argues that social acting involves more than an aggregate of distinct individual actions. A collective action is an authentic and autonomous form of activity created by actors involved in it. Although joint action has a great deal of suppleness and plasticity, it is often tied to pre-existing cultural codes and meanings ingrained in the particular social order. These cultural norms, together with material structural constraints, place limits on individual and group action, but they remain secondary to it: 'It is the social process in group life that creates and upholds the rules, not the rules that create and uphold group life' (Blumer, 1969: 19). All social institutions are a product of joint actions and regardless of how durable a particular social institution is, in the last instance it depends on the existing meanings attached to it through the continuous process of social action. An age-old ritual will be performed only as long as the participants interpret it as meaningful in one way or another. As Blumer emphasizes (1969: 18), 'each instance of such joint action has to be formed anew. The participants still have to build their lines of action and fit them to one another through dual process of designation and interpretation.' The interactions between different social groups are also shaped by particular individual and group perceptions. In addition to individual definitions of the situation, groups are prone to educe a collective definition too. By collective definition of the situation Blumer understands a peculiar sense of group position vis-à-vis other groups – it includes their perception of other groups as well as a self-perception of their own group's position; it incorporates the collective experiences directly in connection to inter-group relations; and it influences the group's courses of action (Blumer and Duster, 1980). For Blumer inter-group perceptions and a collective definition of the situation remain a much more potent source of continuity and change in group relationships than any economic or political factor.

Symbolic interactionism and ethnicity

Among the early Chicago school sociologists, it was Robert Park who devoted most attention to ethnic relations and who, at the same time, was most influenced by Simmel.[3] Park was principally occupied with issues of group mobility, exemplified in his well known theory of 'race relations cycle' along the lines of a human ecology perspective, but his contributions on social distance, group prejudice and the marginal man also contain resilient interactionist-inspired analysis. Park and Burgess (1969[1921]), and others from the early Chicago school, saw ethnic relations as developing along a relatively stable pattern of cycles that include four separate stages of group interaction: contact/competition, conflict, accommodation and assimilation. Studying the structure of group mobility and patterns of immi-gration in American cities, Park and his colleagues argued that the first con-tact of new immigrant groups in the metropolis brings about the state of group competition over 'prized goods or values'. Competition is seen as a universal form of social interaction, largely undetectable as such at the level of the individual consciousness. When individuals become aware of ethnic group competition then, according to Park, one enters the cycle of conflict. Unlike competition, which is a group contest in the broader ecological order, conflict is a more personal affair: whereas 'competition determines the position of the individual in the community, conflict fixes his place in society. Location, position, ecological interdependence – these are the char-acteristics of the community. Status, subordination, and superordination, control – these are distinctive marks of a society' (Park and Burgess, 1969: 574–5). Ethnic groups are able to overcome conflict through processes of accommodation, restructuring the former hierarchy between dominant and subordinate groups by re-negotiating or re-establishing relations of power and status. By its nature accommodation is a temporary and frail arrange-ment loaded with latent conflicts. It is only in the final phase, that of assimi-lation, that ethnic group conflicts can be resolved for good. Defining assimilation as 'a process of inter-penetration and fusion in which person and groups acquire the memories, sentiments, and attitudes of other persons or groups, and, by sharing their experience and history, are incorporated with them in a common cultural life', Park and Burgess (1969: 735) argue that it is only through the development of such common cultural patterns that ethnic group solidarity can loose its grip over individual migrants.

This 'race relations cycle' was seen by Park (1950) as universal, progressive and irreversible. However, since assimilation is a normative ideal which exceeds everyday reality, Park and his colleagues focused most of their attention on the sources of ethnic group animosity, by looking at the patterns of group prejudice and social distance. Unlike the dominant perspectives of his time, Park saw ethnic group prejudice not so much as a characteristic of an individual but rather as an indicator of changing relationships between groups (Lal, 1995). This meant that prejudice was not an attribute of pathological individuals but a universal phenomenon in everyday social relations, which acquires its full sociological meaning when ethnic group relations undergo profound social change. Ethnic group prejudice is amplified when the subordinate group starts to perceive social reality as something which can be changed, and they attempt to change existing social order. This might be perceived as a potential or real attack on the dominant group's monopoly over material resources and its power position, or as a threat to the prevailing values, norms or lifestyles shared by the superordinate group. Ethnic group prejudice is, for Park, tied to the Simmelian notion of social distance. The ethnic groups' social proximity has a direct impact on inter-group relations: the lesser the social distance between the groups the greater is their mutual influence. Park (1950) illustrates this with a paradox that is part and parcel of social relations in the US: while there might be more affection, privacy and friendliness in the interpersonal relationships between 'blacks' and 'whites' in the South than in the rest of the US (e.g., cherished black nanny, loyal black gardener and his white boss, etc.) this is only because the borders of social distance in the South are much clearer and much stronger than in the rest of America.

The most salient example of Simmel's influence on Park is evident in his concept of the 'marginal man'. Just like Simmel's stranger, marginal man represents an outsider who does not belong to any dominant culture. Children from ethnically mixed marriages, first- and second-generation immigrants, just like European Jews and American mulattos, are individuals ambiguously split between two worlds and belonging fully to neither. As the product of a hybrid culture, marginal man epitomizes a new personality 'living and sharing intimately in the cultural life and traditions of two distinct peoples; never quite willing to break, even if he were permitted to do so, with his past and his traditions, and not quite accepted, because of racial prejudice, in the new society in which he now sought to find a place' (Park, 1950: 354). However, being the embodiment of metropolitan city life marginal man is not a by-product of modernity, a residue of the past or present, but rather is seen by Park as a prototype of the future – a cosmopolitan personality with wider horizons and a greater sense of civilization and progress.

Drawing on some of these early Chicago school ideas Blumer (1958, 1969; Blumer and Duster, 1980) has developed the most influential symbolic interactionist account of ethnic relations. Expanding Park's (and indirectly Simmel's) concept of ethnic prejudice as a form of group relationship, Blumer argues that to understand prejudice one has to move from focusing on the individual feelings of 'racists' to a 'sense of group position'. Ethnic group animosities or sympathies are, according to Blumer (1958), for the most part derived from one's sense of one's group's position in relation to other groups. Since individuals tend to see other individuals as representatives of their respective ethnic groups, group prejudice emerges as a symptom of changing positions between the superordinate and subordinate groups. In other words, similarly to Park, Blumer argues that the function of prejudice is to maintain the hegemonic position of the dominant group by preserving the status quo in their relations. The strength of group prejudice comes from two sources: socialization and the role of political elites. According to Blumer the concept of racial or ethnic groups is acquired through primary and secondary socialization and is further articulated by power elites. The leaders of the dominant group aim to maintain the group-centred perception of the social world in order to preserve their privileged position, but they are also able to re-articulate a sense of group position when necessary in order to decrease ethnic tensions. The problem with this position is that it overlooks differences of views within a particular ethnic collective as it relates to collective perceptions of other ethnic groups. To deal with diverse group responses to ethnic group prejudice, Blumer had to further develop this approach by supplementing it with his theory of a collective definition of the situation. By 'collective definition' in ethnic relations, Blumer and Duster (1980: 222) mean

> the basic process by which racial [ethnic] groups come to see each other and themselves and poise themselves to act towards each other; the process is one in which the racial [ethnic] groups are defining or interpreting their experiences and the events that bring these experiences about.

Here Blumer and Duster focus not only on the dominant but also the subordinate groups, by arguing that a group-centred emphasis on ethnic differences is a strategy to improve the collective status of the group. This improvement is seen as being of a symbolic ('status-oriented') rather than of an economic nature.[4] Their focus is on the process of group 'experiencing', which is always prone to change and re-interpretation: from routine personal everyday contacts between individuals within different ethnic groups, to semi-personal transmission of collective myths, stereotypes, rumours and media portrayals of different ethnicities, to impersonal relations in state institutions. Building on Mead's and Simmel's theories, Blumer and Duster see 'variable interpretation of these human experiences' as a starting point of their analysis, and direct their attention on ascertaining 'the kinds of objects racial [ethnic] groups form of one another' (1980: 230). In this way a collective definition of the situation is an ongoing process of collective experiencing that 'can go on in one's home, at work, at meetings, on the street, through the press, over the radio and through television'. According to Blumer and Duster no ethnic group is immune to this process of collective definition. It is also often the case that there are competing definitions of the situation within a single ethnic collective and that some spectacular event (e.g., a highly publicized case of inter-ethnic gang rape) can dramatically affect the dominant collective interpretation of other groups.

The relationship between subordinate and superordinate groups is here more complex than that given by Park. For Blumer and Duster the two groups continually undergo two conflicting principles of collective definition: one concerned with the uniqueness of the group and the other with the group's social status. While the subordinate group is torn between assimilationism (adjusting to the existing social order) and separatism (developing its own institutional structure), the dominant group may polarize around the issue of preserving the status quo (exclusionism) and allowing for more parity between the groups ('the gate-opening orientation'). In the American context of the 1960s, this was a division between, for example, the National Association for the Advancement of Colored People (who advocated slow reforms and integration of Afro-Americans into American society) versus the radical separatist Black Panthers, or between the white supporters of segregation policies in the South versus defenders of multiculturalism and affirmative action. On the other hand, the choices between the two are determined by particular historical settings as well as by collective memory, the groups' economic position and other structural factors. What is crucial for Blumer and Duster is that this dualism allows for ambiguity and constant re-negotiation and re-interpretation of ethnic relations. The relations between ethnic groups are never fixed: they might be shaped by objective conditions such as economic exploitation or institutionalized asymmetry of power, but these factors become meaningful only in relation to definitions ethnic groups make of each other.[5]

Barbara Lal (1986, 1993, 1995) builds on Park's and Blumer's concept of ethnicity as a collective strategy to improve the group's social standing. She finds American society to be a prime example of what she terms 'ethnicity paradox' – a strong emphasis on the uniqueness of the particular ethnic group is a group's strategic device 'for facilitating full participation in economic, political, and social life and a fair share of those resources and values that are sought by members of the wider community' (Lal, 1995: 430). In other words, through successful individual members groups are able to claim higher social status in American society as a whole. The emergence of powerful ethnic networks enable their membership to feel material security (assistance in providing housing, jobs, schools, loans, etc.) and, more importantly, help to build 'a sense of dignity' and to bolster individual and group self-esteem in the context of a fierce inter-ethnic status struggle. This ability to employ ethnic markers strategically indicates that individuals and groups mostly operate with an optional situational concept of ethnic identity. According to Lal (1995: 432) this concept implies that

> the way we see ourselves on any particular occasion is influenced by the situation in which we find ourselves, the presence of real or imaginary significant others, and 'altercasting' as well as the positive or negative value we assume a particular identity will confer in a particular context.

The emphasis here is on the individual and group 'selves': ethnic identities are fluid, flexible, changeable and a matter of consent. Ethnic groups exist as long as membership is voluntary and conscious. Echoing W. I. Thomas and starting from the actor's point of view, Lal argues that ethnicity is what individual and social actors deem it to be; ethnic groups exist when individuals say that they do. For Lal this approach is open and sensitive to changes in the collective definition of ethnic membership, as well as conducive to the emergence of new forms of ethnic identification such as, for example, Black-mixed race.

Richard Jenkins (1994, 1997) shares this situationist vision of ethnic relations. He also interprets ethnic identities in terms of the actor's self-definition of the situation. Ethnicity is a variable rather than a fixed state of being; it is a cultural phenomenon based on shared meanings; it originates and is dependent on social interaction; it is a segment of a broader social identity that every individual holds and as such it is shaped through the 'dialectic between similarity and difference' (Jenkins, 1996). However Jenkins finds some classical interactionist positions limiting in focusing exclusively on internal processes of group identification. Drawing on Barth's (1969) concept of boundary maintenance and Tajfel's (1978) social identity theory, Jenkins argues that in addition to self-definition and self-perception, ethnic group membership owes a great deal to external processes of social categorization. Instead of looking at different cultural contents as a way to detect distinct ethnic communities, Jenkins focuses on the study of ethnic boundaries and on how the imposition of a particular boundary determines whether one is a member of a particular group or not. While the process of group identification takes place inside the ethnic boundary, social categorization occurs outside and across this boundary. In other words, social categorization 'relates to the capacity of one group to successfully impose its categories of ascription upon another set of people, and to the resources which the categorised collectivity can draw upon to resist, if need be, that imposition' (Jenkins, 1997: 23).

External categorization is important because, just as with Goffman's (1961, 1963) prisoners and mental patients, the labels imposed on ethnic group membership can be internalized and made one's own. When categorization is undertaken by the authority which is considered to be legitimate (e.g., the State, a group recognized as superior, and so on) it might foster ethnic group consciousness. For example, the communist state authorities were instrumental in the creation of Moldavian ethnicity in the former Soviet Union and Bosnian Muslim (Bosniak) and Macedonian ethnicities in the former Yugoslavia.[6] They did not create these ethnic groups *ex nihilo*, but their authority of categorization helped to institutionalize a particular definition of ethnic reality that articulated and strengthened internal self-definition. However, what is essential for external categorization is that it often involves the exercise of power and domination: 'the categorised, without the capacity to resist the carrying of identity cards, the wearing of armbands, or whatever more subtle devices of identification and stigmatisation might be deployed, may, in time, come to think of themselves in the language or categories of the oppressor' (Jenkins, 1994: 217). The emphasis on social categorization indicates one of the key sources of ethnic group antagonism: the asymmetrical relations of power. Many group conflicts are fought over the question of social categorization, that is, which interpretation of inter-ethnic reality is the 'right' one as well as who can make such a claim and on what basis. To sum up, for Jenkins ethnic relations are the outcome of ongoing processes of social interaction that involve both external and internal definitions of the situation.

Is ethnicity only a social construction?

Unlike most instrumentalist approaches to ethnic relations, symbolic interactionism is deeply sensitive to individual and group perceptions of social reality and to the changing nature of this reality. Interactionists claim, and with every right, that human beings are profoundly social and symbolic creatures, often governed by their unique sense of the time and space they live in and by what they consider to be a meaningful action. Human beings are also active social agents capable of, and often directed by, feelings of personal and collective empathy. These valuable insights, developed from Simmel's vision of society as a total of individual and group interactions, have been successfully applied to the study of ethnic relations. Symbolic interactionism has more than any other sociological approach made clear how fluid and variable ethnic relations can be, and how unstable and situational are the boundaries of ethnic groups. Interactionists have thoroughly documented cases wherein collective definitions of ethnic reality have been dramatically altered under changing circumstances. Their studies have successfully delegitimized any coherent attempt to make a case for the primordial 'naturalness' of ethnic group membership.

Although social actors still, for the most part, tend to see their ethnic groups as given and static and their cultural boundaries as clearly demarcated, this only tells us something about actors and their beliefs and very little about ethnicity as such. The concept of ethnicity, in all its popular forms and contents, is commonly reified and made eternal precisely because it does not have those features. If human beings are, following Weber (1968) and Geertz (1973), creatures 'suspended in webs of significance' they themselves have spun, then ethnic collectivities represent a quintessence of those humanly created, internalized and institutionalized webs of meaning. In this interactionist emphasis on the plasticity of meanings and boundaries and on the situational logic of social interaction, Simmel's legacy is clear and strong and the argument profoundly convincing. However, in its enthusiasm to deconstruct strong and naïve naturalist claims about ethnic relations and to pinpoint the social construction of ethnic group reality, symbolic interactionism has also demonstrated some Achilles' heels. Out of the three most pronounced weaknesses one is general, while the remaining two are more substantive and directly related to the analysis of ethnicity. These include the following criticisms:

- symbolic interactionism has shaky epistemological foundations, which undermine its analytical claims including its theory of ethnicity
- the theory is too agency-centred and as such is unable to deal with structural constraints in the analysis of ethnic relations
- the theory is too focused on values and meanings in the collective definition of ethnic reality so that it underestimates the impact of material factors such as political power or the forces of economy.

Defining symbolic interactionism as 'subjectivist sociology that concerns itself with the actor's point of view' (Lal, 1995: 421) the theory opens itself to two compelling charges, that is of being intensely relativist and potentially populist. Relying solely on qualitative research methodology, allowing for greater conceptual openness and privileging the agent's viewpoint, symbolic interactionism is not very far from making the statement that all belief systems have equal epistemological validity. While such a position might be perhaps defensible on the level of ontology, it certainly undermines its explanatory ambitions. It is analytically implausible to claim simultaneously that 'there is such a thing as empirical reality' and that symbolic interactionism should continue 'as a science rather than as fiction that can make no claim to being more truthful than any other account', while maintaining the view that 'symbolic interactionists are unlikely to facilely assume that their own understanding of why people behave as they do is necessarily correct and suffices in description and explanation' (Lal, 1995: 436–7). If a researcher's attempt to make sense of a particular social phenomenon is merely of equal epistemological worth to that of the next person, why bother at all? This brings us to the second and related charge, that of populism. Accepting W. I. Thomas' dictum that actors define what social reality is opens the door for an 'anything goes' logic, where particular individual or collective perception is equated with 'universal' truth. There is a thin line between recognizing that there is no universal reality but only particular definitions of the situation, and allowing that every individual and group's standpoint has the same analytical relevance. Although most symbolic interactionists are not far from making such a claim they themselves have to accept their research findings as being more relevant than the claims made by the 'objects' of their research. If this were not the case they would not argue for the situational concept of ethnic identity. For example Lal (1995: 435) claims that her approach is 'grounded in a subjectivist sociological framework that takes into account the point of view of the actor rather than relying on the sense that the sociologist makes of the actor's world', but her analysis of ethnic relations directly contradicts this statement. She convincingly argues that ethnic identities are flexible, fluid, changeable, optional and often instrumental, while most 'objects' of her research (as most ordinary individuals anywhere) cling to a hard primordialist vision of ethnicity in seeing their ethnic group membership as fixed, innate and eternal.[7]

Too much emphasis placed on actors at the expense of social structure is another blind spot for the symbolic interactionist theory of ethnicity. While in principle Simmel's and Mead's legacy was creatively used in analysing the changing patterns of individual and group perception, very little work has been done in accounting for institutional and other structural constraints of human action. The courses of individual and group action are often limited by available information and knowledge, which restrict the development of potentially new and alternative definitions of the situation. As Baert rightly points out: 'even if certain choices are thought as theoretically possible, the internalised generalised other is constraining in that it links particular imaginary choices with particular effects' (Baert, 1998: 74). In the study of ethnic relations this is most visible in an overemphasis on ethnic group self-definition over social categorization. Apart from Jenkins, no other major symbolic interactionist has devoted sufficient attention to the study of external classification and ascription as decisive factors in inter-ethnic relations. This has been systematically avoided because recognizing the power of external factors in shaping individual and group action would automatically mean recognizing the strength of structure over agency.

The students of communist and other authoritarian societies (i.e., Brubaker, 1996, 1998; Malešević, 2000, 2002a) know only too well how all-powerful state apparatuses were able with little or no resistance to create, disseminate and institutionalize particular concepts of ethnicity that in the post-communist period have become a dominant vehicle of social and political action. The Soviet state was responsible for the creation of over a hundred codified and mutually exclusive ethnic nationalities, which were not only statistical categories but also functioned as an 'obligatory ascribed status' (Brubaker, 1996: 18).[8] Focusing exclusively on agency and the actor's defi-nitions of the situation moves us away from seeing the bigger (macro) picture which, in this particular case, is decisive for an explanation of ethnic relations. Furthermore, working solely with an actor-centred view may lead to giving too much attention to one possible ethnic group situation at the expense of other alternatives. Thus Blumer and Duster direct their attention only to dominant and subordinate ethnic groups such as those between Santal and Hindu in West Bengal, Burakumin and Japanese in Japan and 'blacks' and 'whites' in the US, arguing that 'when the respective social positions are upset, and especially when the subordinate racial group chal-lenges the superior social position of the superordinate race, the racial groups enter into conflict' (Blumer and Duster, 1980: 233). This perspective overlooks the possibilities where ethnic groups share similar political, eco-nomic or status position and still suddenly become an object of fierce inter-ethnic struggle (e.g., Serbs, Croats and Bosniaks in pre-1992 Bosnia), or where there are more than two ethnic collectivities involved with each group having a different and non-reciprocal collective definition of the other (e.g., Baya, Banda, Sara and Mandjia in Central African Republic, or Ibo, Hausa and Yoruba in Nigeria). The Bosnian example is indicative since it demonstrates the importance of external structural factors in understand-ing the dramatic change in ethnic relations. As all available research shows (Katunarić, 1991; Pešić, 1995) the three ethnic groups were fairly equally matched in terms of economic, political and social standing and expressed a negligible degree of social distance and animosity towards each other before the war. Yet the outburst of war saw by far the worst cases of inter-ethnic massacres in a European context since World War II. This and similar cases could only be explained by looking at the broader structural determinants, for example, as in this particular case, the break up of the state structures, the collapse of the constitutional system, the disintegration of the existing political and moral order and, most of all, the role of the neighbouring co-ethnic states (Serbia and Croatia) in intensifying the process of ethnic mobilization.

Finally, while symbolic interactionism is right in arguing that through par-ticular collective definitions of the situation individuals and groups organize and make meaningful their experience, this is only one side of the coin. Precisely because meanings, values and perceptions do not float in the air but are tied to specific dynamics of political and economic power are they relevant for inter-group relations. As we can see, both Park and Blumer recognize the role of material factors but find them secondary to individual and group perceptions. As Blumer and Duster (1980: 232) claim: 'It is necessary to bring such objective factors inside of the ongoing process of definition, to see how the objective change has been interpreted. The interpretation may be very different, indeed, from what seems to be the obvious import of the objective change.' While there is no dispute that individual and group interpretation of particular objective change may vary and that this variation might be decisive for the cases in question, one cannot so lightly discard the fact that many forms of objective change will be interpreted quite similarly by ethnic groups living in relatively similar 'ethnic situations'. What is vital here is whether groups share similar socio-economic levels of development, educational standards, possess independent networks of information, have similar collective memories, are exposed to similar state practices and so on. For example, it is more likely to expect that some objective change (say the banning of an ethnic minority newspaper) will have a similar effect on inter-group relationships between Turks and Armenians and Hutus and Tutsis on one hand, and on ethnic groups that do not share a collective memory of genocide on the other. Such a perception-centred perspective is also problematic in its radical situationist view of ethnic relations. Symbolic interactionism makes a valid point in its understanding of ethnicity as a social construction, but exactly because ethnicity is not only a social construction it is a potent source of group action and conflict. Just as rational choice theory (see Chapter 7), interactionism works with a concept of group membership which is too optional: while the former demotes membership to individual instrumentality, the latter reduces it to the question of individual and group volition. Unfortunately, as the world around us shows, ethnicity for the most part has little to do with individual will since collective perceptions of reality are not only intensely shaped and 'contaminated' by the institutions of the State, mass media, educational system or by the interests of political elites, but are also perceived by social actors as real entities. As social researchers we are aware that ethnicity is a social construct, but what is important for us is to find out why most social actors tend to view it as a 'real thing'.

Conclusion

Grounded intensely in Simmel's heritage, symbolic interactionism aims to demonstrate that social life is defined by action: it is always in process, always emerging, becoming, changing. For interactionists individual and collective agents are symbolic and symbol-producing creatures, at all times engaged in interaction and constantly aware of the presence of 'the other'. In this way interactionists analyse ethnic relations as an ongoing, flexible and situational process open to and shaped by the changes in the collective definition of ethnic group reality. An ethnic identity is just a segment of an individual's general social identity, an object of change and negotiation. For Park, as for Blumer and Lal, subjective interpretation of inter-ethnic group reality has precedence over objective changes in social structure, power, or economic relations between ethnic groups. Although symbolic interactionism has contributed a great deal in highlighting the role of individual and group perceptions in governing ethnic group action, it remains too tightly woven in the logic of an idealist and relativist argument that, with the exception of Jenkins' work, has little understanding of the role of force, power, authority and other social realities in ethnic group relationships. By focusing too much on the agent's point of view symbolic interactionism is often unable to deal with the dramatic structural changes that profoundly affect inter-group relationships. An attempt to find micro solutions to macro problems can often end up as a futile exercise. While individual and group perceptions are an important source of action, in the last instance the action itself is dependent on the effects of social, political and economic forces.

Notes

1   It was the Departments of Philosophy and Sociology at the University of Chicago that simultaneously gave birth to Mead's philosophy, Blumer's sociology and Park's human ecology and established foundations for the general perspective of symbolic interactionism.

2   Blumer (1969: 17) defines joint action as a 'societal organization of conduct of different acts of diverse participants'.

3   Park (1950: vi) clearly recognizes his indebtedness to Simmel: 'listening to the lectures of Georg Simmel, at Berlin, I received my only formal instruction in sociology'.

4   It is possible to see here that Blumer and Duster follow Park's general idea, where he argued that 'status, which has to do with self-conception, social control and how one sees one's group in relation to other groups, is usually of greater importance in influencing collective action than the distribution of material rewards' (Lal, 1986: 286).

5   As Blumer and Duster illustrate well: 'The superordinate group may be seen as having noble qualities or as having an evil make-up; it may be seen providing paternal care and guidance or it may be seen as exploitative and to be distrusted' (1990: 231).

6   For more about these Soviet and Yugoslav cases see Brubaker (1996) and Malešević (2000).

7   On results of the social surveys that confirm the view that most lay individuals subscribe to versions of a primordialist view of ethnicity, see Uzelac (1999, 2002) and Bacova and Ellis (1996).

8 As Brubaker (1996: 18) illustrates, '[this category] was assigned by the state at birth on the basis of descent. It was registered in personal identity documents. It was recorded in almost all bureaucratic encounters and official transactions. And it was used, restricting the opportunities of some nationalities, especially Jews, and promoting others through preferential treatment policies for so-called "titular" nationalities in "their own" republics.'

Chapter Six

SOCIOBIOLOGY: ETHNIC GROUPS AS EXTENDED FAMILIES

Introduction

Since the publication of Darwin's *On the Origin of Species by Means of Natural Selection* in the mid-nineteenth century, the theory of evolution has had a very strong impact on the social sciences. Herbert Spencer, Ludwig Gumplowicz, Charles Sumner, Albert Keller, Gustav Ratzenhofer and other early sociologists were deeply influenced by Darwin's ideas and today we know them as social Darwinists. Social Darwinism characterized an attempt to apply the central principles of Darwin's theory of evolution to human societies. This attempt was crude, simplistic and often politically motivated. For the most part it was based on simple analogies between biological organisms and human collectivities: societies are just like organisms – they grow and evolve from primitive to more complex, both are composed of parts that exist to maintain the whole, the growth of population puts a strain on resources which inevitably generates the struggle for survival among organisms, and so on. Social Darwinism gradually developed into a racist movement when the new interpretation of race became attached to physical characteristics and races became seen as biologically and not environmentally shaped entities (Claeys, 2000). Some of the more extreme ideas of social Darwinism (i.e., the practice of eugenics through the sterilization and eventual annihilation of the 'genetically unfit' and 'racially impure'), were adopted and further developed by the Nazis to justify the policies behind the Holocaust. As a result, from World War II onwards there has been a general academic and institutional discomfort and suspicion regarding the use of biological concepts in explanations of human relations.

Nevertheless, with the evermore numerous discoveries and revolutionary breakthroughs in the field of genetics, biology has come to haunt us again. Biological explanations of human behaviour are gaining enormous popularity among the general public as popular biology books sell much better than popular sociology books. However, most of sociology remains stubborn in preserving the post-war consensus and its blunt rejection of any link between the animal and human worlds. This view is all too rigid and often counter-productive, since contemporary attempts to apply some tenets of evolutionary theory to social behaviour have very little if any connection with old social Darwinism. Sociobiology and its more recent derivative, memetics, are not based on simple analogies but are a much more sophisticated attempt to explain human behaviour through the prism of evolutionary theory. In this chapter I will explore the key ideas of sociobiology and especially how these ideas have been applied to the study of ethnic relations.

What is sociobiology?

According to Wilson (1975: 4) sociobiology is 'the systematic study of the biological basis of all social behaviour'. Sociobiologists believe that social behaviour is largely determined by evolutionary strategies and can most adequately be explained by focusing on the evolutionary origins of life forms. Despite their environmental and biological autonomy, individual organisms are not self-sufficient entities that can exist on their own: social interaction is the precondition for their reproduction and survival. Studying ants, termites and bees, sociobiologists have realized that the classical Darwinian principle of individual selection, wherein organisms are seen as being motivated exclusively by self-reproduction, had to be altered to explain altruistic and group-oriented behaviour. In other words, in order to understand intensive sociability, collective solidarity, individual sacrifice for the group, or group behaviour in general, it was necessary to identify the key mechanisms of group natural selection. Drawing on Hamilton's (1964) concept of 'inclusive fitness' Wilson has attempted to explain social behaviour as a process of extending one's reproductive success to the group level, that is, to an organism's closest relatives. Thus, Wilson defines inclusive fitness as 'the sum of an individual's own fitness plus all its influence on fitness in its relatives other than direct descendants; hence the total effect of kin selection with reference to an individual' (1975: 586). However, by broadening the principles of natural selection to the level of a group, sociobiologists also had to abandon the individual organism as the elementary unit of social action in favour of a more basic element – the gene.

A gene is treated as an elementary unit of heredity which is passed from parent to offspring, and whose only purpose is to replicate itself. Genes are molecules made of DNA material. They contain information for making a specific protein and have replicatory potential. For Dawkins (1989: 35–6) the gene is 'a piece of chromosome which is sufficiently short for it to last, potentially, for long enough for it to function as a significant unit of natural selection'. It is a 'basic unit of selfishness'. In the eyes of sociobiology an individual organism serves no more than as 'a vehicle' of gene reproduction: 'the organism is only DNA's way of making more DNA' (Wilson, 1975: 3). Thus, it is the genes that are governed by the principle of inclusive fitness – when a gene cannot replicate itself directly it is programmed to do so indirectly, through its close kin. The principle of kin selection helps explain when and why genes and their corresponding carriers, organisms, are likely to behave altruistically. Individual organisms would favour their close genetic relatives as they are likely to share common genes (e.g., siblings share ½ of their genes, grandparents and grandchildren ¼, first cousins ⅛, etc.). There are many examples in nature that show how animals act altruistically without any apparent advantage to themselves (e.g., a sterile worker caste in honey bees, nest helpers in scrub jays, etc.). An often cited example of kin selection is Sherman's (1977) experiment on squirrels. Sherman's study focused on the probability of male and female squirrels to give alarm calls to other squirrels to warn of potential predators. The key independent variable here was the difference in the nesting patterns for males and females: while females tend to nest near genetic relatives males do not. Although such an alarm call would place female squirrels at apparent risk of attack, they were statistically significantly more likely than male squirrels to give such calls. The experiment was taken as a proof of kin selection in nature.

Applying these principles of inclusive fitness and kin selection to the animal world was largely unproblematic, but extending their explanatory potential to the world of human beings has brought much more controversy. Although recognizing the exceptionality of human beings in developing sophisticated means of communication, languages, systems of beliefs, plasticity of their role playing, rituals, ethics, aesthetics, flexibility of human social organizations and many other forms of cultural behaviour, sociobiologists hold a view that, in evolutionary terms, humans are, just as other animals, created by genes. Moreover, not only is it that they share a genetic make up with the rest of the animal kingdom but the behaviour of human beings is also governed by the actions of their genes. As Dawkins (1989: 2) puts it, 'we, and all other animals, are machines created by our genes'. Most sociobiologists recognize the importance of environment and culture on human behaviour but they still believe that culture has evolved from nature and, as such, it remains subordinated to nature. As van den Berghe (1981) claims: 'There is no denying the importance of culture, but culture is a superstructure that builds on a biological substratum. Culture grows out of biological evolution; it does not wipe the biological slate clean and start from scratch' (1981: 6).

Some sociobiologists stress the limits which genes impose on cultural transmission, while others attempt to explain cultural behaviour by introducing some form of cultural equivalent to the gene. Wilson was always a strong proponent of the idea that 'the genes hold culture on a leash', but for a number of years he has tried to argue for gene-culture co-evolution, describing 'culturgen' as 'the basic unit of inheritance in cultural evolution' (Lumsden and Wilson, 1981: x). Wilson still recommends searching for the 'basic unit of culture' since 'its existence and some of its characteristics can be reasonably inferred' (1998: 147), which could eventually help us achieve 'consilience' – the proof of unity of knowledge through all disciplines that could be explained with the help of a small number of fundamental natural laws.

Others, such as Dawkins (1986) and Blackmore (1999), believe that cultural evolution is much more Lamarckian than Darwinian and can most adequately be explained by introducing the concept of 'meme'.[1] As Blackmore explains (1999: 17), both genes and memes are replicators but while 'genes are instructions for making proteins, stored in the cells of the body and passed on in reproduction', memes are 'instructions for carrying out behaviour, stored in brains and passed on by imitation'. In other words, memes are the cultural equivalent of genes and secure their replication through imitation. The human ability to imitate was seen as crucial for maintaining and passing on cultural traits through space and time. They can include almost any cultural product that can be imitated, from poems, fashion and ways of house building to language, religion, philosophy or ideas in general. Just like genes, memes are considered to be selfish and motivated exclusively by self-reproduction. Memes and genes can strengthen each other (e.g., adopting polygamy as a cultural and religious norm in Shari'a law to transmit religious teachings to youngsters and converts while maintaining male dominance in a patriarchal society that will maximize gene reproduction), but they can also be in conflict (e.g., the celibacy of Catholic clergy is a powerful meme successfully transmitted through generations but it is in direct conflict with the possibility of priests' gene reproduction potential).

Although there is no agreement on whether cultural behaviour should be explained by genes alone or by the interplay between genes, memes and environment, there is a common belief among sociobiologists that sociobiology is capable of explaining standard sociological processes: co-operation, conflict, social divisions, family, kinship, gender relations and so on. However, what is important for this study is the sociobiological contention that it can successfully explain the nature of ethnic phenomena.

Sociobiology and ethnic relations

If humans, as sociobiology claims, co-operate, compete and fight for basically the same reasons as other animals, than following this line of argument it seems reasonable to assume that most social action can be explained by invoking their biological essence. Eibl Eibesfeldt and Salter (2001), van den Berghe (1978, 1981, 1995), Rushton (1999), MacDonald (2000), van der Dennen (1991, 1999) and Vanhanen (1999), among others, start from this general idea in an attempt to develop a neo-Darwinian theory of ethnicity. Although most sociobiological accounts of ethnicity share the central principles of evolutionary theory, not all of them have developed a fully coherent sociological theory of ethnic relations. Thus, for example, Eibl Eibesfeldt and Salter (2001) focus on the biological and psychological predispositions for in-group favouritism. They argue that although ethnic group prejudice have often to be invoked by powerful leaders or by specific social conditions, one has to trace the biologically 'evolved trait of indoctrinability' in order to explain ethnic animosity. Vanhanen (1999) and van der Dennen (1991, 1999) direct their attention to large-scale ethnic struggles and wars in order to identify the biological roots of social conflicts, arguing that the 'universality of ethnic conflicts' should be attributed to 'our evolved predisposition to ethnic nepotism'. MacDonald (2000) attempts to provide an 'integrative evolutionary perspective on ethnicity' by synthesizing some rational choice propositions, social identity theory, genetic similarity theory and a number of other 'compatible' approaches. However, it is only in the work of van den Berghe (1978, 1981, 1999) that one can find a well-articulated sociological theory of ethnic relations.

To fully comprehend the nature of ethnic phenomenon it is necessary, according to van den Berghe (1981), to study human behaviour at three general and deeply interrelated levels: genetic, ecological and cultural. On the genetic level, humans are analysed as a special branch of animals that evolved through the process of natural selection. In tune with the fundamental principles of sociobiology, the emphasis is on human beings as carriers of the genes which are programmed to blindly reproduce themselves. On the ecological level animals and humans are studied by also taking into account their adjusted responses to unpredictable and overpowering changes in environment. Environmental conditions such as the climate, space, light and water, as well as their biotic environment which includes plants and other animals, have a momentous impact on the process of both animal and human development. It is only at the cultural level where humans begin to differ from the rest of the animal kingdom. With the emergence of culture humans have developed their own mechanisms of control, manipulation and adaptation, which are transmitted between individuals and societies as well as through different generations in a non-genetic fashion. Van den Berghe recognizes that cultural evolution is remarkably faster than its biological counterpart. Humans have in many ways acquired a great deal of power over their environment and with the advancement of technology have become by far the most superior species on the planet.

However, in spite of its importance and strength, culture remains subordinate to nature: 'genes are selected through environmental pressures, and they impose limits on culture' (van den Berghe, 1981: 6). Therefore, genetically programmed genes override the forces of culture. Although exceptional in some respects, humans are still, as are the rest of the animal world, guided in their actions by the power of genetics. Following Dawkins, van den Berghe sees genes as selfish 'survival machines' whose only purpose is to reproduce and multiply.

So, if individuals as gene carriers are programmed to be egoistic how can one explain social and altruistic behaviour, the prime example of which is ethnic group solidarity? Drawing on the central sociobiological principle of inclusive fitness, van den Berghe (1978, 1981) has identified the following three factors as decisive in influencing human sociability: kin selection; reciprocity; and coercion.

Kin selection is a direct outcome of the inclusive fitness tenet: the successful reproduction of a gene is not determined only by its own self-reproduction but also by the effects it has on its 'relatives'. When organisms cannot directly reproduce they will aim to replicate through close relatives. Hence, in–group favouritism has biological predispositions: genes will always prefer kin over non-kin and consequently individual organisms, including human indivi-duals, will tend to behave in a nepotistic way. Group solidarity and altruistic actions in general materialize only 'if the cost/benefit ratio of the transac-tion is smaller than the coefficient of relatedness between alter and ego'(van den Berghe, 1978: 403). In other words, in a paradoxical twist, co-operation, individual sacrifice and group solidarity are only possible because of genetic selfishness.

The rule of kin selection applies equally to ethnic relations. In the eyes of sociobiology, ethnicity is no more than a form of extended kinship. Since all human societies tend to be organized on the basis of kinship it seems obvi-ous to sociobiologists that ethnic sentiments should be analysed as kinship sentiments. Ethnic groups are defined by common descent. Ethnocentrism is a type of nepotism that evolved during millions of years as an extension of kin selection. According to van den Berghe common descent can be real or mythical, but even when it is a mere myth it cannot be completely manu-factured. The myth of common ethnic descent has to be believed in and endorsed by a number of generations.

Sociobiologists share the view that ethnic groups are primordial entities dating back to and even before the origins of *Homo sapiens*. In addition to com-mon genetic descent, ethnic groups (or ethnies as called by van den Berghe) are also moulded by the patterns of endogamy and by the territory they populate. For most of human history individuals have lived in small groups not exceeding one hundred members, characterized by inbreeding and inhabiting small and relatively closed spaces. As claimed by sociobiologists, while there was a solidarity and co-operation within the groups they were largely hostile to other groups with whom they were in constant competition and conflict over scarce resources. It was only in the last few thousand years that human groups have expanded in size and complexity. Urbanization, industrialization and modernization have had an impact on ethnicity – the boundaries of ethnic groups have widened, a sense of kinship has become more fictive and ethnic markers more prone to instrumentalization. However, as van den Berghe argues (1981: 35) 'the urge ... to continue to define a collectivity larger than the immediate circle of kinsmen on the basis of biological descent continues to be present even in the most industrialised mass societies of today'.

Nevertheless, not all social interaction is a product of kin selection. Reciprocity is another form of human relations. People co-operate in order to benefit mutually. Such co-operation does not have to be kin-determined. Some animals co-operate through symbiosis such as termites, wood roaches and the protozoa in their digestive system, or leaf-cutter ants and fungi, or a beaver and the water weed and so on. Human animals often behave as self-conscious beings who are able and know how to pursue their interests. The trade and exchange of gifts are examples of conscious reciprocity.

Reciprocity also opens the possibility for free riding, that is, for intentional deceit of one actor over the other. Humans have developed extremely sophisticated mechanisms and strategies of deception, including self-deceit. According to van den Berghe, ideology and religion are prime examples of collective self-deceit. While religion's main purpose is to deny mortality, ideologies justify unequal class positions. Ethnocentrism is seen as a form of rudimentary ideology that originated in pre-modern societies, but it has extended its influence to contemporary mass societies (van den Berghe, 1978, 1981). Reciprocity becomes increasingly important as societies evolve and become more complex. However, even in very complex and highly modernized societies, reciprocity remains a much weaker force than kin selection. This is most clearly visible when comparing the intensity and strength of ethnic and class solidarity. For sociobiologists ethnicity and class belong to two different and often opposing types of collectivities based on very different social relationships. Whereas ethnicity is based on kin selection and is an example of a type I group, which 'tend to be ascriptive, defined by common descent, generally hereditary, and often endogamous', class has an origin in reciprocity and belongs to type II group, which is defined in terms of common interests (van den Berghe, 1978: 402–3). Hence, kinship-based groups (race, ethnicity or caste) remain a much more powerful force than interest-based groups (professional associations, political parties, class or status groups). Reciprocity has developed at a much later stage of human evolution and its appeal is located in cold rationality and instrumentality, while kin selection has a deep emotional appeal of family devotion.

Nevertheless, there is a third and very powerful form of sociability — coercion. Much of human history is based on asymmetrical relationships of power, where only a privileged few have benefited at the expense of the rest. Although coercion is not human invention (lions, baboons and some other species also use force to establish their supremacy), humans have developed very complex and sophisticated techniques of domination. They use coercion not only through individual dominance hierarchies, as is the case with the rest of the animal world, but humans also impose force through group hierarchies. Furthermore, unlike animals humans do not have to rely on physical strength to dominate others. Even intelligence does not guarantee political domination. It is the control of superior technology and the means of violence that has been at the heart of individual and group hierarchy. The human form of parasitism has evolved most successfully through the development of the State and its ideological apparatus. Van den Berghe (1981: 61) defines a State in a fairly economistic way as 'a collectivity headed by a group of people who exercise power over others (who are neither kinsmen nor spouses), in order to extract surplus production for their own individual and collective benefit'. The State is perceived as a prime example of parasitism, where the ruling group uses organized means of coercion to exploit the rest of the citizenry to better their own inclusive fitness. This parasitism is successfully maintained and legitimized with the help of the state's ideological machinery. Nationalism, that is, a dominant set of values expressed by the nation (i.e., the politically conscious ethny), is one such ideology.

According to van den Berghe states are created in two main ways: internally through the centralization of power (by the individual's or group's gradual assertion of control over the rest of the ethny), or externally through conquest of their neighbouring ethnies. Unlike most historical sociologists, van den Berghe does not believe in the modernity of nation-states. On the contrary, he argues that modern states have virtually always been built on the ruins of older state forms. The only significant difference is that throughout history states were either larger (as in empires) or smaller (as in city states) than nations. Although modernity has brought about an increase in the number of nation-states they are, just as in earlier historical periods (and perhaps even more so), primarily organized around a single ethny. Since a nation is no more than a politically aware ethny, the institution of State remains, in his view, generally unsuccessful when attempting to create nations out of an array of ethnies. Belgium is often cited as a typical example of this process – being composed of two distinct ethnies it has been seen as no closer to comprising a single fully fledged nation than it was at the time of its creation in 1830. In van den Berghe's words: 'Flemings and Walloons are almost exactly where their ancestors were in relation to each other just after Julius Caesar wrote De Bello Gallico: straddling an almost static linguistic frontier between more and less Romanised populations' (1999: 31).

In more recent sociobiological writings (van den Berghe, 1999) ethnicity is described as a universal attribute firmly rooted in both genes and memes. Memes, the cultural equivalent of genes, help convey distinct ideas, values, symbols and other cultural artefacts through the process of imitation. Individual cultures are perceived as being composed of 'memetic complexes' that work as cultural filters which help orientate individual and group action. Ethnocentrism, xenophobia or ethno-nationalism are examples of memetic complexes that replicate themselves through human minds. Since they are inherited from one generation to the next these shared memetic values and beliefs help bond members of a particular ethny. Memetic complexes thus often function as ideological supplements to the genetic in-group favouritism. Given that memes replicate in the brain, which is in itself a product of genetic competition in the eyes of sociobiologists, both genes and memes are responsible for ethnic group behaviour. While memes, also referred to as mental viruses, have autonomy, they operate in an environment created by genes and abide by the same evolutionary principles.

Is ethnicity kinship writ large?

Most criticisms of sociobiology and memetics focus on the ethical implications of their propositions. These theories have often been accused of having implicit or explicit conservative, racist or sexist agendas. The arguments put forward by sociobiologists are regularly seen as controversial if not also downright dangerous. It has often been claimed that explaining differences and inequalities in biological terms leads directly to a justification of those inequalities and differences. In this respect sociobiology is seen as giving ideological support for the status quo policies that regularly work against weaker and disadvantaged groups in any given society. Hence making a claim that ethnic groups are no more than an extension of kinship would immediately validate a claim that ethnic conflicts are natural, rooted in human nature and, thus, unavoidable.

Although sociobiological arguments have been occasionally used by racist and sexist individuals and groups, this type of criticism is not only analytically weak but is often very counter-productive. First, any systematic theoretical attempt to explain the motives of human behaviour is open to misinterpretation, simplification, political manipulation and general misuse. If we hold Darwin responsible for racism and sexism, we can, with equal vigour, hold Thomas Aquinas responsible for the Spanish Inquisition, Rousseau for the Jacobin Reign of Terror, Marx for Stalin's gulags or Nietzsche for Auschwitz. Not only is it pointless to condemn or prevent academic inquiry on the grounds of its potential misuse but, more importantly, by avoiding proper analytical engagement with sociobiology and memetics, sociology leaves this important field of research on the motives of human behaviour exposed to monopolistic closure on the part of biologists. In other words, since the study of genes is developing into an increasingly important area of research, recognized academically and publicly, sociology cannot simply disregard these developments as irrelevant. For ignorance might be costly if sociology becomes perceived as a dogmatic discipline that is lagging behind in understanding and accounting for developments in genetics and evolutionary biology.[2] Sociology was conceived as an endeavour to understand and explain (if not dispel) taboos, not to create new ones.

Secondly, not engaging intelligently with developments in modern genetics can lead to crude and simplified notions of 'genes' and 'culture'. Contemporary sociology has come a long way from perceiving 'culture' in an essentialist and unproblematic way, which was an integral part of social science from Plato to Durkheim to Parsons. However, accounting for softer understandings of 'nurture' did not follow any de-essentialization of 'nature': most sociological opponents of sociobiology hold a very essentialist view of genes. Genes are seen as unchangeable and highly deterministic entities. It is believed that accepting the role of genes implies that we are somehow genetically predestined in our actions. However, modern genetics demonstrates that this view cannot be further from the truth: DNA is an extremely dynamic molecule, under constant construction and reconstruction, defined by its variability and tendency to mutate. Genes change under the influence of environment and, in the long term, under the influence of culture. Furthermore genes do not determine human action, they rather provide a potential for a certain course of action. It is a receptiveness to illness which one can inherit, not the illness itself (Steen, 1996). Just as biologists like Wilson operate with an unreflexive and reified concept of culture, so do most sociologists subscribe to an essentialist concept of gene. Reflexive sociology has to engage with a dynamic genetics of today and not with the deterministic biology of yesteryear.

So, as sociologists, we cannot simply discount what humans share in common with other animals – the need to breathe, eat, drink, sleep and, most of all, to procreate. Biology in general and genes in particular do indeed influence our actions. Genes behave as universal replicators and Darwin's idea of 'natural selection' through self-reproduction still holds true for humans as it does for iguanas and houseflies. However, accepting that Darwinian principles of reproduction through individual selection apply to the world of humans with equal strength as to the animal kingdom, does not imply an unquestionable acceptance of its Hamiltonian (1964) extension to group behaviour. While 'inclusive fitness' might play a part in accounting for altruistic social behaviour in humans, it is very far from being a law or even a stable, identifiable pattern of human behaviour as it is for animals. Human beings have, obviously, started from the same evolutionary position, but they have evolved to such an extent that they are now able to interfere and often override genetics. Cloning, the use of GM foods, and the production of stem cells for treating inherited diseases are just some of the more recent examples demonstrating the magnitude of human power over nature. So the really interesting premises and questions here are not those of rigid social constructionism or inflexible biological essentialism that undermine genes or culture, but rather those that attempt to answer when, why, how and under which circumstances culture will act as a more powerful agent than the gene pool, and vice versa. This is a fascinating area of study that needs careful and extensive exploration by sociologists.

So where does this leave us in the study of ethnic relations? First, defining ethnicity in terms of kinship only is an extremely narrow understanding of a much larger phenomenon. Ethnicity is not a fixed and static category; rather it often functions as an umbrella term for many different forms of groupness. It is us, social scientists (and after us journalists and state administrators) who have created and helped institutionalize this term to make sense of very distinct types of group cultural difference. To paraphrase Heisenberg's uncertainty principle, it is the observer as much as the observed that reveals (ethnic) reality. 'Ethnicity' is not real; it is a social concept created to make sense of inter-group difference. As Jenkins (2002b) rightly points out, ethnicity is just one form that collectivity can take and collectivities are not 'things that just happen', nor are they primeval deterministic forces that ultimately set the course of individual action. Nevertheless, saying that ethnicity is an abstract concept does not imply that cultural differences are fictitious: on the contrary, because the cultural and often physical variation among human beings is real the politization of group membership on such a basis is possible. But difference does not necessarily translate into group animosity. Sociobiology is completely unaware of this fact. As we can read in van den Berghe (1995: 365) 'racism, defined as discriminatory behaviour based on inherited physical appearance, can be expected to arise whenever variance in inherited physical appearance is greater between groups than within groups'. The problem with this line of argument is that it equates ethnic difference with conflict. However, what is crucial in ethnic relations, as Weber (1968) was well aware, is not the mere existence of the particular cultural or physical difference that constitutes a group but, rather, collective political action that makes group difference relevant and sociologically meaningful.

Secondly, van den Berghe's view of ethnicity as being a universal, omnipotent, primordial force based on common descent, rooted in the principles of inclusive fitness and kin selection is too static and analytically limiting. While inclusive fitness and kin selection might have played a greater role in the organization and behaviour of human collectivities at the dawn of humanity, when our ancestors indeed lived in very small and genetically compact groupings, this dramatically changed from the moment humans started developing even rudimentary forms of technology, science and political and social institutions. Among other things, these developments resulted in an exceptional scale of migration and 'interbreeding'. Van den Berghe recognizes how profound this change was but still minimizes its relevance for the nature of ethnicity. This is a crucial problem for any sociobiological account of ethnic relations. Whereas van den Berghe agrees that in modernity common descent can be fictitious and is often open to manipulation, he still maintains that most people continue to identify with groups that claim biological descent. However, claiming genetic kinship and actually possessing such a kinship are two very different things. If one rigorously follows the sociobiological interpretation of social behaviour then you cannot have it both ways. If the argument is that humans are carriers of their genes, then any reference to symbolic kinship and behaviour determined by the belief in common descent is simply not good sociobiology. As contemporary genetics has proven on many occasions (Cavalli-Sforza et al., 1996), with the possible exception of Basques, Icelanders and a few other ethnic collectivities, there is very little genetic intra-group similarity among the ethnic groups worldwide. The great majority of human groups are genetically hybrid populations. So what we are left with today is very little genetics and a lot of culture – that is, a belief in common descent. It is true that this belief is an exceptionally strong aspect of ethnic politics but what is crucial here, and at the same time defeating for any sociobiological account, is that it is only a belief, it is not a biological fact.

Thirdly, this conflation of real and fictive kinship when discussing ethnicity is just a symptom of a wider problem present in sociobiology and memetics. Both Wilson and Dawkins, just as van den Berghe or Blackmore, attribute to genes and memes anthropomorphic features. The often-heard syntagms 'selfish gene' or 'egotistical meme' imply that genes and memes possess a will of their own. They are personalized and given properties that only thinking creatures can have: consciousness, purposefulness or motivation. This is again a case of poor genetics – genes are not only very far from being fixed and static entities (the concept 'gene' is used in a number of different ways by geneticists for changing sections along the DNA) but, more importantly, if they are governed by laws of genetics and biology they could never be egoistic or altruistic since these are moral qualities. Morality is a product of culture *par excellence*. The mere fact that genes manage to survive for much longer periods than other biological entities and that some genes endure longer than others, tells us only that they are stronger and more persistent – but it does not tell us anything about their 'character'. Midgley (1980) nicely illustrates this by depicting genes as a group of travellers who had independently crossed a horrible desert. 'It might happen that in doing so they had unknowingly often removed resources which would have saved the lives of others – but this could tell us nothing about their characters unless they had known that they were doing so, and scraps of nuclear tissue are incapable of knowledge'(1980: 128). With memes this is even more so, since memes are no more than a mental creation: there is no material, physical equivalent of DNA. In both cases there is an extensive reliance on metaphor, which is a sign of feeble science.

The perception of ethnicity as an extended family is a powerful image but it is an image based solely on the use of metaphor – people inhabiting an island like Ireland might believe in the myth of common descent but genetically they are not related; biologically they do not constitute a single super family. People do indeed use and project the family and kin-related metaphors onto large-scale ethnic groups, such as depicting Mustafa Kemal Ataturk as 'the father of all Turks', speaking of 'the sons and daughters of the eternal mother Russia', indicating that one shares the same German 'blood', and so on, but very few individuals actually believe that they are related in a biological sense. As Smith (1998) points out, the myth of common ethnic ancestry does not have to imply belief in common biological roots: the Roman myth of common descent stressed their diverse origins (Sabines, Latins, Etruscans) as does the English myth of common ancestry (Briton, Anglo-Saxon, Norman). In addition, there are often situations when there are two or more competing ideologies of ethnic origin at work. For example, the competing Greek myth of ethnic descent that emphasizes either ancient Hellenic roots (supported by pro-Western secular intelligentsia) or the myth of the chosen people of true faith tied to Byzantine Orthodoxy (propagated by clergy and other anti-Western conservative groups). What is relevant here is that these myths of ethnic descent historically change as the socio-political environment changes.

Fourthly, being grounded in Wilson's essentialist biology van den Berghe's theory of ethnicity also operates with an unreflexive concept of 'nature'. Van den Berghe does not problematize the concept of gene, he simply takes it for granted. This approach, which builds on analogy with physics (the gene as an equivalent to an atom or quark), is based on a naïve view (long surpassed in contemporary physics) that one can identify an 'elementary unit' of analysis governed by universal physical laws. The recent research in physics, chemistry and astronomy has established that the fundamental goal of Newtonian mechanistic science to identify the ultimate element of analysis to which all matter can be reduced was a utopian project: there is no 'elementary unit' in physics, there is only a temporary stability of fields (Malešević, 2002a: 80–1). This is even more apparent in biology and culture – genes are extremely dynamic sets of molecules, while searching for the 'basic unit of culture' as Wilson now advocates would sound rather humorous to most contemporary anthropologists and sociologists. This extremely posi-tivist approach leads van den Berghe (1995: 360) to a conclusion that 'all social organisms are biologically programmed to be nepotistic'. While one can agree that nepotism is an important part of human sociability there is no evidence which indicates that nepotism is all (or at all) genetic. Humans internalize values that prevent us from acting on nepotistic impulses, but we are also socialized to be nepotistic – a mother who abandons her baby is a social outcast in any society. As child psychologists tell us, small children do not differentiate between 'races' and 'ethnic groups'; we learn to be racist. The simple fact that levels of nepotism differ in different societies is a good indicator that ethnocentrism is not entirely genetic. As argued and docu-mented by Weber (1961, 1968) and Schumpeter (1942), societies also differ in their perception of nepotism: whereas nepotism is a backbone of social solidarity in traditional society, nepotism is largely seen, in theory if not in practice, as being harmful to capitalist meritocracy.

Finally, the most serious problem with sociobiology and memetics in gen-eral, and van den Berghe's theory in particular, is that it cannot provide what it promises in the way of a biological explanation of social phenomena. Van den Berghe's theory of ethnicity works very well when it moves from inclu-sive fitness and kin selection to social, political and cultural explanations of ethnic relations. As we can see even the formal, biological part of this theory, kin selection, for the most part operates on a symbolic level – social actors believe in the myth of common descent and that belief governs their nepotis-tic behaviour.

The remaining two building blocks of the sociobiological account of eth-nicity, namely reciprocity and coercion, are both outside the domain of biology. Reciprocity is rooted in an instrumental logic of trade and exchange, while coercion is associated with asymmetrical power relations and justifi-cation of such a situation by state rulers through a dominant ideology. While both reciprocity and coercion are important elements for explaining group behaviour in van den Berghe's theory, their connection to kin selection is largely provisional and unnecessary. In other words, sociobiology cannot explain ethnicity within biology and without invoking non-biological processes such as trade, exchange, political manipulation and ideological justification. Instead of digging deep into the research of contemporary genetics, van den Berghe rather adopts a crude Marxist interpretation of state coercion, where the state is defined in very simplified economistic and conspiratorial terms and reduced to a group of manipulating agents, whose only aim is to 'extract surplus production' from their subjects.[3] Instead of providing a subtle analysis of the relationship between culture and heredity when discussing ethnocentrism, van den Berghe simply shifts between cultural and biological interpretation: while in kin selection ethnocentrism is biologically rooted, in reciprocity and coercion it is no more than a set of sophisticated lies. So, the principal problem in the sociobiological theory of ethnicity is that it is more social than biological and what sociobiology can explain (i.e., reciprocity, coercion, etc.) other sociological theories can explain just as well if not better without invoking genes or biology. Until the time sociobiology can provide a biologically or genetically more potent and coherent theory of ethnicity we will have to look for more persuasive explanations elsewhere.

Conclusion

The main contribution of sociobiology to the understanding of human behaviour is its rehabilitation of the largely depreciated connection between biology and society. Sociobiologists rightly emphasize that human beings are part and parcel of nature, that we also follow Darwin's principles of variation, selection and retention in that we have much more in common with the rest of the animal kingdom than we would like to think. Van den Berghe (1990: 175) is right when he argues that there is a certain 'specieswide anthropocentrism' that dominates contemporary sociology. The new and ever-increasing discoveries in biology highlight the importance of an analytical engagement of sociology with genetics. Sociology cannot remain deaf to these developments. However, current sociobiological interpretations of ethnic relations are for the most part futile and limited in explanatory terms. Ethnicity is explained either solely through reference to social and cultural categories (as in the concepts of coercion and reciprocity), or by shifting between biological and metaphorical versions of kin selection. In addition, just as in rational choice theory (see Chapter 7), sociobiology is tautological and circular and thus unfalsifiable.[4] Memetics, for its part, reduces culture to mere imitation while accounts of genes and memes both oscillate between unreflective positivism and a constant reliance on metaphors. For the sociobiological model of ethnicity to be taken more seriously it needs a much stronger genetic and biological interpretation of social behaviour than it currently possesses. Ethnicity can occasionally be 'kinship writ large', but is obviously much more than that, as any reference to fictive kinship indicates. Human beings have a great deal in common with other species but what is crucial in explaining ethnic relations is not their similarity but their difference from the animal world. While all have developed to the evolutionary stage of being animals capable of survival, only some of us have also developed into political animals – and that is what is at the heart of ethnic relations.

Notes

1   Unlike Darwinism, Lamarckianism is grounded in a belief that traits that an organism acquires during its lifetime can be passed directly on to its offspring. In other words for Lamarckians evolutionary changes proceed at the much faster pace.

2   Whereas psychology and anthropology have significantly engaged with evolutionary biology and genetics, sociology, as van den Berghe (1990: 175) points out, has managed to purge biology 'even from the two specialties where its relevance would seem most glaringly obvious: demography and ecology'. However, there are a few emerging but influential sociological voices that call for sociology's re-evaluation of the 'natural world', such as those of Jenkins (2002a) and Archer (2000).

3   Van den Berghe's definition of the state is not only deeply economistic in reducing a complex system of institutions and agencies to groups of people who benefit from the extraction of surplus production, but it is also extremely vague. Such a wide definition could accommodate anything from business enterprises to the Catholic Church.

4   Van den Berghe agrees that his theory is unfalsifiable (1986: 250), but does not see it as a major problem since 'insistence on a test of instantaneous falsifiability is based on a naïve perception of the development of scientific theory'.

Chapter Seven

RATIONAL CHOICE THEORY: ETHNIC GROUP MEMBERSHIP AS AN INDIVIDUAL GAIN

Introduction

Rational choice theory (RCT) has its philosophical roots in Hobbes' and Locke's theory of social contract, and Bentham's and Mill's utilitarianism and the view of human nature as being intrinsically selfish, greedy and largely unchangeable. Its economic and mathematical origins can be traced to Adam Smith and neo-classical economics as well as to increasingly popular game theory. However, what is most important for us is its sociological background. Although this background has never been fully explored one can find rational choice type arguments in some of Weber's and Pareto's works. Weber's (1968) theoretical and, to a lesser extent, his empirical emphasis on methodological individualism, as well as his accent on the fact that only individuals are capable of 'meaningful social action', and Pareto's theory of social action (1966) with an emphasis on individual rationality in the process of justification of *residuas* through *derivations*, all indicate a strong presence of RCT-type thinking among the classics of sociological theory. This legacy of the classics, with their emphasis on individual self-interest and motivated action, features strongly in RCT's take on ethnicity.

There seems to be something paradoxical in the study of ethnic relations within the theoretical framework of rational choice theory. The rational choice approach is by its methodology and epistemology ultimately an individualist position of analysis, while ethnic conflicts and ethnic relations in general are regarded as having a distinctly collectivist character. Rational choice theory draws its explanations from the central assumption of an individual's rationality, whereas ethnic hostilities and conflicts are often perceived by many as examples of collective irrationality. However, ethnic relations and ethnic group solidarity have been one of the phenomena where RCT analysis has been shown to be a very popular and applicable paradigm. In the realm of the contemporary sociology of ethnic relations, RCT is one of the more influential approaches. The aim of this chapter is briefly to interpret and critically evaluate some of the RCT postulates, particularly in the way they have been used in the field of ethnic relations. The purpose of the chapter is to explore the strengths and weaknesses of RCT in terms of its explanatory power for the sociology of ethnic relations.

The foundations of rational choice theory

Rational choice theory is based on the simple assumption that human beings are rational and motivated by self-interest in their everyday actions. The notion that individuals tend to behave as rational and egoistic creatures also includes assumptions that their actions are predominantly intentional as well as that they have a stable and relatively consistent set of preferences. It is argued that although the actions of actors may be restricted by their experience and social norms, their behaviour can regularly be explained in reference to their need to try to maximize their advantages. Unlike structuralism or functionalism (see Chapter 3), where the elementary unit of analysis is a social system, a collective, in rational choice theory that place is always reserved for an individual. Individual actors are seen to be the point of departure for analysis, while group and collective behaviour is interpreted as co-operation driven by the primacy of self-interest.

Unlike most other contemporary sociological theories, rational choice theory is exclusively focused on human behaviour. Its theoretical postulates as well as its methodological and empirical studies are concentrated on explaining and predicting individual and group behaviour, whereas attitudes, beliefs, cultural values and ideologies are mostly neglected or simply perceived as a 'second order reality'. The analyses of behaviour are also distinct in a sense of overemphasizing maximization over optimization. In other words, unlike neo-functionalist explanations that see human beings as *homines sociologici* whose actions are predominantly norm-oriented, for RCT an individual is actually the opposite – *homo economicus* – whose actions are almost universally seen and explained as utility-oriented. In RCT analyses one can clearly find Smith's and Hobbes' legacy that states that 'only desire can motivate action'.

Although there is a strong common link between various rational choice theories, one can still identify significant differences between the three leading rational choice sociologists, Jon Elster, Raymond Boudon and James Coleman. While all three share an emphasis on methodological individualism, the primacy given to the actor's intentionality and to rationality, they all differ in their theoretical and political leanings: whereas Elster develops a Marxist theory of rational choice and Boudon builds on the Weberian tradition, Coleman's aim is to provide a theoretical synthesis of micro and macro positions by using rational choice theory.

Elster's work is unique in his interpretation of Marx as a methodological individualist. Although Marx is commonly perceived as a methodological holist whose explanations focus on structural factors such as the 'capitalist mode of production', 'social formations' or 'social classes' and, as such, has been traditionally 'hijacked' by structuralist Marxists such as Althusser, Poulantzas or Godelier, Elster (1985, 1990) has attempted to demonstrate that Marx was, first of all, concerned with explaining the unintended consequences of human action. Unlike structuralist-oriented Marxists, Elster's analytical Marxism aims to show that what is good and worth preserving in Marx's work was his economistic model of social action. What is needed, according to Elster, is to set the micro foundations for Marxian macro analysis and to introduce game theory in order to explain the strategies of the individual actors and their motives and necessities in the formation of collective organizations such as social classes. For Elster, Marx's emphasis on class struggle indicates that he was primarily concerned with agency (proletariat and capitalist entrepreneurs as social agents) and not with structure, as is commonly believed.

In contrast to Elster, Boudon's ambition is to develop a rational choice theory of the Weberian type. Although Weber is traditionally seen as an idealist, a neo-Kantian, whose explanations of value systems and world religions are derived from his *verstehen*, interpretative-driven methodology, Boudon's aim is to show us another, more materialist, face of Weber. As Boudon tries to demonstrate, Weber was not only a self-declared methodological individualist but also one whose many explanations focus on the rationality of individual actors (i.e., the Roman soldiers' affinity towards Mithraism or the impact of magic on aborigines). What also distinguishes Boudon's approach from most other rational choice positions is his significantly wider understanding of rationality. Instead of pure means–ends utilitarian rationality, Boudon (1987, 1989), following Weber, argues for the introduction of at least two other types of rationality: axiological and situated rationality. While axiological rationality refers to social action that is related to values and not to ends (in accordance with Weber's value-rational action), situated rationality includes, as Boudon explains, the set of an individual's 'good reasons' for undertaking certain action. Thus, the rationality of action according to Boudon can be accessed not only through utilitarian motives, but also through social action driven by particular strong beliefs (i.e., hero sacrifice) and through an actor's own internal motives for pursuing a particular course of action.

Unlike Elster and Boudon, Coleman (1990; Coleman and Fararo, 1992) is less interested in grounding his position in reference to the classical works.

Rather, his main aim is to defend rational choice against accusations of being too micro and too individualist. For that purpose his theory aims at integrating the micro and macro levels of analysis. However, integration is achieved by giving clear primacy to the micro level, which is a position neatly summed up in Collins' (1981) phrase as the 'microfoundations of macrosociology'. Coleman recognizes the fact that individuals very often behave in a non-economic way by seeking to realize collective interests at the expense of their self-interests, as well as the fact that they are institutionally and normatively constrained in their actions. He explains this situation in terms of granting the authority held by one individual to another, in which the authority that is granted leads to subordination of one actor to another and where a newly resulting entity (i.e., structure) begins to operate independently of the will of the actors. In this way actors are occasionally in a situation that leads them to behave in a way that accomplishes the interests of others or of the collective unit. Nevertheless, what is crucial for Coleman is that an individual's 'transfer of control' over their actions to others is initially motivated by self-interest. For Coleman (1990: 292) norms are nothing more than a result of an individual's 'giving up of partial rights of control over one's own action and the receiving of partial rights of control over the actions of others'. And as such, norms are 'initiated and maintained by some people who see benefits resulting from the observation of norms and harm stemming from the violation of those norms'.

Although these three positions differ greatly they also share many common themes, such as the assumption of an individual's rationality and methodological individualism. However, what is more important is that all three are similar in accounting for a solution to the two central questions for RCT: an individual's decision-making process, and the nature of co-operative behaviour. In other words, they all give similar answers to the questions: How do individuals make their choices? And how are society and collective action possible if everybody acts as a selfish individual?

The process of decision making is the key problem of RCT analysis. Individuals make decisions that may lead them to attain certain goals. They have more or less stable preferences and an available set of alternative behaviours. RCT states that in most cases individuals would behave rationally – acting so as to obtain the maximum net advantage. According to Elster (1986) there are three distinct elements in the choice situation:

1   A feasible set of all courses of action that are rationally believed to satisfy various 'outside' constraints.
2   A set of rational beliefs about the causal structure of the situation that controls the courses of action as well as their outcomes.
3   The subjective ranking of the feasible alternatives (often deduced from a ranking of the outcomes to which they are expected to lead).

RCT analysis claims that individuals 'will engage in collective action only when they estimate that by doing so they will receive a net individual benefit' (Hechter, 1986: 271).

The question of collective action is also answered in reference to individual motives. Thus, according to RCT, when one observes collective behaviour in practice this can always, in the end, be explained as a situation where actors integrate for the purpose of benefiting as individuals from the collective good, and where collective action only serves as a most rational means available to make the 'price' less costly. The famous 'prisoner's dilemma' game is for RCT a typical example of how individuals can lose if they blindly follow their own self-interests at the expense of altruistic behaviour that would prove to be a beneficial outcome for all of the actors involved. Co-operative behaviour in RCT analysis is analysed also with reference to game theory's models of assurance and chicken games. Therefore, group formation and group behaviour is explained in terms of cost-benefit calculations. To understand the RCT argument about collective action and group solidarity more clearly, let us take a look at how RCT explains ethnic relations.

Ethnic relations and rational choice theory

We should clarify from the outset that most rational choice theorists do not believe in the existence of anything called 'ethnic phenomena'. For Hechter (1986, 1995) ethnic relations are no qualitatively different from class, religion or status relations. Similarly to class, religion or status, in his view, ethnicity can be analysed and explained by reference to the ordinary sociological categories such as social and individual action, rationality, assimilation, group formation and so on. What makes ethnic groups different is only the fact that in this case cultural or physical differences are used by the actors themselves to demarcate individuals and social groups with the single aim of maximizing individual advantages.

Rational choice sociologists look at individuals as actors who are in a state of permanent competition over limited resources, economic advantages, wealth, power or status. In this process of competition, ethnicity, that is, shared meanings and cultural resources such as language, customs, accents, skin colour or even eating habits, can and very often do serve the function of making the price of group membership significantly cheaper. In other words, in the situation of group conflict or an imminent threat of such conflict, individuals are more likely to amplify the importance of their ethnic group membership. In these circumstances, according to Hechter (1986: 271), ethnic groups perform two functions: they are the central source of private rewards as well as punishments, which motivate actors to take part in collective action; and since the actor's cost-benefit calculation depends heavily on his/her estimation of the probability of success of that particular collective action, ethnic groups play a crucial role by controlling information and thus limiting the scope of choices available to individual actors. To put it more simply, individuals are, on the one hand, offered the benefits of ethnic group membership and, on the other, are restricted in their choices by the ethnic groups which prevent 'free riding' by monitoring and controlling their membership.

Although physical and cultural differences are closely related to ethnic animosities, since conflicts of this nature are perceived by the actors themselves as real group conflicts, they are in themselves insufficient for the formation of the groups. As Banton (1983) points out, it is only when these differences are granted cultural significance and used by individuals for their own ends that social groups form. For example, people may differ in the types of clothes they wear or what kind of flowers they like, but they would only under very exceptional circumstances organize themselves (perceive in-group/out-group membership) on such a basis and attribute cultural and political significance to this type of group membership.

To succeed in attributing cultural significance to groups it is necessary, as Barth (1969) was already aware, to tow the line between the groups and to demarcate the ethnic group boundaries. Only when groups manage to establish relatively firm boundary markers do cultural differences become sources of group identification. As long as actors compete on an individual basis the ethnic boundaries are largely irrelevant, but when collective action takes place the situation becomes completely different. In Banton's (1983) words, 'when people compete as individuals, group boundaries are weakened but when they compete as groups, boundaries are strengthened'. Thus, in rational choice theory ethnicity, just as any other form of collective membership, functions primarily as a source of benefits that compel individual actors to participate in collective action.

According to Hechter, collective action on an ethnic basis depends not only on a group's monitoring capacity but also on its organizational resources, the intensity and form of solidarity, the adoption of non-violent tactics, the history of equitable distribution of collective benefits and a group's size, as well as the capacity of individual and institutional 'opponents' to punish possible participants. Although Hechter recognizes the importance of the impact of structural factors on potential ethnic social action, it is his belief that individual motives are central for such an action to happen. Ethnicity is no more than a social resource that can be mobilized and manipulated for individual gain.

Although the strength of ethnic ties in more exceptional situations such as wars and conflicts is recognized, these are largely explained in reference to situational factors. Banton (1994) argues that individuals have a number of social roles within society and these roles are visualized as being arranged on a scale – from so-called basic roles (i.e., gender) at one end to those roles 'which are largely independent of other relationships' (i.e., fan club) at the other. As Banton claims, in more extreme situations 'ethnic roles that have been towards the middle of the scale have been pushed up to the basic end'. In other situations and under different circumstances, they are likely to be replaced with other social definitions – class, family, religion, etc.

In rational choice theory ethnic identity is perceived as one of the elements of a general social identity that every individual holds. RCT underlines the multiplicity of social identities. An interesting example is Basque ethnic identity (Lyman and Douglass, 1973). A Basque living in the US, in contact with another Spanish Basque, would stress his regional sub-ethnic identity (Vizcayan); in contact with a Basque from France he would stress his national ethnic identity (Spanish Basque); in contact with a non-Basque he would stress his general ethnic identity (Basque); and in contact with a Basque in the Basque region he is an American. This situationality and changeability of ethnic identities has been demonstrated by rational choice sociologists on numerous occasions. Since ethnicity has been identified as a social and cultural resource that actors can occasionally rely on in the pursuit of their own individual benefit, the researchers were eager to show how individuals use the strategy of so-called 'ethnic identity switching' in a rational and self-interested manner. A typical example is Duijzings' (1992) report on the appearance of a relatively large ethnic group in Kosovo and Macedonia in 1991 who claimed to be Egyptian and demanded to be registered as such in the Yugoslav census.

As Duijzings explains, in the previous census these people mostly declared themselves to be Albanians, while in fact, Duijzings thinks, they belonged by ethnic origin to the Romany Gypsy population. The reasons for their frequent 'identity switching' is the fact that after 1981 (the time of the previous Yugoslav census) Albanians lost their political dominance and Serbs took over the political hegemony and control of all strategic institutions in the province of Kosovo. In 1991 being Albanian was a clear disadvantage, so in order to gain some benefit from this position they demand to be a separate and distinct ethnic group – Egyptians. Here again one can see how RCT emphasizes fuzziness and circumstantionality of ethnic identities.

What is crucial for this perspective is the view that ethnicity is not a primordial or static feature but rather a dynamic, changing process. In other words, ethnicity is to be analysed principally in terms of inter-group and inter-individual relationships, not in terms of fixed cultural contents. As

Banton (1994) precisely states: 'change in ethnic relations often comes about not because people change the value they place upon association with co-ethnics, but because they change their ideas about which relationships are to be governed by ethnic norms'.

Since RCT is primarily concerned with social change and, unlike structuralism or functionalism, claims to be able to explain such change, the analysis of the changing nature of ethnicity is the main focus of its study. The change in the importance attributed to ethnic identity is hence explained in line with the cost-benefit calculations of individuals. In Hechter's view ethnicity should be analysed in relation to the individual's changing circumstances and his/her perception of this change:

> changing relative price leads to corresponding changes in behaviour: the more costly it is for people to choose a traditional course of action to achieve a given benefit, the more likely it is that they will consider an innovative alternative to reach the same end. (Hechter, 1986: 277)

Is ethnicity just a free riding trick?

The main epistemological strategy of rational choice theory is pragmatic reductionism. By pragmatic reductionism is meant that although the researcher is aware of the limitations of his/her theory and methodology, he/she is still committed to the activity of providing scientific explanations. However, these explanations are now possible, according to RCT, only if one analyses social phenomena by reducing them to individual actions, beliefs and properties. In other words, by applying the doctrine of methodological individualism. As Elster (1985: 5) argues, 'if the goal of science is to explain by means of laws, there is a need to reduce the time-span between explanans and explanandum – between cause and effect – as much as possible, in order to avoid spurious explanations' and 'in this perspective reductionism is not an end in itself, only a concomitant of another desideratum'. Hence, if sociology wants to remain an explanatory science then it has to opt for pragmatic reduction and methodological individualism.

The position of pragmatic reductionism clearly has its merits. On the one hand it aims at rescuing sociological research from the paralysis and irrationality of some post-essentialist approaches (see Chapter 10) and, on the other, it wishes to preserve sociology's explanatory potentials. Unlike postmodernism's reluctance to engage with 'real life issues' by overemphasizing the 'social construction' of reality such as gender, class and ethnicity, by arguing for the multiplicity of truths, and by avoiding singular explanations through playing with meta-narratives, rational choice theory does indeed provide a practical and reliable alternative of explanatory certainty. However, how plausible and certain is this certainty?

Unfortunately, this certainty is built on false and analytically sterile assumptions. First, there is a certain circularity in RCT explanations that leads towards explanatory dead-ends. If we assume that every individual action is rational and motivated by self-interest, then what is the point of analysis when we already know what our research results will be? In other words, RCT explanations seem very often to resemble some die-hard Marxist and feminist analyses that presuppose their findings by simply looking for and then finding their explanans and explanandums in patriarchy and capitalism. In rational choice theory these factors are assumed to be rationality, intentionality and the egoistic motives of actors. This circularity and tautology of analysis leads towards post hoc types of reasoning. As Baert (1998: 166) rightly points out, rational choice theorists 'conceive of their task as demonstrating the fact that social practices which are *prima facie* irrational are actually rational after all'. In this sense they are very similar to the early functionalist arguments of Malinowski and Radcliffe-Brown regarding the universal functionality of certain 'savage' customs, rituals and practices. What was functionality for Malinowski and Radcliffe-Brown is now rationality for Elster and Boudon. Since the circular and post hoc explanations are based upon propositions that are not empirically validated and which often aim at supplying mutually exclusive observations (i.e., explaining with the same level of conviction why people engage in ethnic conflicts and why they do not), this type of reasoning is therefore, as Baert (1998) and Smelser (1992) confirm, not falsifiable.

The deficiency of this type of argument is clearly visible in the study of ethnic relations. A finding that ethnic behaviour and ethnic conflicts are not products of collective madness but of individual rationality does not really tell us much. This circular form of reasoning only tries to rationalize events in an *ex post facto* manner. The RCT sociologist wants us first to accept the idea of individual rationality, and then this assumed rationality is used as an explanation for the particular type of behaviour – such as social action in ethnic conflicts. The outbursts of mass killings on an ethnic basis are explained in reference to group competition in imperfect markets: the individuals make a choice to participate in such actions because all other options are more costly. For example, Hechter claims that

> it is not difficult to interpret events in Bosnia as the by-product of a cool, calculating land-grab by Serbs and Croats against their weaker Muslim victims, for grabbing land, like other forms of looting, is profitable in the absence of effective state authority. (1995: 54)

In other words, taking part in an ethnic massacre was seen by actors as the most rational choice. This type of reasoning is not only ethically problematic (exemplified in the often used cynical and euphemistic RCT phrase 'the exit costs have been raised'), but it is also deficient in explanatory terms. It is a typical case of post hoc explanation that presupposes individual rationality and then explains the massacres by referring to that rationality. When an individual is forced to choose between taking part in the massacre or being massacred himself than we can hardly say that he had any real choices to make. It is certainly more fruitful to look at the structural and situational determinants that had an impact on the development of such a situation. Additionally, looking at the variables such as fear, conformity with rules, shared values and memories, ideological convictions and so on can probably give us more information that would yield better explanations (Malešević, 2000, 2002a).

Or let us take a less extreme example. Hechter aims to explain the persistence of the traditional Romany Gypsy and Amish populations within fully modernized societies as examples of group rational behaviour. He states that

> by *controlling education*, intentional communities not only maximise their chances of *moulding children's preferences* – giving them a taste for community-provided benefits and an aversion to those provided in the outside world – but also raise their exit costs by denying their children access to the kind of training that would enable them to compete successfully in the external labour market. (1986: 276, italics added)

Here again we have the case of presupposed rationality that produces a very weak explanation. Taking into account that all traditional communities try to 'reproduce an archetype' and maintain the traditional way of life, the real question is why the Romany Gypsies and Amishes have been able to do this where other traditional communities have not. In addition, to avoid the circularity of rational choice explanation, Hechter is forced to move from methodological individualism and a presupposed utility-oriented explanation towards concepts borrowed from the enemy camp of structural-functionalism, such as internalization of group norms and socialization (community that shapes children's preferences) and structural determinants of individual action (community and education system). A similar strategy is employed in Banton's work, who now agrees that 'ethnic ties may be inculcated' and 'that individuals frequently acquire a preference for association with co-ethnics as people who share the same norms as themselves' (2000: 487).

Secondly, there is a clear problem with the way the notions of rationality and intentionality are used. Although most rational choice sociologists recognize the simple fact that not all human actions are rationally motivated and that people do not always behave in such a way as to realize their interests, they argue that the assumption that people do behave in this way allows us to identify the role of other motivations in their behaviour. The main problem with this line of thinking is that rationality and intentionality are too vaguely defined and are often stretched to the extremes. If one considers every form of social action as being rational, intentional and meaningful, then again our analysis becomes useless. The point of explanatory activity is to discriminate between those factors that are somehow more substantial and those that are less important in highlighting the reasons, motives and origins of certain types of action or event. By overstretching the notions of intentionality and rationality our emphasis shifts from the internal and situational understanding of the roots of social phenomena towards looking for external justifications for our presupposed rationality. In other words, instead of focusing on the social problem itself, we focus on the question, 'How can I demonstrate that behind this action were the individual's rational motives?' Thus, we become much more political than analytic: our aim is no longer to explain but to convince. If one treats all human action as rational and intentional then we end up with findings of very little explanatory relevance.

In addition, as Baert rightly points out, most sociological theories do recognize the role that individual intentionality plays in social action but, unlike rational choice theory, they do not postulate the regularity or typicality of its occurrence. In Baert's view rational choice theory does not make a distinction between acting rationally from acting as if one is rational. Although one could agree with the idea that individuals generally tend to act within the realm of principles of rationality, this does not mean that this can be used as empirical evidence that individuals generally act rationally. As he concludes, 'for individuals to act as if they are rational does not necessitate any rational decision process remotely similar to the one attributed to individuals by RCT' (Baert, 1998: 168). Furthermore, as Chivers (1985) and Dex (1985) have also emphasized, social action can shift from being rational at one time to becoming inertial or even habitual at a later stage. However, more importantly, although the assumption of an individual's rationality tells us that there will be a certain consistency in people's behaviour, it does not tell us anything about the substance of their concerns (Hindess, 1988).

When such a wide notion of rationality is applied to the study of ethnic relations then we end up with all-but identical explanations. Rational choice sociologists want to convince us that people will generally tend to use their ethnic membership in order to achieve some individual gain. Their ethnic group behaviour is explained in reference to intentional choices that are optimal in a particular situation. Behind ethnic group solidarity we can find no more than individuals motivated by self-interest, who rely on their ethnic markers to maximize their advantages. Hence, ethno-mobilization, separatism, ethnic revival, xenophobia, ethnic wars and ethno-nepotism are all explained as the best available choice under situational constraints for a rational individual. For example, in discussing ethnic conflicts and nationalism Hechter makes the following strong statement: 'the state authorities are always interested in suppressing nationalist groups' (1995: 62). However, there are numerous empirical examples demonstrating when and how State authorities can be interested in promoting various forms of nationalism, from the nationalisms of the majority ethnic group (i.e., Han in China or Serbs in Milošević's, Yugoslavia), over the state-sponsored nationalisms (Swiss, American, Nigerian) to the nationalisms of minority ethnic groups, of which the most recent example was President Yeltsin's strong support for Baltic state nationalisms in the last two years of the USSR's existence.

The problem with this type of explanation is twofold. On the one hand, by overstretching the notion of rationality it does not allow us to discriminate between the subtleties of various ethnic situations, while on the other hand, the extreme voluntaristic concept of an ethnic group undermines a deeper understanding of the processes involved in ethnic relations.

When we demonstrate that separatism, xenophobia or ethnic nepotism can all be traced back to the individual's rational and self-interest motivated behaviour, what do we know more about group relationships than we knew before the analysis was undertaken? We might know more about individual motivations, but we know very little about the specificities of group relationships. From RCT analysis we can learn little about the differences between macro events, such as the break up of the state, and micro actions, such as favouring to shop in a store owned by a co-ethnic. When the analysis is exclusively focused on the individual's rationality, the macro variables such as the role of the State, ideology, historical legacies, collective memories and so on are completely left out of the picture. Because of its overemphasis on the individual's rationality and intentionality, rational choice theories very often do not see the wood for the trees.

By giving primacy to the individual's choices, RCT has to adopt an extremely voluntaristic concept of ethnicity. In these studies ethnic groups differ very little from philatelic societies. For example, Banton (1980: 476) explicitly states that 'any approach from rational choice theory must treat all groups as coalitions or alignments of individuals, influenced by the consequences of choices made in earlier periods'. Ethnic membership is here seen as a matter of simple choice, whereas in reality it seems to be just the opposite. This approach is almost exclusively focused on the internal aspect of ethnic group definition and has little analytical patience with the ascribed (external) aspect of ethnicity. For example, Hechter (2000: 97) argues that 'different heights, weights, hair and eye colour ... might serve as a basis for the development of a social identity'. Unfortunately, as many anthropological studies show, the ascribed ethnic categorization often has a much more profound effect on inter-group relationships than the internal one. What Hechter ignores here is that the crucial problem is whether a particular ethnic collective is perceived as a 'legitimate' group by others. It is very often the case that certain group actions and state policies are governed by the belief that some communities do not constitute a separate ethnic or national unit. A great number of ethnic conflicts are fought over the question of whether a particular community is a 'real' ethnic or national group. A typical example is Bosnian Muslims (today known as Bosniaks) who have, until very recently, been categorized by Croats and Serbs as a (presumably ethnically unconscious) religious group that is a part of the Croatian/Serbian ethnic community. By viewing ethnic groups as independently created by the voluntary action of individual actors, RCT has difficulty in explaining the enormous strength of ethnic ties throughout history in forms of collective memory, as well as the persistence of so-called ethnic cores or, to use A. Smith's (1981) terminology, *ethnies*. Stating that ethnic group membership is no different from that of class or status groups, rational choice is unable to explain the simple question: Why do ethnic attachments regularly prove to be more potent than any other type of group membership? Why are so many people ready to die, or (even more strikingly) to kill for their ethnic kin, and so few for their trade union or golf club?

Thirdly, rational choice sociologists simply ignore the cultural aspect of individual choices. Rationality, as well as an actor's choices, are always far from being culturally free. Although many rational choice theorists assume that preferences are stable across cultures (i.e., Becker, 1976), as numerous ethnographic studies demonstrate this view could not be further from the truth. Despite some universal features of human rationality a great deal of social action is shaped by the specificities of individual cultures.

RCT treats preference formation largely as an unproblematic process because it starts from the presupposition that all human beings are driven by similar motives. For example, Hechter (1986: 269) says: 'it can be expected that everyone will prefer more wealth, power and honour to less, because attaining these goods often makes it easier for individuals to attain other (perhaps more idiosyncratic) goals'. This statement overlooks the fact that individual preferences do not have to be connected with possession, not only in psychological terms (i.e., idiosyncratic values) but, more importantly, in terms of dominant norms and cultural values. Actors may have aspirations and preferences that do not fit utilitarian measures, which means that their preferences cannot be hierarchically ordered and measured in terms of 'less or more value'. The problem with this line of thinking is that it reduces the complexity of human values and motives to hierarchically ordered 'preferences'. Individual action is not only driven by the content of ends but also by the content of means.

On the psychological level some individuals may prefer simple hard work, without material benefits, as their intrinsic, psychological need, which enables them to achieve self-fulfilment; or they may prefer things such as security or serenity over any material benefits; or they can act completely on an emotional basis (anger, fear, anxiety); or they can be motivated by categories such as glory, heroism, altruism, saving-face or social justice. The studies of ethnic relations are full of examples that show how individuals are often willing to sacrifice intentionally for ethno-nationalist, religious or ideological reasons. How can a rational choice sociologist explain mass self-immolation of Kurds in front of Greek embassies after the capture of the PKK leader in 1999? Or what about Japanese *kamikaze* pilots in World War II, or Hamas suicide bombers? Hechter's response to this is the following: 'social sources of emotional action are not well understood'; 'very little is known about the salience or intensity of values'; 'it is impossible to tell which of them [religious beliefs or the fear of sanctions] is responsible in the usual case' (1995: 55, 56). In other words, the RCT argument is: since we know little about emotions and values one should rule them out as an explanatory device. How convenient!

This problem is even more pronounced on the cultural level. Through the process of primary socialization individuals can internalize or develop preferences where they despise material goods, power, or honour. There are many anthropological studies showing how some ethnic groups support egalitarianism and reject individualist values. A nice example is given by Levi-Strauss (1989) in the case of Gahuku-Gama of Papua New Guinea, who have learnt football but who play for several days – as many matches are necessary for both sides to reach the same score. Because of the predominance of egalitarian values the game is not perceived in its original European sense as a competitive contest, but is rather treated as a ritual around which collective values are reaffirmed. To demonstrate the cultural diversity of individual preferences we do not have to go to Papua New Guinea. As sociological research shows, collectivist values prevail in some European societies as well. For example, Croatian sociologist Županov (1977, 1985) has repeatedly demonstrated in his empirical work that former Yugoslav society was characterized by the predominance of a collectivist ethos, which he termed 'egalitarian syndrome'. Hence, not all human behaviour takes place within a context of competitive individualism. RCT also omits the significance of collective memory as a value-driven form of social action. Armenian animosity towards Turks cannot be explained without reference to collective memory of the 1915 genocide, nor can dislike or distrust of Tutsis towards Hutus be understood without knowledge of the 1994 massacre.

Fourthly, rational choice theory does not only neglect culture, values and ideology but also politics. RCT analysis reduces political action and political actors to economics. Perceiving social actions only in terms of individual utility maximization, RCT is not only unable to account for non-economic and non-materialistic sources of individual motives, but also for the structural determinants of collective action.

Even when one agrees that human beings are often guided by their self-interests and situational rationality, these factors are frequently of little relevance in explaining macro phenomena. RCT treats all individual choices as equal, while complex societies are full of situations where the 'structural' conditions of choices are very unequal. For example, an individual can do little in resisting the social influence of institutions such as the school (which is obligatory in all modern mass societies), mass media (owned by the State or huge business corporations), the army (obligatory in countries with conscription), police and immigration office, courts or the party (in one-party states). He or she can certainly make individual rational choices, but the impact of structures can, and often is, decisive for the outcome of individual and collective action.

Coleman's (1990) attempt to explain structure in reference to the individual's initial rationality in granting authority to another individual, and then becoming unintentionally placed in a situation to pursue the interests of another actor, is very problematic. On the one hand, it states the obvious – as Hobbes and Rousseau taught us long ago, in every society individuals do indeed transfer a part of their will and liberty to joint institutions. The hypothetical social contract exists whenever one finds 'the state of law' operating. Although individuals often do pursue (rather unintentionally) the interests of other actors (i.e., leaders, ruling elite, etc.), most of the time they simply obey and follow the inertia and 'irrationality' of institutional logic and bureaucratic mechanisms of action. The 'state' and 'the school' certainly have no will of their own but still operate as independent social agents and in accordance with non-individual logic.

On the other hand, Coleman's argument falls short of providing an explanation of how and why the structure becomes perceived as an independent entity by individuals themselves. Since the individuals reify social relations and see 'the State' or 'the nation' as real entities, their behaviour is also guided by such beliefs. As we can learn from Weber (1968), social action is not only guided by instrumental rationality but also by value rationality. Individuals are more often than not directed by their strong beliefs and commitments. Unlike other RCT sociologists (i.e., Hechter, 1997, who explicitly rules out both emotional and value-rational motives), Boudon has acknowledged this fact. However, when one recognizes that values are often as important as interests, he undermines the principles of pragmatic reductionism and places their explanation out of the RCT frame of reference.

The importance of political institutions, and institutions in general, for the understanding of human action is perhaps most visible in the study of ethnic relations. One cannot properly explain the recent outbreaks of ethnic animosities and wars in the Balkans or Caucasus, as well as the break up of former communist federations, without making reference to the institutions of the communist state. As Brubaker (1996) rightly points out, it was the Soviet and Yugoslav states that institutionalized ethnic differences at the level of territorial and political entities. The concept of the ethnic nation was largely reified in the minds of Soviet and Yugoslav citizens through particular policies and practices of the communist state. As a result the break up of the former federations run along the lines of ethnic republics that were governed by 'institutionally constituted national elites'. Without an understanding of structural changes such as the decentralization of federal power on an ethnic basis, one is not able to explain ethnic relations in the post-communist world. The rational and self-interested behaviour of individuals in the situation of state collapse might be an ultimate result of these changes, but without an understanding of the State's role in communism our micro explanation would certainly remain banal. Although one can look at the individuals as rational creatures, as Hindess (1988) makes clear, they cannot be treated 'as social atoms that can be picked at random from their groups, because it makes no difference who they are' (p. 29).

This weakness of RCT is implicitly acknowledged in the more recent works of Banton (2000) and Hechter (2000), who now both explain ethnic and national conflicts more in terms of politics than economics. Instead of focusing on any individual actor 'who can be picked at random' Banton strongly distinguishes between the role of political elites and the rest in the explanation of ethnic conflicts, whereas Hechter 'limits nationalism to the realm of politics'. So we can, for example, read that ethnic mobilization 'can also be a form of collective action by which members of elites pursue their individual ends with the sometimes reluctant support of followers who have less interest in the desired outcome' (Banton, 2000: 489). A much more prominent role is now given to elites and their 'definition of the situation', who are seen as 'ideological mobilisers' of ethnic action and who 'can impose their definition of the situation upon a person contemplating an exit option' (2000: 490). It is even acknowledged that 'ethnic preferences can be changed by the eloquence of mobilisers or by the messages of the mass media' (2000: 493).

Although one could easily accept these explanations, they clearly belong to different theoretical traditions in the sociology of ethnic relations, that is, to elite approaches and symbolic interactionism (see Chapters 5 and 8). The shift to elite theory and to symbolic interactionism shows not only that RCT is unable to deal with the unequal positions of different social actors but it also demonstrates, through its retreat into eclecticism, the explanatory powerlessness of pragmatic reductionism and methodological individualism.

Even more importantly, the introduction of explanatory apparatuses from other theoretical traditions often contradicts the basic postulates of rational choice theory. If the leader can impose his 'definition of the situation' on his co-ethnics, then what is the role of the individual's free choice? And, finally, if symbolic interactionism or elite theory can successfully explain ethnic relations, why do we need rational choice theory at all?

Conclusion

The main quality (as well as the main weakness) of rational choice theory is its simple methodology. Its analyses are plainly too crisp and too good to be true. Because of its simplicity the theory can be questioned and attacked on almost every aspect of its explanation: methodological individualism, the micro position of analysis, the economic deterministic approach, its neglect of the affective sphere of human action, choice formation, the lack of attention to 'structural reasons' of human behaviour, its failure to explain the preference formation, its neglect of values and so on. Even the main axiom of individual optimization is tautological, and it cannot be tested nor falsified. All these deficiencies are also reflected in the study of ethnic relations. Using an extremely voluntaristic concept of ethnicity, and reducing politics and culture to economy, rational choice analysis is unable to explain the obvious strength and persistence of ethnic ties, both historically and geographically.

However, the application of RCT to ethnic relations has had some positive outcomes. Taking into account that strong feelings of ethnic attachments, ethnic hostility and ethnic conflicts were, until quite recently, mainly explained as irrational, primordial and atavistic behaviour, the most important contribution of RCT to the study of ethnic relations is its demystification of ethnic irrationality. Rational choice analysis has elaborately shown that phenomena such as racism, inter-ethnic group hatred or nationalism can be based on very rational motives. In market situations and in market-oriented societies competition over jobs, housing, or educational possibilities may develop into ethnic group struggle if ethnicity is available to be used to advantage. On the other hand not all human behaviour is intentional and utilitarian, and not all actions on the part of individuals are driven by personal will. The questions of power-distribution, the role of values, choice and preference formation, as well as that of emotionally determined behaviour remain unanswered by rational choice theory. Therefore, even if one agrees with RCT theoreticians that social relationships are very often based on market relations, that does not mean that every society and every individual, at every time and in the same way, applies this 'the best means to given ends' schema. Society is much more than a market-place.

Chapter Eight

ELITE THEORY: ETHNICITY AS A POLITICAL RESOURCE

Introduction

Classical elite theory, articulated most comprehensively in the works of Mosca, Pareto and Michels, is perhaps the only prominent sociological tradition that does not have a direct contemporary progeny. Apart from Wright Mills who attempted a peculiar synthesis of Marxism and elite theory, there was no significant theoretical attempt to build a coherent contemporary sociological elite theory.[1] This is even more pronounced in the study of ethnic relations. There are no comprehensive contemporary sociological theories of ethnicity that trace their roots to Pareto, Michels or Mosca. However, despite this lack of connection with the classics, influential sociological accounts of elite action have re-emerged indirectly in the neighbouring disciplines of political anthropology, social psychology and political science. Moreover, these approaches have been particularly focused on identifying the origins, causes and mechanisms of ethnic group mobilization. While sharing the central tenets of this position, contemporary elite theory of ethnicity has developed around two broad approaches: one more symbolist and the other more instrumentalist. The first approach, developed in the works of Abner Cohen and Tuen van Dijk, comes from anthropology and psychology respectively, and is focused on the analysis and interpretation of symbols, and the ideologies and discourses used by political groups and elites to sway mass support as well as to capture the public imagination in order to generate social action. The second approach, associated with the works of Paul Brass and Ted Gurr, comes from political science and is more concerned with the study of instrumentalist logic as used in strategies and tactics deployed by political elites for the manipulation of the masses. Nevertheless, what is common to both approaches is the view that ethnicity is first and foremost a political phenomenon. Or in the words of Cole and Wolf (1974: 283), 'ethnicity is politics'. However, before one engages more intensively with these contemporary theories, it is necessary to skim over the key principles of classical elite theory. My aim here is to show that in spite of their nescience, the classics have created an adequate theoretical apparatus which could provide a nucleus for the development of a potent and coherent elite theory of ethnicity.

Classical elite theory: no place for ethnicity?

The common theme of Mosca, Pareto and Michels is an idea that, regardless of the political and social system one lives in, it is always a minority that dominates the majority. Moreover, they argue, there are no mechanisms that would allow for true control of majority over minority. Although modernity has brought about remarkable technological and organizational changes that have nominally increased popular participation, in reality social structures remain resolutely hierarchical, and change is little more than a camouflage for the elite's tighter grip on political power. Just as with premodern, so modern societies are based on the domination of the elite over the masses, and social and political order is shaped around the elite's perpetual attempt at subordination of the masses. Drawing on Machiavelli, classical elite theorists argue that this subordination is achieved in two principal ways: through force and through deception. A combination of the two was seen as the most potent weapon in preserving the hold on power. Thus Machiavelli, and Pareto after him, make a distinction between two types of rulers – lions, epitomizing strength and determination, and foxes, embodying cunningness and the skills of persuasion – arguing that the most successful rulers are a combination of the two:

> [the ruler] should be able to assume both that of the fox and that of the lion; for whilst the latter cannot escape the traps laid for him, the former cannot defend himself against the wolves. A prince should be a fox, to know the traps and snares; and a lion, to be able to frighten the wolves. (Machiavelli, 1997: 67)

This interplay between the elite's use of sheer force and the force of persuasion is a key factor in the explanation of their dominance over the masses for all three classical elite theorists. Vilfredo Pareto sees human beings as, for the most part, governed by irrational ('non-logical') motives – residuas. Residuas are deeply rooted sentiments and impulses which are the paramount and stable source of individual action. However, to maintain a social order most human actions are encoded and formulated as reasoned and rational, that is, as derivations. Unlike residuas derivations are intellectual constructs developed and displayed for the use of 'significant' others, to enable the functioning of societies. In other words a derivation is a form of rational justification for deeply irrational motives. Official elite claims, such that they struggle 'to safeguard democracy', 'to protect the Islamic way of life' or 'to preserve socialism', amount to nothing more than justification of the personal or group drive to hold or acquire power. In this process more successful elites are able, through the use of supple derivations, to intensify mass residuas.[2] The popular support of leaders is reflected in a ruler's ability to meet mass sentiments. Pareto (1963: 2031) defines an elite as a 'class of the people who have the highest indices in their branch of activity', and makes a distinction between the ruling elite and elites in waiting. He sees circulation of elites as a driving force of social change: history is a 'graveyard of aristocracy', where elites in their competition for power, status and material resources aim at acquiring popular support by manipulating the masses. While Pareto does not discuss ethnic relations in any comprehensive way, it is not difficult to deduce from his theory that ethnic group-centred ideologies such as ethno-nationalism or racism are no more than a particular kind of derivation used by political elites to invoke popular sentiments in order to mask their self-interests. In fact Pareto explicitly saw racism and anti-semitism as 'blind revulsions with no more reason in them than in the action of a child belabouring the inanimate object it has stumbled against' (1966: 121).

Gaetano Mosca shares Pareto's pessimistic view of human kind and the elite's need to justify their privileged position. He argues that every ruling class, if successful, rules in accordance with a particular set of values and principles that are accepted by the masses as legitimate. These principles, termed by Mosca a political formula, have to be grounded in the dominant ethical and legal order of a particular society if they are to be acceptable to the general public. While different societies are governed by different political formulas, no political elite will stay in power for long if unable to utilize an adequate political formula. Mosca differentiates between two types of political formulas – rational (such as belief in self-determination and popular sovereignty), and supernatural (such as the belief in the divine origins of monarchs) – but finds both deeply flawed. Although manipulative and useful to elites, political formulas are not simple tricks created by elites to mystify the masses. For Mosca (1939: 71) they 'answer a real need in man's social nature' to be governed by a particular set of ethical principles. The main reason why elites are more successful in the articulation and exploitation of the particular political formula is their organizational ability: 'an organised minority, which acts in a co-ordinated manner, always triumphs over a disorganised majority, which has neither will, nor impulse, nor action in common' (Mosca, 1939: 53). Just like Pareto, Mosca does not discuss ethnicity. However, his theory allows for the interpretation of situations wherein the demands of ethnic groups are ideologically articulated, that is, as political formulas rooted in a set of moral principles (i.e., human rights, preservation of tradition, minority protection, etc.) which are ambiguous enough to provide for elite manipulation for their own gains.

Mosca's emphasis on the importance of organization and organizational skills for elite minority rule are further explored by Robert Michels. For

Michels (1962) elite rule is not so much rooted in the personal psychological qualities of individuals as in the structure of bureaucratic organization. Analysing the organizational structure of the German Social Democratic party, he convincingly came to the conclusion that, regardless of their proclaimed aims, organizations tend towards the development of oligarchic hierarchy. His 'iron law of oligarchy' is built around the following findings:

- any attempt to develop an effective mass organization leads to the selection of experts and those with valuable organizational skills as leaders
- to be effective, leadership has to function as a cohesive group which at the same time helps the leaders to keep themselves in power
- the rank-and-file members of the organization lack cohesion and as a result tend towards apathy and subordination to elite authority.

In other words, any attempt to build successful mass organization in order to achieve a particular goal will end up with the organization becoming an end in itself. For Michels all remedies are thus futile. For example, instead of controlling and preventing oligarchic tendencies, the increase in popular participation only serves to disguise the oligarchic nature of the organization. When applied to the study of ethnicity the 'iron law of oligarchy' reads as: any attempt at the institutionalization of ethnic group membership (e.g., creating an ethno-national movement, establishing a cultural or territorial autonomy, or implementing a consociational arrangement) will inevitably lead to the institutionalization and strengthening of the elite's dominance over the (formally co-ethnic) masses.

Although neither Pareto and Mosca nor Michels have discussed ethnic relations, their respective theories of elite rule provide a stable stepping stone for the analysis of ethnicity in the spirit of elite theory. Basically, for classical elite theory ethnicity is a second-order reality, an ideological mask used by the leaders for their own political ends. Let us now explore to what extent the contemporary theories of elite rule build on these earlier ideas in their attempt to develop a more complex and more comprehensive argument regarding the link between ethnicity and political domination.

Culture and political control:
ethnic relations as power relations

Contemporary elite approaches take their cue from the classics by seeing politics as the main arena of social action. However, unlike the classics they also attribute an important place to culture. Abner Cohen (1974a, 1977, 1981) argues, more specifically, that social action is best understood by focusing on power relations and symbols. By symbols, Cohen means 'objects, concepts, or linguistic formations that stand ambiguously for a multiplicity of disparate meanings, evoke sentiments and emotions, and impel men to action' (1974a: 23). While symbols are essential as building blocks in the development of personality and in dealing with the existential problems (i.e., in helping differentiate between good and evil and in comprehending key dichotomies such as life and death, fortune and misfortune and so on), their intrinsic ambiguity leaves them open to instrumentalization. Symbols possess indefinite and uncertain meanings but are, at the same time, indispensable for social action and communication. Collective action and, indeed, human societies more generally are inconceivable without the use of symbols. However their indispensability on the one hand, and their elusiveness on the other, make symbols both objects of and for political action: people love and hate, kill or die, for and because of symbols. In other words, Cohen (1974b, 1979) argues that symbols are 'essentially bivocal, satisfying both existential and political ends'; they are 'expressive' and instrumental at the same time. 'The ceremonials of authority do not just reflect authority but create and recreate it.' Symbolist ('idealist, altruistic, non rational') man is also political ('shrewd, calculating, utilitarian') man. Hence symbols are an integral part of power relations. Power is 'an aspect of nearly all social relationships' and refers 'simply to relations of domination and subordination' (Cohen, 1979: 88).

He is critical of classical sociological traditions that analyse power as state power expressed in domination of one class over another (Marxism), or as one of the three dimensions of stratification along with status and class (Weberianism). Cohen finds the Marxist view too narrow and the Weberian too extensive in stating that power relations incorporate economic relations. There are only two dimensions that 'pervade all social life', power and symbolism, and, paraphrasing Marcuse, Cohen writes about 'two dimensional man'. This strong link between symbolism and power relations is most clearly expressed in collective rituals and other social activities aimed at group mobilization. What is important here, according to Cohen, is the fact that most people are not aware of this ambiguity and bivocality of symbols. When they participate in a ritual of any kind they rarely see its political implications. This situation provides a space for intentional manipulation by political leaders. As he underlines, 'it is this ambiguity in their meanings that forges symbols into such powerful instruments in the hands of leaders and of groups in mystifying people for particularistic or universalistic or both purposes' (1979: 103). Symbols are effective weapons in power struggles because of their 'irrationality' and their connection to the real or imaginary objects and acts that deeply affect human feelings.

Since power and symbols permeate all of social life, they are also an integral part of ethnic relations. Cohen (1974a) treats ethnic groups as 'informally organized interest groups' who share a common culture and 'who form a part of a larger population, interacting within the framework of a common social system like the state' (1974a: 92). In operating with such a wide definition he extends the meaning of ethnicity to any politically conscious status group. Hence he labels London City stockbrokers as an ethnic group. According to Cohen, City stockbrokers are an interest group who share a 'high degree of trust' and similar values, 'who speak the same language in the same accent, respect the same norms and are involved in a network of primary relationships that are governed by the same values and the same patterns of symbolic behavior' (p. 99). Stockbrokers are compared to Nigerian Hausa traders living in Yoruba towns, and Cohen argues and documents how 'city men are socio-culturally as distinct within British society as are the Hausa within Yoruba society'. Since ethnic groups are analysed as interest groups and interest groups are, by definition, political associations, ethnicity is essentially seen as a political phenomenon. Thus the revitalization of ethnic attachments as experienced in Africa or the West has little to do with the protection of specific cultural traditions. On the contrary, ethnicity far from being a pre-modern and parochial feature is essentially a vehicle of modernization: the emphasis on ethnic group difference and symbols are dynamic instruments in the process of power-seeking. The new forms of ethnic symbolism are selectively borrowed from the past, and re-arranged to meet new social situations. Ethnic groups use and re-formulate cultural tradition as a resource in a power struggle. People do not kill each other because of the difference in their customs, but because these cultural differences are coupled with deep political divisions. As Cohen emphasizes:

> Ethnicity in modern society is the outcome of intensive *interaction* between different culture groups, and not the result of a tendency to separatism. It is the result of intensive struggle between groups over new strategic positions of power within the structure of the new state: places of employment, taxation, funds for development, education, political positions and so on. (1974a: 96)

Although seldom specified, Cohen uses the notion of instrumentalization of ethnic symbols in two ways: first as political symbolism of various interest groups that are in a state of competition with each other and with the State, and, second, as symbolism of elite power. What differentiates elites from other informal groups is their privileged positions 'in some important sphere of social life'. On the one hand they behave in a similar way as other informal collectives in preserving their particular interests, and on the other they must, in order to remain an elite, legitimize their privileged status by promoting some universalistic goal. In Cohen's words: 'They validate their elite position in terms of an ideology, or a "theory" which is designed to convince the ordinary members of the society, as well as themselves, of the legitimacy of their status' (1974a: 102). Ethnicity usually serves as the factor with the widest appeal in mobilizing the masses for the elite's particularistic goals, that is, to gain or remain in power. Therefore, an elite constantly attempts to present its particular interests as the universal, common interests of the community as a whole. That is why power struggles between political elites are very often publicly presented as a confrontation over politically marginal, but communally vital matters – rituals and symbols. The emotional appeals to potent symbols such as the common ethnic ancestry or ethnic hero worship is the most expedient device for elites in achieving their ends.

Teun van Dijk (1991, 1993) focuses even more strongly on the link between power and cultural reproduction. Analysing the dominant political, corporate, academic, educational and media discourses in Western societies, he argues that ethnic antagonisms and racism are, for the most part, a product of subtle symbolic reproduction controlled and directed by elites. He claims that since power elites dominate the key means of symbolic reproduction, such as the education system, mass media, business corporations, the churches, political institutions, trade unions and even welfare offices, they are in a position to control the content and structure of messages disseminated in the public arena.

Van Dijk (1993: 44) defines elites broadly as 'groups in society that have special power resources', such as 'property, income, decision control, knowledge, expertise, position, rank, as well as social and ideological resources such as status, prestige, fame, influence, respect, and similar resources ascribed to them by groups, institutions, or society at large'. However, what is decisive for van Dijk is the elite's privileged access to 'systems of sociocultural discourse', i.e., control over symbolic resources. Here he highlights the role of symbolic elites (mass media editors and directors, politicians, columnists, scholars, textbook authors) as principal opinion makers and groups involved in the creation and legitimization of policies towards ethnic minorities. Building on the wider research of cognitive psychology, van Dijk sees ethnic antagonism as being collectively reproduced through the process of social cognition. Thus, socially shared values, norms and attitudes provide for the possibility of out-group discrimination: the language and rules of ethnic group animosity have to be first learned. To oppose multiculturalism or Affirmative Action policies, one has to have some level of knowledge regarding what these policies stand for. Van Dijk's (1993) argument is that the social reproduction of ethnic animosity is based on the reproduction of its social cognitions ('through processes of inference, learning, and sharing within the group'), which are executed through public discourses, and since elites control most of these discourses then elites are essential for the cognitive and ideological reproduction of ethnic group hostility. Analysing representative texts and the speeches of elites from the world of politics, media, education, academia and business, van Dijk has been able to identify how elites are able, by using subtle ideological and discoursive means, to impose their own definition of the ethnic situation. In this way, according to van Dijk, elites have 'manufactured ethnic consent', which has helped to legitimize majority group discrimination over ethnic minorities as well as upholding (white) minority domination in the societies of the West.

Ethnicity, politics and elite behaviour

Although both contemporary elite approaches see ethnic relations through the interplay of culture and politics, the works of Brass and Gurr are more focused on perceiving cultural markers as instruments of political action. Paul Brass sees ethnicity as a powerful political resource for generating popular support in competition between political elites. Ethnic identities are not innate or given, they are social and political constructs. Moreover,

> they are creations of elites who draw upon, distort, and sometimes fabricate materials from the cultures of the groups they wish to represent, in order to protect their well being or existence, or to gain political and economic advantage for their groups and for themselves. (Brass, 1993: 111)

For Brass cultural difference becomes an object of inter-group dispute only when it represents a particular political conflict of interests. Even here, culture does not stand for authenticity of a group's essence, since it only includes selected cultural traits, but is rather used as a source for the political mobilization of groups. Such selective mobilization of cultural difference is possible because ethnicities are variable, dynamic and fuzzy: religious attachments can change, bilingualism is rampant in today's world, kinship ties are weakening or narrowing to include only closest relatives, massive migration diminishes feelings of attachment to the place of birth, and so on. Therefore the politicization of culture is not inevitable, rather it is determined by a set of social circumstances. What one can witness when ethnic groups are politically mobilized is not a struggle over the cultural foundations of each ethnic collective (i.e., an ethno-nationalist claim of protecting 'our' heritage and identity), but conflict over symbols whose contents are shaped by a changing social and political environment as well as by intentional intervention of political elites. In the period of group mobilization, traditional culture does not 'awaken', but is instead transformed and reduced to a few cultural markers – symbols loaded with intense political meanings. Brass' research on South Asia (1991, 1997) demonstrates how selected symbols such as Urdu language, cow sacrifice and Shari'a law were consciously used by Hindus and Muslim elites in political competition with each other, and with elites within their own ethnic corpus. He shows how new meanings were attached to old symbols in order to create greater inter-ethnic cohesion. However, the elite's behaviour and the choices they make are constrained and limited by existing sets of beliefs shared by members of the group. Regardless of how influential leaders might be, they will not be followed if the ideas they promote stand in stark opposition to the collective values and principles shared by the group: the most popular Israeli leadership would quickly loose all support if it were to start preaching that all Israelis should convert to Islam, just as Pakistani leaders would if they were to argue that Kashmir should remain part of India. Nevertheless, what is crucial for Brass is that 'the process by which elites mobilize ethnic identities simplifies those beliefs and values, distorts them, and selects those that are politically useful rather than central to the belief systems of the people in question' (1991: 16). To use Brass' own (1979) example, a simple inversion of the statement 'Hindus revere the cow' into 'those who revere the cow are Hindus' illustrates an elite's power to transform the existing cultural markers into forceful political symbols for ethno-mobilization.

According to Brass, ethnic group mobilization and social conflicts based on ethnicity are more likely to occur in societies that undergo intense social transformation. As a result social and ethnic group transformation go hand in hand. Apart from elite competition and manifest cultural differences, there have to be three other criteria met in order for there to be successful ethnic group transformation. These include the adequate means of symbol communication to all social strata within the group; the absence of immense class divisions; as well as the existence of a socially mobilized population which is open to symbol communication. The stronger inter-class connection and communication is dependent on objective factors of social development that include the existence of mass media, the level of local vernacular standardization, literacy rates and the extent to which schools provide the curriculum in the native language. All these factors influence the scope and direction of ethnic group transformation.

Ted Gurr is more interested in the violent forms of ethnic group competition, that is, in the study of ethnic conflicts, wars and genocide. More specifically, he focuses on issues such as the reasons for ethnic group mobilization, the rationale behind violent outbursts between ethnic groups as well as between particular ethnic collectivities and governments that claim to represent those collectivities. Following a very rigorous process of conceptualization and operationalization, Gurr (1993, 2000a; Gurr and Harff, 1994) has undertaken a number of empirical studies to demonstrate that a combination of externally imposed disadvantages (e.g., discrimination, political environment, the extent of state violence, external support and international economic status) and an intensive sense of ethnic group identity are the most likely sources of ethnic group mobilization. However, the role of political elites remains central: 'the extent and intensity of the resulting conflict depend upon the strategies followed by ethnic groups' leaders *and* those followed by governments' (Gurr and Harff, 1994: 79). Unlike other elite approaches, Gurr is especially interested in the strategies employed by elites to mobilize popular support. For example, in his work on genocide he differentiates between elites with a history of using violence to repress dissent and to hold onto power, and elites that use their power for granting differential group rewards in exchange for loyalty (Gurr, 1986). The potential success of elites in influencing ethnic group mobilization depends on the degree of inter-group and inter-elite cohesion. This cohesion is based on the extent of interaction and communication between elites and the masses. As Gurr and Harff point out, the impact of leadership on the followers is also dependent on the number of divisions and potentially conflictual splinter groups within the ethnic collective; the number of competing group leaders; the cultural traditions that tolerate strong leadership and even the number of mass media outlets in ethnic group possession. Taking into account the institutional constraints in democratic political orders (e.g., the protection of human rights), they argue that autocratic leadership is more likely to succeed in ethnic group mobilization than its democratic counterpart. Thus Gurr's view (2000b: 64) is that although ethnic conflicts are complex and multi-faceted phenomena, in the last instance responsibility for wars lies with dominant ethnic elites: 'Ethnic identity and interest per se do not risk unforeseen ethnic wars; rather the danger is hegemonic elites who use the state to promote their own people's interests at the expense of others.'

Is ethnicity just an object of elite manipulation?

Elite theory is unique among contemporary sociological approaches to ethnicity in having a very specific target of its analysis. No other sociological approach concentrates so resiliently on the study of a particular type of social agent. Whereas symbolic interactionism, neo-Marxism and the other approaches that we have encountered so far attempt to provide a holistic theory that would be able to explain social life in its totality, elite theory singles out a concrete group of social actors whom it deems to be decisive for generating social action, and examines them, and only them, extensively. This mode of analysis is simultaneously a source of its strengths and weaknesses. On the plus side elite theory provides a relatively simple analytical framework, which is not only theoretically tight but is also realistic in its focus on tangible, actually existing people and, as such, is empirically very useful. Elite theory bestows us with a simple but potent predictor of ethnic group conflict. An analytical focus on the role of leadership, the motives of power holders, the links between rulers and their followers, the strategies and tactics of group mobilization employed by political elites and so on are essential in understanding any specific case of ethnic group animosity. What elite theory does is to provide us with research tools for identifying concrete 'sources of trouble'. With its use one is able to pinpoint individuals and groups most responsible for enacting or preventing a particular social change. If, for example, when trying to explain ethnic separatism among Muslims in South Asia, one is in a position to demonstrate empirically how Ulema's particular interpretation of Shari'a law is strategically employed to transform their position of religious authority into one of political hegemony over their co-ethnic brethren, then such a finding can have direct explanatory, ethical and policy implications. We know who to blame and, potentially, how to contain such an episode. In this sense the elite theory of ethnic relations is the embodiment of Occam's razor principle that the most simple solution is often the right one. On the minus side, although elite theory provides us with a realistic and practical account of ethnic relations, that account is incomplete and occasionally problematic. This incompleteness is pronounced in three major ways: a) elite approaches to ethnicity have a weak theoretical foundation; b) they underestimate potential and actual action of the masses; and c) they operate with an inadequate understanding of culture.

The contemporary elite theory of ethnicity lacks strong epistemological and general sociological foundations. This is most apparent in the weak or almost non-existent link between classical and contemporary elite approaches. While Pareto, Michels and Mosca did not discuss ethnicity, they did provide much wider and epistemologically stronger fundamentals for generating a sociologically coherent and thorough elite theory that is able, as I previously indicated, to encompass ethnicity. They elaborated general principles of individual and collective action, provided historical analyses of social change and social structure, developed methodological and conceptual apparatus for analysis, and so on. Unlike the classics, the contemporary elite theory of ethnicity, as it now stands, hangs in the air – it is too narrow in its focus on ethnicity and, as such, is unable to supply a comprehensive theoretical framework that would be able to articulate ethnic relations in the wider social context of social change and social structure. Thus, instead of surpassing and overcoming the shortcomings of the classics as, for example, neo-Marxism or neo-functionalism attempt to do, contemporary elite theory is a long way from the classics and it remains theoretically much more limited than its classical predecessors. The main reason for this is the fact that the most influential contemporary elite positions do not have a sociological background but come from political anthropology, social psychology and political science. As such their primary goal is not to ground their analysis of ethnic relations in a wider understanding of social reality, or to link it to a firmer sociological tradition, but rather to provide effective and a relatively simple account of power relations that could have direct policy implications.

However, such a quick fix has a number of negative consequences. The simplification of ethnic group realities may lead to an essentialist understanding of what is, in fact, a dynamic process, this leading to an extreme reification of the variable 'ethnicity'. Both Cohen and Gurr operate with a very hard and collectivist notion of the ethnic group as an interest/normative group. Thus Cohen (1974a: 92) perceives ethnic groups as 'people who share some patterns of normative behaviour', while ethnicity 'refers to the degree of conformity to these collective norms'. For Gurr an ethnic group 'consists of people whose identity is based on shared traits such as religion, culture, common history, place of residence, and race' (Gurr and Harff, 1994: 83). These definitions are not only static and essentialist but are also vague and misleading. This view implies that those individuals who do not conform to collective norms, or whose 'identity' is not based on 'culture, common history, place of residence, and race' cannot be regarded as members of a particular ethnic collective. Does this not mean that any resistance to dominant collective norms entails expulsion from group membership? Following this logic, any ethno-nationally conscious German who opposed the dominant Nazi interpretation of Germaness in the late 1930s could not be regarded as (a proper) ethnic German. Similarly, do individuals who share 'culture, common history, place of residence, and race' with two or more groups count as members of a particular ethnic community? Definitions such as these tend to treat social agents as entities with singular and clearly defined wills by attributing individual characteristics to collections of different people. Such essentialism has no roots in classical elite theory. As Femia (1998: 2) rightly points out, for Mosca and Pareto (just as for Machiavelli) 'there were no unconditional values or norms, no universally valid modes of conduct, no supra-historical "essences" distinct from the observable attributes of human beings'. No collectivity, and hence no ethnic group, has an essence.

Furthermore, simplified understandings of elite behaviour do not take into account what both Machiavelli (1997) and Pareto (1966), and especially Weber (1968), identified as the unintended consequences of purposive individual and collective action. It is only in the work of Brass that we see the recognition of constraints and limits within which elites have to operate. However, even here there is little understanding of structural changes brought about by the unanticipated consequences of conscious decisions made by elites. Elites, just as other social actors, are restrained in their actions by a constantly changing social environment and by the inability to control the consequences of their own actions as well as of those undertaken by other social agents. For example, many former communist apparatchiks (e.g., Kravchuk in Ukraine, Illiescu in Romania or even General Jaruzelski in Poland) have attempted to play an ethno-nationalist card in the dying days of communism to maintain themselves in positions of power. However by unleashing the force of ethnic nationalism which they could not control, they ended up loosing power to new and more radical right-wing nationalists.

This brings us to the second set of problems associated with the contemporary elite theory, which partially explain a conscious ignorance of elite approaches in contemporary sociology at large. This relates to the perceptions of the masses. Both classical and contemporary elite theory treat non-elites as passive creatures prone to easy manipulation. Unlike elites, who seem to be heterogenous, often in conflict with each other, creative and skilful in their power struggle, the masses are largely viewed as homogenous, ignorant, dependent conglomerates, with child-like qualities. While elites are the prime subjects of social history, the masses are no more than mere floating objects, or as Machiavelli put it: most men are 'ungrateful and fickle, dissemblers, avoiders of danger and greedy of gain' (1997: 65). Such a pessimistic perception of non-elite groups, coupled with the late Pareto's flirting with Fascism, has led to a superficial and unjustified identification of elite theory with extreme right-wing politics. The dominance of an alternative conflict paradigm, that of Marxism, which seemed to offer a much more optimistic vision of mass behaviour, further prevented the development of a sociologically mature elite theory. However, classical elite theory and Marxism (see Chapter 3) have much more in common in their treatment of collective manipulation than is generally recognized. Just as in Marxism, elite theory operates with the 'false consciousness' thesis, which implies that most individuals internalize and hold on to distorted perceptions of social reality and as a result act contrary to their own self or group interests. This state of falsified reality is justified by dominant ideology in Marxism or by derivations or political formulas in elite theory, and is seen as directly benefiting the rulers. The only significant difference here is that Marxism ties this condition to the structure of capitalist order, and believes that individuals will overcome this state by becoming conscious of their true (class) identity, whereas elite theory sees this process as linked to 'human nature' and, as such, inevitable in all societies regardless of their economic, political or social organization. In this sense both theories see strong ethnic group attachments as artificial products of elite manipulation. Such a position is too crude to understand the subtlety of ethnic relations.

While the actions of elites are in most cases decisive for the direction of inter-ethnic group interaction, this has little to do with 'human nature', class consciousness, or individual talents of respective elite groups, but much more with the structural position of minorities maintaining control over the institutions and mechanisms of power. Michels' work is more instructive here, since he links sources of domination to the structure and functioning of bureaucratic organizations, and reading this through Weberian glasses this means modernity as such. The elites are in a position to direct the masses not because they have superhuman abilities but because the institutions of modern society allow them to do so, and the masses themselves give tacit consent for such processes to take place. For example, Milošević's sudden and dramatic rise to power on the wings of ethno-nationalism in Serbia had very little to do with his intellectual or leadership qualities and a great deal with the historical contingencies that grew out of the very peculiar and contradictory nature of Yugoslav federalism. Intensive decentralization on the federal level and even stronger centralization on the micro-state level, coupled with the institutional monopoly left in place by the decentralized and disintegrating Yugoslav communist party machine (including its tight grip on the mass media), provided an ideal environment for the rise of demagogic leadership (Malešević, 2000). Such an environment was also a fertile ground for overt expressions of mass ethnocentric sentiments.

As Gouldner (1970), Giddens (1984) and others have convincingly argued, modern human beings are self-reflexive creatures whose actions are embedded in and created through social practices. Although individuals might operate with limited conceptual apparatuses (discursive consciousness), most are well capable of using tacit forms of knowledge which are seen as relevant and meaningful to the actors themselves in everyday life (practical consciousness). In this way many individuals are aware of the hegemonic position of elites in articulating particular ethnic group demands, but nevertheless see it as meaningful to go along with the process of ethno-mobilization. Their motives might be purely instrumental, or they can act on the basis of emotion, habit or value rationality (Weber, 1968; Malešević, 2002a). Both classical and contemporary elite theory tend to underestimate the motives of the masses.

The third limitation of the elite perspective is deeply related to its ignorance of the masses: despite their nominal emphasis on symbolism and the role of culture, elite theory works with an extremely instrumentalist concept of culture. Brass (1993: 111), for example, speaks of ethnic identities as mere 'creations of elites', whereas Cohen extends the concept of ethnicity to any politically conscious status group (e.g., London City stockbrokers). This view is in clear discrepancy with classical elite theory where, as Pareto was well aware, derivations can be intensified by elites but cannot be created *ex nihilo*, since they cannot run against already existing emotions. Such a hard instrumentalism is unable to explain the potency of ethnic ties over other forms of group bonds. As Eriksen (1993: 55) rightly points out, 'if ethnic identities are created wholly through a political process, then it should have been possible to create any identity at all'. There is certainly more to ethnic relations than politics. While both Cohen and Brass highlight the force of symbols, their analysis of symbolism and culture remains subsumed under the instrumentality of power relations. In other words, symbols appear as an epiphenomenon to power struggle where culture has no autonomy. As a result elite positions operate with a rudimentary and basically un-sociological theory of symbolism, which either leans directly on cognitive psychology (as in van Dijk) or remains on an almost primordialist level, as in Cohen, who gives explanations such as 'the cult is powerful principally because it is also *mystically* related to *something rooted* in their very *human nature*' (1979: 93, italics mine). The non-utilitarian and non-cognitive dimensions of symbolism hang about completely unexplained.

Although ethnicity is a political phenomenon *par excellence* it is only in the interplay between culture and politics that sociologically meaningful action arises. Symbols in particular, and culture in general, are partially *sui generis* phenomena; they are dynamic and perpetual and have life of their own and it is exactly because they have such autonomy that they are open to political instrumentalization. Through the intentional and structural process of politicization, cultures which have some features of timelessness become transformed into ethnic attachments which clearly are political and as such provisional, temporary and passing. Since elite theory lacks a historical dimension in its explanation, and explains social relations exclusively from the perspective of current social conditions, it overlooks situations when symbols are not used as political tools. It is only under particular social conditions and in the specific historical moments that culture and symbolism can be politically activated. To explain the power of symbol manipulation one has to look at issues such as the impact of collective memories, the strength of real or fictional pre-modern ethnic ties, or at the intensity of value-rational and emotional group allegiances.

The reduction of culture to politics comes also from elite theory's conception of an ethnic group as a minority group. Cohen, van Dijk and Gurr define and use the concept of ethnicity as a minority within the frame of 'non-ethnic' nation-state. This is a one-dimensional approach that overlooks the fact that from the perspective of a social actor, every individual is ethnic: minority ethnicity is possible only if there is an 'invisible' majority ethnicity. If 'minority groups' emphasize their cultural distinctiveness it is only because there is a distinct dominant culture from which to differentiate themselves. To focus our analysis only on the 'minority' group as a source of the problem is not only to miss the point of the study, but it may also indicate that the researcher is speaking from the majority standpoint.[3]

Conclusion

The study of elite motives, behaviour and interaction is a key facet in understanding ethnic relations. No other group of social agents is so decisive for the direction of social action and any sociological account that omits the role of a power-holding minority is bound to be reductionist. The strategies and tactics of ethnic group mobilization, the ideological appeal of ethnic symbols or the circumstances of ethnic group homogenization cannot be identified or understood fully without meticulous analysis of the individual and collective action of elites. The study of political instrumentalization of ethnic group membership is equally important in understanding and explaining the force of ethnic politics. The politics of ethnic symbol mani-pulation, and especially the ability of elites to simplify and select potent ethnic symbols, remains a high point in any fruitful inquiry of ethnic relations. However, the elite approaches, as they stand now, are incomplete and as such unable to provide a more comprehensive theory of ethnic relations: while contemporary elite theory of ethnicity is epistemologically and conceptu-ally too thin, classical elite theory, which operates with a more structured sociological account of social reality, has little to say about ethnic relations as such. A more nuanced elite theory would have to build upon the episte-mological heritage of the classics, aiming on the one hand to overcome their 'naturalism', determinism and ignorance of ethnicity and, on the other, to provide a more balanced view of culture and politics. Moreover, a more powerful elite account would also have to offer a broader analysis of ethnic relations that would secure ample treatment of both elite and non-elite action. Although ethnicity is a potent political resource in inter- and intra-group relations, it is a compelling social force precisely because it is more than a political resource.

Notes

1 Among a very few attempts to build on classical elite theory are those of Field and Higley (1980), and Higley and Burton (1987, 1989). But theirs is much more an empirical than theoretical attempt.

2 However, as Pareto (1966: 44) recognizes, derivations cannot create residuas which are not already there. They can only provoke and strengthen already exist-ing sentiments.

3 Such a view has its roots in the melting pot ideology which, in short, follows this reasoning: there is one nation-state, and ethnicities are viewed as obstacles which suddenly appear and restrain the functions of the state; the emphasis on cultural difference and the formation of ethno-political institutions is a collec-tive strategy to overcome economic or political deprivation. Hence an ethnic group is seen primarily as an interest group that is formed for political purposes.

Chapter Nine

NEO–WEBERIAN THEORY: ETHNICITY AS A STATUS PRIVILEGE

Introduction

Since Weber was the only classic writer of sociology who formulated a comprehensive theory of ethnicity, the postulates of which are still resonant in many approaches that otherwise have little in common with Weber, one would expect to find a proliferation of neo-Weberian positions on ethnicity in contemporary sociology. However, this is not the case. Although Weber's analyses have had a tremendous influence on the contemporary study of ethnicity and thus, as Stone (1995: 403) claims, 'we are all Weberians now', there are very few sociologists who explicitly claim to be Weberian, and even fewer of those whose theoretical articulation of ethnic relations can truly carry that title. The main reason for this is the sheer depth of Weber's general theory of society, which has been incorporated into contemporary sociological discourses on ethnicity only very slowly and in a rather segmented way. Most sociological accounts of ethnic relations have employed some aspects or particular insights from Weber with little regard for the theoretical and historical context these insights were a part of, that is, with little attention paid to Weber's integral theory of social action. As a result one can encounter rather obscure and distorted interpretations of Weber's position on ethnicity, such as the assumption that his theory is profoundly primordialist and hence similar to sociobiology (van den Berghe, 1981), or else deeply instrumental and thus akin to the rational choice position (Hechter, 1976b).

Even more comprehensive and analytically coherent positions suffer from the neglect or disregard of some important aspects of Weber's general theory of society, which tends to make their particular interpretations of Weber's account of ethnic relations one-sided and incomplete. Nevertheless, two contemporary neo-Weberian approaches to ethnicity have distinguished themselves as providing powerful explanatory models that imaginatively extend Weber's original concepts. Whereas both of these positions start from the conceptualization of ethnic relations as a peculiar form of status privilege, they develop distinctive paths of interpretation. One strand of contemporary neo–Weberianism is represented in the works of John Rex and Frank Parkin, who build on Weber's concept of monopolistic social closure to provide a more economistic account of ethnicity, while the other strand is articulated in the writings of Randall Collins and Michael Mann, focusing on the issues of state prestige and military power to develop a geopolitical and state–centric interpretation of ethnic relations.

Ethnicity and the monopolistic social closure

John Rex follows Weber's and Kant's view of social science as being causally limited and hence more idiographic and interpretative than nomothetic and exact. Although social science is unable to generate ultimate truths of decisive ontological importance, its value lies in its capacity to engage with and detect the courses of human action. Thus, the essence of sociology is social action, which can be studied through social relations. These social relations constitute social structures that have to be analysed 'in a quasi-phenomenal way as organised in terms of humanly-imposed categories of action', where the knowledge of these social structures can serve as a guide to practical action (Rex, 1980: 119). However, recognizing the primacy of agency over structure does not mean that structures can be reduced in any way to the motives of individuals as rational choice theory claims. On the contrary, 'structures are seen as arising from the continuity in time of interlocking patterns of interaction' (ibid.). Although strategic and intentional intervention can and does influence their direction, they are very far from being open to persistent forms of redefinition and re-articulation – as claimed, for example, by symbolic interactionism. This implies that external constraints are creations of human beings and as such can be changed by human action.

Drawing on Weber's distinction between open and closed social relationships, Rex (1986a: 8–9) sees groups as entities which involve closed social relationship, where individual actors are imputed to possess a sense of responsibility and representativeness. In other words, social action is impossible unless actors are 'held responsible amongst themselves both to themselves and to outsiders'. This feature of group membership is crucial not only to generate social action but also to formulate and create a social entity as a group. Since ethnicity is often popularly perceived as an epitome of a group, Rex aims to emphasize that such a view, based only on the external attribution of in-group responsibility and representativeness, is deeply flawed. Unlike the case of proper groups and communities, ethnic attachments do not create groups in themselves. Rather, they provide a skeleton around which a group can be formed. Ethnic groups are not self-evident and fully formed collectivities; in Rex's view they are analogous with classes, estates or status groups, in the sense of quasi-groups, groups of an amorphous type whose formation and articulation is dependent on social action.

The process of monopolistic social closure over social relationships is for Rex, just as for Weber, a key variable in explaining group dynamics, and especially the changing character of ethnic relations. In market situations, which are a nearly universal feature of social relations since they arise always when there is a clear disparity in the distribution of possessions or special-ized services, in-groups will be inclined to close off access to out-groups. Although social closure can involve prohibiting entry to symbolic rewards, Rex sees this group mechanism of control as most influential in curtailing economic benefits for the out-group. Although ethnic bonds in themselves are fairly weak in generating social action in the economic sphere, the process of monopolistic social closure can make them a potent device of social exclusion. Here Rex finds a degree of similarity between the views of Weber and the early Marx. This is particularly evident in Weber's analysis of ethnic difference and segregation in the example of sexual relationships between 'blacks' and 'whites' in the American South. In this analysis Weber explains antipathy to biracial marriages on the part of both groups as a dis-tinctively recent development, which is related not to 'natural' animosity of the two groups but, primarily, to the practices of monopolistic social closure on the part of 'whites', and the ever-increasing emancipation on the part of 'blacks'. Rex concludes that Weber, just as Marx, shares a 'belief that racial and ethnic exclusiveness is not effective as an intractable force in itself in creating racial separation and conflict. And with Marxists he [Weber] would be predisposed to look for its origin in the attempt to close off economic opportunities by one group as against another' (1980: 122).

However, unlike Marx, who ties social relations to the ownership of the means of production and sees classes as dominant forms of group member-ship, Rex follows Weber in defining classes as quasi-groups composed of individuals who share a similar market situation. Challenging the Marxist view Rex (1986b) argues that by distinguishing between status orders and class relations, one can locate ethnic group animosities in areas other than the relations of production. Such a broader understanding of class situations allows for more subtlety in empirical analyses that document cases wherein ethnicity overlaps with status in one situation, and with class, caste or estate in other cases. If, for example, group inequalities arise on the basis of legal or political rights instead of property or social pedigree, one has to speak of estates rather than classes or status groups. Therefore, Rex perceives ethnic groups as relatively loose associations that can acquire the characteristics of status groups, classes, castes or estates. In other words, ethnic groups 'may be arranged in a hierarchy of honour, they may have different legal rights and they may have different property rights' (Rex, 1986a: 14). Although caste and estate relations are rare in modern social environments (as they typically disappear with the processes of modernization), status group affiliations remain strong, if not stronger, markers of contemporary ethnic relations. Rex sees the US as being the embodiment of a status-dominated society where the patterns and time of immigration determine an ethnic group's social standing, and an individual's advancement in profession, education, housing or possession of material commodities makes him/her 'less ethnic'. Although Rex concurs with neo-Marxists that group inequalities in capitalism should (also) be analysed through the prism of class relations, class analysis remains weak in its explanatory capacity to account for non-capitalist societies and situations where ethnic group interaction takes non-economic form.

Although his work is predominantly focused on the study of immigrant minority groups, Rex (1996) views ethnicity in universalist terms, not only that 'we all have ethnicity', and ethnic bonds as such are 'part of the human condition', but also that as individuals we are born into 'an ethnically structured world'. In order for ethnicity not to become an object of deep social conflict it is necessary, according to Rex, to maintain a strong distinction between the public and private domains. In his view multiculturalism is to be differentiated from the concept of a plural society which stands for the (largely unequal) institutionalization of ethnic group differences, and which is more likely to perpetuate social divisions and ethnic group conflicts. Instead, a multicultural society is to be understood as one where the public sphere, incorporating such areas as politics, economics, professional education and law, would be based on single and universal cultural principles whereas the private sphere, which involves areas such as religious beliefs, moral education and primary socialization, would allow for greater diversity between ethnic groups. While differential treatment in the public domain would lead to segregation and inequality, a degree of difference in the private domain is a precondition for avoiding crude and severe assimilation as well as the economic, political and status hegemony of the dominant ethnic group.

Frank Parkin (1979) also builds on Weber's concept of monopolistic social closure in his attempt to explain the impact of ethnicity on social stratification. Parkin extends Weber's original idea in arguing not only that social closure represents the key mechanism of social control in modern societies, but also that this mechanism operates in three distinct ways – as exclusion, as usurpation and as a combination of the two. In all three situations class and ethnic cleavages are analysed as being intensely interdependent, that is, instead of treating them as separate or sporadically related phenomena, Parkin argues that study of the mechanisms of group social closure indicate that ethnicity and class are 'aspects of a single problem'. Since the concept of social closure refers to the maximization of in-group benefits by the restriction of out-group access, in fact it generates two distinct processes – exclusion on the part of the monopolistic in-group and, its direct consequence, a counter-exclusion (or in Parkin's terms, usurpation) by those who were originally excluded. The two processes of social closure operate in a different but mutually determining way.

Exclusion, which is seen as a dominant form of social closure in stratified societies, involves the exercise of power and control from the top down through restricting entry and resources to groups with less power. Two strategies of exclusion have proved most successful – through property and through professional qualifications and credentials. Both strategies provide for in-group diffusion of collective privilege from one generation to another: property rights are maintained through inheritance and credentials through cultural capital. When exclusionary practices are employed according to individual achievement then society is more likely to create status group segmentation, but when exclusion is practised in accordance with ascribed group features such as ethnicity then it generates deep communal in-group/out-group divisions. Examples of such ascribed social exclusion include South Africa under the apartheid system and the deep American South.

Usurpation is a form of social closure that works from the bottom up, reflected in the attempts of excluded groups to change their subordinated position or to acquire more resources from the dominant group. This form of social closure is regularly dependent on mass mobilization (e.g., strikes, demonstrations, marches, etc.) and is often defiant towards the existing legislative system. Parkin argues that usurpation is more likely to succeed when defined in class rather than in ethnic terms, since class-based protests can withhold labour in order to hinder the process of production, and in that way it can affect the general wellbeing of all groups and classes in a particular society. Ethnic forms of usurpation are seen as relying more 'upon collective mobilization of a purely social and expressive kind', such as through the use of moral persuasion which highlights discrepancies in the normative ideology of the dominant ethnic group (i.e., the official commitment to equality). Since, in Parkin's view, ethnic minority groups do not occupy 'strategic positions in the division of labour', or are 'dispersed throughout the labour market', they are seen as being too weak a force to disrupt a particular social and economic order (Parkin, 1979: 85).

In cases where exclusion and usurpation are combined, Parkin speaks of 'double closure'. This is a situation when initially subjugated groups have made their particular collective benefits a means to exclude other less organized or even more disadvantaged groups. Typical examples would include the double closure of South African 'white' workers vis-à-vis 'white' elite on the one hand and 'black' workers on the other, or Protestant workers versus Protestant middle class and Catholic workers in Northern Ireland. In both cases the hierarchical position of the middle group ('white'/Protestant workers) relies on both strategies of social closure – usurpation towards the dominant group and closure towards the less powerful group. What is important here, according to Parkin, is that exclusionary criteria cannot be invented at random as Weber (1968: 342) implies, but are grounded in historically or legally shaped definitions of group inferiority. 'Ethnic subordination, to take the commonest case, has normally occurred as a result of territorial conquest or the forced migration of populations creating a sub-category of second-class citizens within the nation-state' (Parkin, 1979: 96). This fact explains why there were no successful attempts at group exclusion by subjugated groups even when they form a majority.

The geo-politics of cultural difference: ethnicity and the state

For Randall Collins (1986, 1999) the secret of ethnicity lies in the nature of the State and the geo-political relations among states. The strength of a particular state, which is dependent on its ability to permeate (civil) society and to mobilize its population for military purposes, determines simultaneously the State's geo-political standing as well as the character of its inter-ethnic make up. Collins focuses on ethnic group mobilization which is, in his view, moulded for the most part by the policies as well as the reputation of the State in the wider geo-political environment. To fully understand the consequences of the State's image and actions regarding the processes of ethnic group mobilization, one has to move beyond the events that constitute an ethnic group's present and look at the macro history or the 'history of the long-run' which set the trajectories for present-day events. Macro–historical analysis indicates that ethnic groups are not only reproduced but often created in the process of political mobilization. As Collins (1999: 72) puts it: 'conflict creates the framework that is projected backward into a primordial past. An ethnic group is not merely, or even primarily, a community that shares a common culture and identity. Its identity is constituted by dividing lines, by contrast with others.' Echoing Weber he sees ethnic groups as meta-communities, 'communities of communities' that are constituted by social action and the 'cultural labelling of group boundaries'. Just as in Weber's original formulation, ethnic groups are formed as groups by the active participation of individuals as well as by the institutionalization, and later internalization of group markers that serve the purpose of setting group boundaries. Although any cultural marker can enhance group mobilization, Collins finds language and what he calls 'somatotypes' as the key factors for the process of social construction of ethnicity.

Somatotypes are socially constructed group differences based on physical markers. Although physical group differences are variable and in reality determined much more by social interaction than by biology, they are important markers of in-group identification and out-group categorization. However, the somatic group differences acquire their full meaning only in the context of broader historic changes. They mirror directions of migrations, invasions and conquests from past epochs and, as such, are 'geopolitical markers inscribed on the bodies of human beings' (Collins, 1999: 74). In other words, the attribution of physical markers has little to do with biology and a great deal to do with geo-political history. The nineteenth-century ethnic Swedes sneered at all those who were very blonde, had fair skin and blue eyes and regarded them as ethnic Finns, that is, a group with low ethnic status. The basis of such an ethnic stereotype cannot be explained without reference to macro history which locates the source of this stereotype in Sweden's two centuries of domination over Finnish lands and, especially, seventeenth-century control of the Swedish aristocracy over Finnish peasants. Thus it is primarily through the geo-political domination that somatic differences become indicators of social inferiority or supremacy.

In addition to somatotypes, language is also a powerful ethnic group marker. However, it is not the language in itself that is a potent predictor of social action, but rather its geo-political function. The interplay of historical contingencies determines which dialects transform into standardized vernaculars. The process of creating linguistic similarities goes hand in hand with state expansion: 'strong states foster linguistic uniformity, and highly mobilised linguistic ethnicities strive for an autonomous state' (Collins, 1999: 77). Thus, just as somatotypes, linguistic differences do not constitute ethnic groups as groups, but are socially constructed through relatively long historical periods of time. For Collins ethnicity is a 'real-life ideal type', which is socially constructed by the actions of individuals in their everyday lives. It is constructed from a number of cultural markers such as somatic and linguistic differences, family names and so on. However it is only small, well integrated and relatively isolated communities that can possess a high degree of cultural similarity on the basis of these markers. Modern complex societies can never be ethnic communities in the same sense. Nevertheless, this is where the paradox of ethnicity lies:

> the more locally anchored such patterns are in practice, the less likely they are to be important for social action. It is the larger, looser metacommunities that

THE SOCIOLOGY OF ETHNICITY

> group strangers into categories for political action, as well as for acts of discrimination and hostility or sympathy and support. In these larger ethnic metacommunities, the generalised notion of ethnicity becomes a social reality in itself in its shaping of macrodivisions in society. (Collins, 1999: 78)

Drawing on Weber's concepts of the State's power prestige, Collins locates the sources of state legitimacy in the degree of military experience among its population. The power prestige of the State does not only work externally, affecting the State's geo-political status and influence, but (according to Collins) it simultaneously has an impact on the internal legitimacy of the rulers. Put simply, military victories raise the prestige of state rulers while military defeats tarnish their status and diminish their legitimacy in the eyes of their citizens. When the dominant ethnic groups identify with their rulers the power prestige of the rulers directly translates into the geo-political prestige of the dominant ethnic group. Consequently, military defeats and diplomatic humiliations of the State affect the social standing of the dominant ethnic group in a broader geo-political context. Starting from this idea Collins (1999) formulates a set of propositions that allow for the prediction of the long-term ethnic dynamics. First, a high degree of ethnic group mobilization is dependent on a state's organization and its capacity to penetrate its society – while, for example, the Ottoman millet system of collective separation and elite control prevented stronger state penetration and hence broader meta-ethnic group mobilization, the large war coalitions of Greek city states against Persia helped create broader and highly mobilized forms of ethnic solidarity.[1] Secondly, the State's dominance in a wider geo-political environment is bound to advance the group status of the dominant ethnicity vis-à-vis other ethnic collectivities within the State – the military conquests of the British Empire in the nineteenth century fostered the linguistic assimilation of regional and other group identities and has helped create a fairly homogeneous (English) public culture and educational system. Thirdly, the State's weakness in a wider geo-political arena directly decreases the social standing of the State's dominant ethnic group – the military retreat of Austro–Hungary diminished the prestige of German ethnicity and with it its integrational capacities, just as the break up of the Soviet Union reduced the power prestige of a Russian ethnic collective in the eyes of Georgians, Kazakhs or Latvians. Finally, geo-political stability and the balance of power over longer periods of time weakens ethnic mobilization and increases a cosmopolitan atmosphere and appreciation of cultural differences – the influence of 'multiculturalism' and 'political correctness' in contemporary public discourse is a form of trans-ethnic cosmopolitanism.

Michael Mann (1999, 2001) also focuses on the links between ethnicity and the State, attributing a significant role to military and political factors in explaining the direction and intensity of ethnic conflicts. However unlike Collins, who places more emphasis on the prestige of the State in the international arena, Mann is predominantly concerned with the macro-historical explanation of extreme forms of ethnic group violence – ethnic cleansing and genocide. Mann argues that although ethnicity is popularly defined in terms of common descent and culture both are largely fictional, since large groups of individuals such as 'English', 'Russian' or 'Croats' can neither have common ancestry nor can they maintain a singular way of life. Thus resonating both Weber's and Collins' definitions, Mann (2001) believes that what is commonly referred to as an ethnic group is actually an array of 'socially constructed macro aggregated ethnicities', where aggregation stands for group markers such as language, religion, 'race' and so on, around which groups can be mobilized. Although ethnic descent is for the most part mythical, it is an enormously powerful source of group action in the contemporary world. So powerful that between 60 and 120 million people have been killed as a result of ethnic cleansing and genocide in the twentieth century alone. Even though mass killings on such a large scale are commonly perceived as an anti-modern exception, a throwback to a pre-modern era of barbarity and savagery, Mann's argument is that the intensification of ethnic forms of group animosity and ethnic mass murder are, in fact, products of modernity – and in particular its main organizational form, the modern nation-state. Since in feudal and other traditional orders, states were more or less the private property of rulers who exhibited more cultural similarity and group solidarity with other ruling families than with their 'co-ethnics', there was no rationale for ethnically motivated mass murder. It was only with the process of modernization, the rationalization of state institutions, development of military technology, democratization and spread of citizenship rights that ethnic violence has become rampant. The practice of ethnic cleansing intensified with the expansion of the infrastructural powers of the State,[2] with the articulation of the State as a 'moral project' and with politicization of ethnicity in the process of nation building. The motto of the Enlightenment and modernity – 'in the name of the people' – has in its historical reality blurred the right of *demos* with the right of *ethnos*. Hence projects of democratization have often come only after intensive forms of ethnic cleansing. Historically speaking, the more representative governments have been, the more ethnic violence one can witness.

Modern, politically liberal, economically capitalist and socially welfare-providing states have also a distinctly 'dark side': 'capitalist class compromise, liberal democracy and tolerance among the European settler people were all built on top of terrible atrocities committed against the indigenous "others" – for this was *Herrenvolk* democracy' (Mann, 1999: 25). According to Mann, the extreme forms of systematic ethnic violence have much more to do with the process of democratization and liberalization than with the behaviour of authoritarian regimes. Whereas, for example, authoritarian Ottoman rulers, concerned with stability, promoted quasi-consociational arrangements (via the millet system) and avoided large-scale killings of civilians, the modernizing secular Young Turks movement organized the first twentieth-century genocide on an ethnic basis. The genocide of Armenians was not undertaken in the name of Allah or imperial Ottoman glory but in the name of a people conceived in modern ethno-national terms. The invitation of people into history, to use Tom Nair's (1977) phrase, and the aspirations towards political democracy often brought mass murder as its corollary. 'By claiming legitimacy in the name of "the people" genocidal regimes claim kinship to movements which are usually recognised as the bearers of true modernity, like liberalism or social democracy' (Mann, 1999: 19).

Are ethnic groups status groups?

As we saw in previous chapters, most contemporary sociological theories of ethnicity were formulated as endeavours for adapting classical postulates to a dramatically changed modern environment. Contemporary accounts of ethnic relations are, for most part, engaged in reworking or repairing the shortcomings of the classics. Thus neo-Marxism emerged as an attempt to elucidate the puzzle of why ethnic bonds have proved to be a more compelling basis of group solidarity than class, as predicted by Marx. Similarly neo-functionalism was born out of the effort to account for Durkheim's hasty judgement that ethnic group attachments will decline under the grindstone of Reason, Enlightenment and Modernity. The neo-Weberian project is very different in this respect. Instead of repairing explanatory deficiencies neo-Weberianism is more of an extension than a reformulation or modern adaptation of Weber's ideas. Since Weber's analysis of and arguments on ethnic relations remain highly edifying and applicable in their original form even today, there is very little theoretical intervention or any serious attempts at their re-articulation for present-day social conditions. This is not to say that there are no criticisms of Weber's theory of ethnic relations – as with any sociological account this one is also the object of stern critique from Marxist, functionalist and other positions – but that such critique is for the most part external, that is, outside the Weberian framework of analysis. Unlike most other contemporary sociological theories of ethnicity, neo-Weberianism is more geared towards supplementing than modifying Weber's original position. However, being grounded in such secure footsteps does not mean that one is immune to analytical flaws. Although the neo-Weberian theory of ethnicity is extremely productive and pertinent in explaining the dynamics of ethnic group relations, it is also beset with omissions and problems that need to be addressed more thoroughly. Since neo-Weberian arguments have developed as a creative addition to Weber's articulation of ethnicity, any criticism of these arguments is quite often simultaneously a challenge for Weber's original stance.

There are four sets of problems expressed in neo-Weberian accounts of ethnicity:

1   the fragmented nature of explanation in the analysis of ethnic relations
2   the neglect of the cultural dimension in accounting for the strength of ethnic ties
3   the lack of a coherent political interpretation of the patterns of ethnic group mobilization
4   recurrent exaggeration in the conceptualization of ethnic groups as status groups.

Weber was probably the only classic of sociology who successfully attempted to integrate macro and micro levels of social life, by simultaneously focusing on the individual motives of social action on the one hand, and by pursuing analyses of large-scale phenomena such as his comparative study of world religions or the origins and forms of capitalism on the other. However his theory of ethnicity seems to be, for the most part, unconnected or only sporadically related to his main macro concepts such as domination, legitimacy, charismatic authority or bureaucracy. Although Weber makes a rather patchy link between ethnic groups and nations and states in a very short section of *Economy and Society* (Weber, 1968: 921–6), there is no theory of (ethno-)nationalism or ethnic group mobilization here. Weber's model of ethnic relations remains a profoundly micro-centred affair. This has led directly to the situation where contemporary neo-Weberianism has fragmented into two distinct and mutually almost incomprehensible approaches; the micro sociology of ethnicity epitomized by the works of Rex and Parkin, and the macro sociology of ethnic relations represented in the writings of Collins and Mann. The main problem with these positions is that they almost exclusively concentrate on one level of social life, giving the explanatory primacy to one group of factors at the expense of others in their interpretation of ethnic relations. Thus, while Collins and Mann provide a wide, historically sensitive analysis of ethnicity that identifies geo-politics and the logic of the State as the master keys of explanation, and thus neglecting the micro foundations of individual and group action, Rex and Parkin offer micro-centred and largely ahistoric analyses that are mainly preoccupied with individual and group motives behind the use of mechanisms of monopolistic social closure.

The lack of systematic, coherent and well integrated accounts of ethnic relations which, if not going so far as to bridge individual and group action with the impact of historical structural changes, would at least relate one to the other in some comprehensive way, deeply affects the explanatory potential of both Weber's and neo-Weberian positions. This is an especially peculiar development since Weber's general theory of society as a whole is well able to accommodate the micro and macro dimensions of social life, as his analysis of the relationship between protestant ethics and capitalism (Weber, 1958), or rationalization and disenchantment (Weber, 1948) demonstrate. In both of those cases broader historical and structural change has been closely related to individual and group motives and beliefs in order to provide an articulate, consistent and systematic explanation of particular social phenomena. Therefore, while both these classical and contemporary theories of ethnicity share a Weberian identity, neither exploits the explanatory logic or potential of this tradition to the full.

The second, equally surprising weakness of neo-Weberian theories of ethnicity is their grave underestimation and corresponding lack of analysis of the cultural dimension of ethnic relations. Taking into account that, with the possible exception of Simmel, Weber was the only classic of sociology who devoted an exceptional amount of attention to the study of individual and group ideas, values and beliefs and as a result was often seen as a father of 'idealist' sociology (i.e., particularly in Parsons' reading of Weber), it is astonishing that leading neo-Weberian accounts of ethnicity are all profoundly materialist. All four leading neo-Weberians operate with a very instrumentalist view of ethnicity. For Rex and Parkin, even though ethnic groups are a particular type of status group they are in themselves too weak a force to generate social action. For Collins and Mann, ethnic groups are social constructs where culture or ethnic descent are only used as group markers to initiate group mobilization. Just as in elite theory culture has been subordinated here to economics and politics, and ethnicity is again perceived as an object rather than being an autonomous or semi-autonomous subject of group action. This represents a significant departure from Weber's (1968) original view, since he defined ethnic groups in terms of shared belief – if there is no group belief in common descent there will be no ethnic group. Weber's analysis was much more sensitive towards ideas and group beliefs. However, to reiterate once more, although ethnic relations are predominantly political relations where the instrumentalization of group difference is an important, if not a decisive, factor of social action, such an action is inconceivable and nearly impossible without the autonomy of culture. In other words, human action is not only, and on some occasions not even predominantly, governed by individual self-interest, but rather is composed of a variety of motivational causes – traditional, habitual, emotional and value rational.

While this is fairly clear in Weber's theory of social action, it is for the most part neglected in neo-Weberian accounts. However, by undermining cultural factors one is unable to deal intelligibly with non-instrumental aspects of group action, or to establish a connection between the sudden changes in dominant values and the corresponding forms of ethnic group behaviour. This is clearly apparent in Collins' treatment of cultural markers. Collins only identifies two such markers as vital for the social construction of ethnicity: language and somatotypes, which, in itself, is a severe omission (what about religion, customs, eating habits, etc.?) and these two are not even understood and explained on their own terms. Instead they function as a second-order reality to support the explanatory master key that is geo-politics. This approach leads to a vague and conceptually empty understanding of ethnicity, with almost bizarre statements – such as 'people who belong to an ethnic group tend to look alike' (Collins, 1999: 73), or treating simulta-neously and at the same level 'Scandinavians' and 'Swedes and Finns' as an ethnic group (1999: 73). A more culturally nuanced analysis would be able to differentiate between different layers of cultural difference, which would help to establish the explanatory links between, for example, the collective perceptions of such a difference with the sources of individual or group value rationality (Malešević, 2002a).

The third and perhaps most serious weakness of neo-Weberianism is a lack of coherent political articulation of ethnic relations. Although both Weber and neo-Weberians see politics as the main source of social action and define ethnic relations in those terms, they do not really provide a compre-hensive political theory of ethnicity. While Weber was well aware that cul-tural difference was sociologically relevant only when articulated in political terms, that is, the existence of a political community is a prerequisite of ethnic group action, he did not really develop a politically ample account of ethnic relations. In other words Weber's political analysis of ethnicity is rather rudimentary and remains more on the level of a statement than apt analysis. Neo-Weberians such as Collins and Mann do operate with much more politically refined models of ethnicity, but these models are formulated on and deal almost exclusively with the macro level of analysis, where above all they directly or indirectly draw on Weber's studies of the State and nation, and very little on his work on ethnicity as such. In this way they overemphasize the role of external factors such as the nature of the State or its geo-politicial standing, at the expense of internal factors such as indivi-dual and group motives, beliefs, values and interests. They also make very little connection between ethnicity and the other main concepts of Weber's theory such as domination, legitimacy or rationality. Rex and Parkin are focused much more on micro relations but here ethnicity is too tied to eco-nomics. Both Parkin and Rex attribute a great deal of importance to class analysis and to the inter-connections between class and ethnicity. Their pre-occupation with the monopolistic group closure as a main source of ethnic group dynamics leads them to the situation where they overlook the broader theoretical context of which this concept is an integral part. Rather than being solely an instrumental device for the economic benefit of in-groups, social closure is a much wider category related also to symbolic domination and political control, to group status arrangements, and to social relations in general.[3] But, more importantly, neither Weber nor Rex and Parkin attempt to link this concept with the rest of Weber's general theory of society. Hence, although Weberianism and neo-Weberianism define ethnic relations in political terms, they do not really explore them in these same terms. Despite being key concepts of Weber's political sociology, 'domination', 'legitimacy', 'charisma' and 'rationalization' find very little or no place at all in their theory of ethnicity.

Finally, there is the problem of the Weberian conceptualization of ethnic groups as a particular form of status group. Even though ethnic groups, just as other social groups, are seen as amorphous and ajar collectivities with fuzzy boundaries, and notwithstanding their ability to relatively quickly transform into classes, estates or castes, Weberians generally work with a status-centred concept of ethnicity. Although there is a clear and intensive emphasis on the multiplicity of forms that ethnic attachments can take when confronted with empirical analysis, Weberians tend towards concep-tualization of ethnicity in status terms. As Rex (1986a) recognizes, estates and caste systems usually diminish with the process of modernization, and what characterizes contemporary societies are social struggles on the basis of ethnicity as a group status privilege. For Collins it is the status of the State's dominant ethnic group that determines the level of prestige and honour that a particular state enjoys. In other words, just as neo-Marxists do with 'class' so neo-Weberians often attribute a privileged position to social status.[4]

The problem with this view is that it is often analytically too static and group-centric. As Banton (1987: 122) rightly asserts, status-focused analysis 'makes little allowance for interaction between individuals and does not link up with the analysis of motivation'. The root of this problem can be traced to Weber's (1968) definition of ethnicity which is only inward looking ('human groups that entertain a subjective belief in their common descent'), and does not take into account how others perceive and categorize a par-ticular group. Since the definition is too idealistic it omits the decisive impact of changing inter-group realities that directly affect their individual and collective status positions. The key element in understanding ethnic relations is the nature of group dynamics. We rarely focus on the study of stable status relations between different ethnic groups; what attracts our attention are sudden and dramatic group conflicts that typically arise when particular status (class, etc.) arrangements are challenged. The conceptualiza-tion of ethnic groups as status groups averts the focus of an analysis from what is really important – the mechanisms of ethnic group mobilization. That is, status-centred analysis is often unable to deal with the sudden ruptures, with the dramatic transformations of status orders. In this way status-focused analysis minimizes individual and micro group differences within a particular collective. For example, concentrating on status distinctions between Croats and Serbs may forestall the fact that there are decisive status group differences between Slavonian Croats, Dalmatian Croats and West Herzegovinian Croats. Furthermore, the static nature of status-centred analysis fails to get an analytical hold on swift transformations in in-group/out-group perceptions among individuals and sub-groups ('sub-ethnicities'). As a result it is unable to explain how groups with a traditionally inferior status, such as West Herzegovinian Croats, can become, status-wise, in times of ethnic war the most superior grouping within the Croatian ethnic corpus. To deal with rapid status enhancement in the context of war one has to work with much more open models of ethnicity. This is not to say that ethnic groups do not act as status groups. On the contrary, they very often do. But the point is that they are not only status groups. Ethnic groups can simultaneously have features of status, class, caste, estate, etc. and be neither status groups, nor class, caste and so on. In fact the group dynamics provides for hybrid forms of group social structure.

Conclusion

More than in the case of the other sociological classics, Weber has left a compelling legacy in the study of ethnic relations. Weber has not only provided theoretical models and research devices such as 'monopolistic social closure', 'ethnic honour' or the concept of ethnicity as a status group, but with his emphasis on the multiplicity of ethnic group relations or the perception of ethnic groups as belief-based political communities, he has also set the directions of contemporary research. When successful, neo-Weberianism is for the most part a creative extension of this rich legacy. However, the fragmented nature of this legacy, which in its original form already lacked a clear and transparent connection to Weber's other main concepts and thus to his general theory of social action, has created a contemporary situation where leading neo-Weberian accounts of ethnicity have become deeply polarized. Instead of creating a comprehensive and relatively integrated theory of ethnic relations, neo-Weberianism has emerged in two structurally diverse forms – as a macro-historically conscious perspective that focuses on the impact of geo-politics and state formation on ethnic relations, and as a micro-economistic standpoint that concentrates on the in-group monopolization of status privilege. The main drawback of these positions is not the nature of their analyses, which are extremely effective within their own framework, but rather their incompleteness, which comes from dealing with only one layer of social reality. In other words, over-emphasizing the micro over the macro structure or vice versa can never provide a complete picture of the social world. Such polarization is more likely to strangle that what is most distinctive in Weber's position – the attempt to relate successfully agency to structure. Therefore, neo-Weberianism as such is not problematic as a general position in the study of ethnic relations. On the contrary, this is conceptually and empirically the most fruitful of socio-logical approaches on ethnicity. What is problematic with the contemporary neo-Weberian accounts of ethnicity is that they are not Weberian enough.

Notes

1 The millets were semi-autonomous administrative units organized on the basis of ethno-religious affiliation for the non-Muslim subjects of the Ottoman empire.
2 On the distinction between the infrastructural and despotic power of the State see Mann (1988) and Hall and Ikenberry (1989).
3 Although Rex operates with the concept of social closure which is more in tune with Weber's original position, his view of ethnic relations is still too economistic.
4 Mann's theory is clearly an exception here since he does not attribute such a privileged role to social status.

Chapter Ten

ANTI–FOUNDATIONALIST APPROACHES: DECONSTRUCTING ETHNICITY

Introduction

Most 'conventional' sociological approaches, and even sociology itself, have recently come under sharp criticism from a corpus of perspectives loosely termed 'anti-foundationalist'. Although internally diverse, ranging from reflexive feminism and social psychoanalysis to post-modernism, post-structuralism or post-Marxism, these new approaches share a common theoretical ground which is aimed at challenging universalism, positivism and the totalizing objectives of 'conventional' sociology. The anti-foundationalist perspectives also emphasize the authoritarian and destructive outcomes behind totalizing aims of science, and agree on the impossibility of a single universal truth promised by the Enlightenment project. The 'conventional' sociological approaches such as neo-Marxism or functionalism have been perceived as 'hegemonic meta-narratives' (Lyotard, 1984) whose claims to truth are seen as misleading and potentially dangerous since, in the view of anti-foundationalists, truth is always provisional, contingent and discursive. Instead of universal grand Truth, anti-foundationalists such as Foucault (1980) speak of multiple, plural and particular truths: the regime and grammar of truth lies always in the domain of a particular community or society.

Such a radical view has had a direct influence on the study of ethnic relations. Instead of searching for the source of ethnic group animosity, for the essential explanatory variable or the ultimate cause which would explain ethnic relations, anti-foundationalists, following Derrida (1976), aim rather to deconstruct ethnicity itself. By deconstruction it is meant that there is no master key to unlock the secrets of social relations, including ethnic relations. There are no ultimately privileged individual or group discourses and there is no unequivocal domination of 'one mode of signifying over another'. Anti-foundationalists argue that there are no essential meanings, and hence no group identity is real or definitive: ethnic group membership is always discursive, open and conditional. The aim of anti-foundational analysis is not to explain but rather to deconstruct, that is, to pinpoint discrepancies, arbitrariness and hegemonic practices that are integral to any process of discourse construction. Focusing in particular on language and textual analysis, anti-foundationalists aim to recreate meanings from that which is left out, ignored or suppressed within and by a particular discourse. Anti-foundational analyses of ethnic relations can be broadly classified into two relatively distinct approaches; those that have their origins in 'conventional' sociology and have developed as a critique of these origins, such as post-modernism, post-structuralism and post-Marxism, and those that have origins outside 'conventional' sociology, such as reflexive feminism and social psychoanalysis.

De-centring identity claims: post-modernism, post-structuralism and post-Marxism

Anti-foundationalists such as post-structuralists, post-modernists and post-Marxists argue that the disintegration of meta-narratives such as Marxism, structuralism or functionalism has created a contemporary situation where social reality is fractured and fragmented, social events are disjointed and incomprehensible outside of their own frame of reference, and individual action is isolated and void of any meaningful content. Any attempt to privilege one group identity over another (i.e., class over ethnicity or gender over class) is equally flawed since all language games have equivalent legitimacy. In a world of incommensurable discourses of truth and dissolved social subjects all group identities are multiple, contingent and changeable. Unlike Marxism, functionalism and other modernist positions that aim to locate the ultimate essence of social reality by identifying the fundamental principles of social action, anti-foundationalism sees such attempts as utopian and counterproductive, and intends to preserve the differences and discontinuities that social reality is made of.

In the eyes of post-Marxists such as Laclau and Mouffe (1985), identities share with discourses the quality of being relational. Individuals are dispersed throughout different discursive formations where their social positions and their collective identities remain only partial fixations, never complete and never finished. The collective and individual attempts to impose a particular form of group identification as the dominant one encounters other similar hegemonic attempts. In their own words: 'any discourse is constituted as an attempt to dominate the field of discursivity, to arrest the flow of differences, to construct a centre' (Laclau and Mouffe, 1985: 112). As Kellner (1995) emphasizes, anti-foundationalism has reclaimed the relative freedom of identity from structures, but primarily as an 'orgy of unconstrained voluntarism, assemblage and self-styling'. For anti-foundationalists, and particularly for post-modernists, human subjectivity is not wholly created or determined by institutional mechanisms. Rather, in the fragmented reality of a post-modern condition, individuals are forced to 'cobble together their own biographies' (Beck, 1991) out of the multiplicity of incomprehensible sets of meanings, ideas and practices. Instead of expressing the essence of who one is, identities are provisional, fluid and flexible attachments to ever-changing collective entities. Post-modernism, poststructuralism and post-Marxism see identities not only as being dissociated from structural constraints, but the structural constraints themselves are perceived as dynamic and variable: one's identity is constantly reconstituted, as are the collectivities one defines oneself against.

Post-structuralist analyses of ethnic relations build primarily on Foucault's theory of discourse. Foucault's discourse analysis starts from the assumption that there are no essential structures of knowledge and reality. All meanings are constructed historically through discursive practices. Goldberg (1993) has concentrated in particular on the processes of constructing racial and ethnic discourses. Seeing race and ethnicity as historically changing discursive objects, he argues that there is no possibility of creating a singular understanding of these concepts. Instead 'race is whatever anyone in using that term or its cognates conceives of collective relations' (Goldberg, 1993: 81). No reference to race and ethnicity is neutral or socially detached. Overt, popular expressions of racism and academic analysis of ethnic relations equally constitute specific fields of discursivity. What Foucaldians such as Goldberg attempt to do is to deconstruct a 'grammar' and the internal set of rules that constitute a particular discursive formation.[1] In other words, Goldberg is interested in analysing the archaeology of specific discourses by identifying their internal practices and strategies of categorization, hierarchy and order. 'Ethnicity' and 'race' have no essential or fundamental features; rather they are discursive devices through which individuals are constituted as members of particular social groups. Echoing Barthes (1993) and Althusser (1994), Goldberg argues that the discourses of race and ethnicity help to naturalize the groups they identify in their own name. These group-centred discourses articulate, or in Althusserian terminology interpellate, human beings not as individuals but as 'Germans', 'Serbs', 'Blacks' and so on. Thus, there are no universally acceptable criteria to categorize social groups: 'the range of reference has largely turned on characteristics like skin colour, physiognomy, blood or genes, descent or claimed kinship, historical origin or original geographical location, language and culture'. But all of these quasi-parameters are rooted in a particular historical condition and, consequently, they 'could have extended and could extend beyond these' (Goldberg, 1993: 82). Hence, in the view of post-structuralists there cannot be a universal theory of ethnicity that identifies a single master cause to explain ethnic relations. Since one can encounter only distinctive, historically particular and multiple forms of ethnicity, their interpretation necessarily has to be multiple.

Carter (1997) supplements Goldberg's archaeology of ethnic and racial discourses with intensive study of the genealogy of such discourses. In other words, to understand ethnic discourses Carter argues that one has to move from Foucault's early emphasis on the archaeology of discourse to his later genealogical analysis. This implies the strategy of tracing the origins of discourses and the processes in which they construct human subjectivity. As Carter points out, genealogy 'examines the ways in which discourses and practices generate an experience of "race" and make "race" a truth for us, an experientially valid means of interpreting social relations and negotiating the everyday social world' (1997: 131). Thus, when analysing particular ethnic and racial discourses, Foucaldian analysis is more interested in questions of 'How?' than in questions of 'What?' Since all truth claims are perceived as contingent and provisional, post-structuralism finds it more fruitful to look at how particular discourses have been constructed than at what constitutes a particular discourse or whether such discourses are true or false. Rattansi (1999) extends this line of reasoning by arguing that ethnic identities are for the most part 'decentred, fragmented by contradictory discourses and by the pull of other identities'. As such, ethnic collectivities are truly 'imagined communities' (Anderson, 1991), which are articulated through a particular historical experience. However the process of ethnic identity construction is not only shaped by historical and structurally hegemonic macro discourses, but also 'the variety and contradictions of ethnic and racialised discourses, as constitutive of the social, are particularly highlighted, painting up the complexity and relative contingency and openness of the processes by which identities are constructed in "routine" everyday practices' (Rattansi, 1999: 84).

Post-modernists such as Bhabha (1990, 1994) or Bauman (1991, 1993) broaden this analysis to include not only the archaeology or genealogy of specific discourses – the entire Enlightenment-induced concept of social order is put under intensive scrutiny. They trace the totalizing ambitions of modernity to Enlightenment's attempt to order and regulate and, in that way, to transcend cultural difference. The Enlightenment conception of modernity was that of 'essentially orderly totality' (Bauman, 1987), which aimed to absorb the individual and collective self together with the Other. However, as Bhabha (1994) argues, cultural difference is always incomplete and as such open to a variety of cultural translations, which intrinsically prevent hegemonic sequestration of diversity. Ethnic homogeneity, which in the last instance is formulated as cultural homogeneity, is rooted in a modernist ambition to incorporate cultural difference including the Other, but since the process itself is dependent on the very existence of the Other it can never succeed. In other words, any endeavour to create an ethnically pure collective is an illusion since the concept of the ethnic self can be articulated only in opposition to the ethnic Other. All identities are hybrids composed of competing narratives of 'the people'. Post-colonial immigration, the arrival of refugees, and greater mobility of individuals have exposed the myth of cultural homogeneity and undermined the traditional narratives of uniform ethno-national culture. Thus Bhabha opposes the conceptualization of cultural difference as 'a free play of polarities and pluralities in the homogeneous empty time' of a particular collective. Rather, cultural difference is conceived as dialogical and dialectical: 'it is constituted through the locus of the Other which suggests both that the object of identification is ambivalent, and, more significantly, that the agency of identification is never pure or holistic but always constituted in a process of substitution, displacement or projection' (Bhabha, 1994: 162).

Modernity's attempt to transgress hybridity and the fragmented nature of ethno-national narratives often results in devastating consequences. Bauman (1989) identifies the Holocaust as an epitome of modernity's drive to impose order on a world 'devoid of reliable foundations'. Rather than being an anomaly of modernity, Bauman sees the Holocaust as the very product of modernity. The Enlightenment obsession with order, classification and the elimination of randomness and ambivalence leads to intolerance of difference. Modernity has not only created the environment and means for the realization of ethnic genocide, such as the efficient bureaucratic apparatus, science and technologies with the capacity to implement grand projects and blue-prints, but it has also created a technocratic and instrumentalist culture that can adapt to that purpose. The 'Final Solution' was rooted in a profoundly modern (utopian) project of creating an ethnically pure community. It was a product of modern 'dull bureaucratic routine' governed by the principles of instrumental rationality and a hierarchical delegation of tasks where, through the concept of professional honour, 'discipline is substituted for moral responsibility'. The modern state has concentrated and monopolized the means of violence and, as a result, has transformed violence into a mere technique. The State's monopoly on violence has also created a situation where its ambitions towards social engineering (often formulated 'in the name of the people') have rendered it infallible. Thus, 'genocide arrives as an integral part of the process through which the grand design is implemented. The design gives it the legitimation; state bureaucracy gives it the vehicle; and the paralysis of society gives it the "road clear" sign' (Bauman, 1989: 114). The Holocaust could not be accomplished through pre-modern outbursts of irrationality such as pogroms, periodic destruction of Jewish shops and property, or random killings. Mass extermination on such a scale requires distinctively modern means – systematic division of labour, efficient bureaucracy and cold and calculated rationality of ends.

While post-structuralism and post-modernism are focused on a broad critique of the Enlightenment heritage and exhibit a very pessimistic interpretation of the contemporary situation, post-Marxism aims to balance a critique of the hegemonic discourses of modernity with concrete proposals for the direction of social change. Just like post-structuralists and postmodernists, post-Marxists see group identities as relational and contingent. They are especially critical of classical Marxism in its privileging of class identity at the expense of other forms of collectivity. However, unlike other anti-foundationalist positions they show a greater degree of belief in human agency and the possibility of meaningful collective action. The recent work of Hall and Gilroy, among others, indicates how post-Marxism approaches ethnic relations.

Recognizing the fact that identities are multiple and dynamic does not rule out the empirical possibility that the inclusiveness of a particular ethnic identity could allow for heterogeneity of origins and, at the same time, foster an 'integrated' counter-hegemonic movement. Thus, Gilroy (1990, 1992) sees the idea of 'being black' as an umbrella concept which, although incorporating very distinct individuals and groups, nevertheless often acts as a potent generator of political action (i.e., the black consciousness movement in the 1960s). However, this strategy is often risky since there is an inherent danger of essentializing and reifying group identities. As Gilroy argues, identity politics often rely on Euro-American concepts of modernity which 'condition the continuing aspiration to acquire a supposedly authentic, natural and stable identity'. This view is deeply problematic for Gilroy since it operates with 'over-integrated conceptions of culture', which 'masks the arbitrariness of its own political choices in the morally charged language of ethnic absolutism' (Gilroy, 2000a: 491). That is why he now strongly opposes the concept of race. Although the concept itself is an image with a compelling strategic mobilizing force, 'race' has for the most part been essentialized, and within popular culture it has been commodified. Cultural authenticity has been articulated as a resource in the service of corporate interests, linked to the market need for supplying new and ever-increasing visual technologies with novel forms of cultural expression (Gilroy, 2000b).

Stuart Hall (1991) follows a similar line of argument. Unlike classical Marxism he sees class identity as being just one among many forms that group identification can take. Since in Hall's view an identity is not a state but a dynamic process, individual and group attachments are always partial and incomplete, and often shaped by distinctive discursive practices and contingent events. However, he also differentiates his position from post-structuralism in reaffirming the concept of agency. As Hall (1996b: 2) explains, this does not mean a return to the subject as a 'centred author of social practice', as present in many modernist positions, but rather a 'reconceptualisation – thinking it in its new, displaced or decentred position within the paradigm'. Hence the emphasis is more on the process of identification than on identities as such, more on the potential of decentred subjectivity than on the unresisted power of discourses. This process is characterized by persistent attempts at splitting and dividing (us from them, me from you) and corresponding feelings of ambivalence, uncertainty and hesitation over choices being made, since the process of defining and redefining oneself rests on defining and redefining the Other. Since all identities have a narrative structure no identity is coherent, stable or permanent. Instead, as Hall argues, 'as the systems of meaning and cultural representation multiply, we are confronted by a bewildering, fleeting multiplicity of possible identities, any of which we could identify with – at least temporarily' (1992: 277). Identities are 'points of temporary attachment to the subject positions which discursive practices construct for us' (Hall, 1996b: 6).

Enjoyment thieves and ethnic patriarchs: psychoanalytic and feminist readings of ethnicity

In addition to post-structuralism, post-modernism and post-Marxism there are two other influential anti-foundationalist perspectives on ethnicity: social psychoanalysis and reflexive feminism. While both of these perspectives share the post-modernist criticism of 'meta-narratives' and express scepticism towards the totalizing projects, positivism and essentialist claims of modernist approaches, they still maintain some explanatory ambitions. Although these ambitions are now scaled down, more reflexive and ajar, both psychoanalysis and feminism operate with a particular set of interpretative devices developed with the aim of shedding an explanatory light on ethnic relations. In other words, unlike post-structuralism or post-modernism, which see any attempt at explanation as a process of imposing a particular (hegemonic) discourse on diverse and constantly changing realities, feminism and psychoanalysis uphold the belief that not all meta-narratives are equivalent, and to understand and explain the particular on its own terms one has to engage with the univeralist claims, which are the condition of possibility for particularism as such. Whereas for feminists this interplay between particular and universal is to be found in the analysis of gender, for psychoanalysts it is the concept of the unconscious.

Sociologically, Žižek (1989, 1993) develops the most articulate psychoanalytic theory of ethnic relations. Drawing on Freud's early works and on Lacan's understanding of the unconscious as the ego's reaction to the Other, Žižek analyses ethnicity through the dissection of one's desires and passions as being primarily located in the Other. Lacan's concept of *jouissance*, formulated as enjoyment, is identified as the key generator of individual and group action. Human unconscious is geared towards enjoyment. However, since enjoyment is not mere pleasure but *'lust im unlust'*,[2] and since it is always to be found in the Other, it can never be fully achieved. Hence it operates as a perpetual attempt of acquiring enjoyment which is always outside of oneself, thus creating a state of traumatic irrationality. To fulfil this constant lack of enjoyment one develops fantasies. Ethnic group animosity, xenophobia and racism are all forms of fantasy scenarios aimed at satisfying this lack of enjoyment (to fix it in place). Through these fantasy scenarios one not only projects one's pain onto the Other, but these fantasies also function as a mask for attempting to achieve real but impossible essence. In a nutshell, for Žižek ethnic enmity is about the theft of one's enjoyment. Since in his view the ethnic collective is linked together by a shared belief in possessing a common 'Thing',[3] that is, an ethnic essence which is supported by the individual and collective fantasy scenarios, any real or potential attempt by outsiders to interfere with 'our' Thing is conceived as a threat. Ethnic antagonism is located in different perceptions of the collective organizations of enjoyment – the eating and drinking habits, the mating practices, the ceremonial rituals and feats. Others are perceived as always experiencing an excess of enjoyment. In Žižek's words:

> what really bothers us about the 'other' is the peculiar way he organises his enjoyment, precisely the surplus, the 'excess' that pertains to this way: the smell of 'their' food, 'their' noisy songs and dances, 'their' strange manners, 'their' attitude to work. To the racist, the 'other' is either a workaholic stealing our jobs or an idler living on our labour ... the basic paradox is that our Thing is conceived as something inaccessible to the other and at the same time threatened by him. (1993: 205)

In his view an ethnic group exists as long as its particular form of enjoyment remains vital and ample in its social practices and is successfully conveyed through ethnic myths that sustain those practices. While ethnic mythology might for the most part be invented or imagined, to be successful it has to rely on 'some real, nondiscursive kernel of enjoyment'. However, the theft of enjoyment, and, hence, group conflicts, do not arise from mere cultural difference or from ethnic groups living next to each other, but are the product of an 'inner antagonism inherent in the communities'. There is no need for the actual physical presence of the Other to set this animosity in motion, as Lendvai's (1971) phrase 'anti-Semitism without Jews' illustrates so well. Inner-group antagonisms are not only displaced by being projected on to the Other, but also, through this displacement, one's desire is constituted. Following Lacan, Žižek argues that if our enjoyment is, at the end of the day, always enjoyment of the Other, then our hatred of the enjoyment of the Other is also hatred of our own enjoyment. Ethnic enmity is rooted in the collision between distinct modes of ethnic enjoyment, that is, between different styles of organizing one's enjoyment, but it is ridden with ambivalence: while the Other's enjoyment is a threat to our enjoyment we are also enthralled and fantasize about the enjoyment of the Other.

Reflexive feminism has also provided influential anti-foundationalist analyses of ethnicity. Most of these studies focus on three topics – the historical interaction of ethnicity and gender, symbolic and ideological uses of women in ethno-national projects, and the role of (gender and ethnic) marginality in the universalist discourses of modernity. bell hooks (2000), Guillaumin (1995) and Fenton (1999), among others, have traced historically diverse patterns of ethnic and gender subordination. In most cases the question of sexual relations between dominant and subordinated ethnic groups was a predictor of all social relations between groups: whereas subordinated men were generally perceived as a threat to superordinate women, subordinated women were regularly seen as sexually accessible to superordinate men. Such a state of affairs indicated not only the degree of dominance of superordinate over subordinate groups but it also demonstrated the gendered structure of this domination where superordinate women were also subordinate to superordinate men. This is clearly spelled out in hooks' analysis of ethnic relations under the conditions of slavery in the American South:

> In most instances, the white mistress did not envy the black female slave her role as sexual object; she feared only that her newly acquired social status might be threatened by white male sexual interaction with black women. His sexual involvement with black women (even if that involvement is rape) in effect reminded the white female of her subordinate position in relationship to him. For he could exercise his power as racial imperialist and sexual imperialist to rape or seduce black women, while white women were not free to rape or seduce black men without fear of punishment. (2000: 386)

These links between gender and ethnicity are also visible in contemporary Western societies with the emergence of 'the feminisation of labour opportunities' (Fenton, 1999; Phizacklea, 1999), that is, with the advent of women immigrants such as baby-sitters, maids or prostitutes who are demarcated and exploited on the basis of both their 'ethnic' and gender identity.

Feminists such as Anthias and Yuval-Davis (1983; Yuval-Davis and Anthias, 1989) also provide elaborate and detailed studies of ethno-national narratives where women are depicted as central to ethnic projects. As Yuval-Davis (1993: 627) argues, women are often 'given the social role of intergenerational transmitters of cultural traditions, customs, songs, cuisine, and of course, the mother tongue'. Their behaviour is communally postulated as a moral compass that sets the boundaries of an ethnic group. The sexual promiscuity of women is often invoked as a parameter that delineates 'our' women, and thus our morally superior community, from 'their' women and 'their' morally inferior community. Being sexually dissolute doesn't only make a particular woman an immoral individual but, more importantly, it makes her less of a Sikh, Serb or Irish because it is the behaviour of women that sets the parameters of what it means to be a (good) Sikh, Serb or Irish. Not only is it that women often symbolize ethnic collectives, but women are regularly conceived of as biological reproducers of ethnic groups (i.e., ethnic groups are seen as being composed of family units). In this way they are attributed the role of being ideological reproducers of their ethnic group, since the ethnic group's culture is structured around gendered institutions such as marriage, family and sexuality. The fact that ethnic territories are often described as the 'motherland' indicates, according to Yuval-Davis (1997), that through the use of such a hegemonic discourse women are chained to patriarchally conceived notions of purity and honour, where the motherland, just as actual mothers and daughters, is viewed as a passive object that needs to be defended and protected by the active subjects, that is men, their husbands and sons.

Finally, reflexive feminism also builds on post-essentialist and psychoanalytic notions of the Other where the female subject is analysed as patriarchy's Other. Julia Kristeva (1984) focuses on the 'place' from which women are to represent themselves. Instead of the discourse of marginality from which both women and non-dominant ethnic groups were historically designated to speak, she aims to enfeeble the centrality of any discourse and, in particular, she attempts to 'undermine the phallocentric order that defines women as marginal in the first place'. In its attempt to decentralize the subject of History, which pretends to be neutral while, in fact, was for the most part Male and White European, reflexive feminism shares a great deal with postmodernism or post-structuralism: just like these two positions, feminism asserts difference and resists totalizing narratives of modernity. Both women and minority ethnic groups, being the Other of the European Enlightenment male subject, are to transcend the place of marginality by deconstructing the master narratives of modernity which legitimize some collective representations (Western, phallocentric, upper or middle class) and block or invalidate other narratives (colonized, female, working class, etc.).

Deconstruction or destruction of ethnicity?

Anti-foundationalism has, in many ways, undermined the certainty and security of 'conventional' sociological approaches. Its dissection and deconstruction of grand meta-narratives has brought an awareness that science (including social science) and modernity, just as any attempt to extract a pure, context-free knowledge, are always in the last instance power-driven and thus never innocent, and it has also greatly contributed to the recognition that there is no master key to unlock the secrets of social reality. Postmodernism, post-structuralism and post-Marxism have helped us to realize that any attempt to single out the essential unit of social analysis, to identify the decisive actor of social change or to uncover the ultimate layer of social structure will always remain a futile exercise. Social psychoanalysis and reflexive feminism have also highlighted the complex nature of the human psyche, patriarchy and other hidden forms of domination, which are largely invisible, and collectively unrecognized, but which are deeply interwoven in everyday social relations. More than anything, anti-foundationalism has demonstrated not only that cultural difference is always incomplete but, more significantly, for the study of ethnicity, that as such it can never be transcended. Any attempt to eradicate, segregate, separate or integrate cultural difference is simultaneously a process of creating new forms of cultural difference.

Focusing on the deconstruction of hegemonic discourses, anti-foundationalists have rightly signalled that in the study of social reality what often matters is not the question of whether particular discourses are true, but rather how they have been constructed, who they address and what they aim to achieve. In other words, to paraphrase Foucault, the analysis of ethnic relations benefit more from its focus on the 'how' instead of the 'what' of particular truth claims. With their criticisms of scientism, universalism and hard essentialism which characterize most foundationalist positions, anti-foundationalists correctly indicate that one has to work with much more open models of ethnicity. Post-structuralism and post-modernism justly challenge the totalizing ambitions of some 'conventional' theories of ethnicity. It is epistemologically unsustainable to attribute a special and privileged role to one single social actor, be it class, gender or ethnicity, as it is to one 'meta-narrative'. Anti-foundationalism is very forceful indeed in demonstrating that the basis of narratives with privileged agents of social change are quite weak, and that reality in itself is both multiple and discursive.

However, recognizing that there are no universally privileged social actors does not mean accepting the view that all 'language games' are equal, and that the social actions of all actors have an equivalent impact on social relations. On the contrary, by acknowledging the idea that there are no general and omnipresent social actors one can better focus on particularly shaped asymmetrical relations of power. One can now concentrate on questions when, why and how interpretations and articulations of concrete social (ethnic) reality by these particularly privileged social agents become hegemonic, shared or trusted by many. In other words, although 'meta-narratives', 'discourses', or 'language games' might be epistemologically of equal worth, their structural position (i.e., whether a particular discourse or meta-narrative is dominant and institutionalized or not) makes them contextually and ontologically very different and unequal. The root of this problem, which affects the entire anti-foundationalist understanding of ethnicity, lies in three major pitfalls: a) radical relativism, which often leads to nihilism and analytical paralysis; b) cultural determinism in treating social actors as being created through discursive practices; and c) the dissolution of ethnic relations through the use of vague and largely non-analytical concepts of 'identity'.

Anti-foundationalist perspectives, and especially post-modernism and post-structuralism, have often been criticized for their relativistic understanding of social reality. Starting from the idea that any attempt at explanation is ultimately motivated by the quest for domination, they consciously opt for conceptual looseness and deconstruction instead of methodologically rigorous explanation. Since the idea of deconstruction is a form of attack on all conceptual systems, models and definitions, anti-foundationalists oppose theory building and rely on metaphors, wordplay and alinear interpretations of discourses and events. Despite its critical appeal, such a position is logically unsustainable since any form of deconstruction – regardless of how loose it might be – is ultimately dependent on the process of argumentation. To deconstruct and uncover invisible forms of domination, as well as to demonstrate to others the results of this deconstruction one has to operate within the parameters of reason and rationality. As Habermas (1987) and Taylor (1984) have rightly emphasized, in rejecting the possibility of individual freedom and logic, anti-foundationalists cut the ground from under their own feet. In other words, the epistemological criticisms of hegemonic meta-narratives, language games or discourses are diluted when there is no epistemological or normative 'axis' to build upon. Such radical relativism is problematic on both epistemological and normative grounds. On the one hand, in recognizing the equivalence of all truth claims anti-foundationalism is unable or unwilling to differentiate between different types of power, thus equalizing, for example, the more benign forms of ethnic animosity such as the use of ethnic slurs or jokes with the extreme types of inter-group conflict such as ethnic cleansing or genocide. On the other hand, the position is analytically constraining in its inability to distinguish between different 'regimes of truth'. For example, it is not clear at all how one can distinguish between concrete 'meta-narrative' and non-'meta narrative'. In order to move from the metaphoric level of analysis towards useful empirical analysis of the 'regimes of truth' one has to offer more superior criteria on who and how one is to decide that particular discourses are incommensurable.

Anti-foundationists do not offer an adequate conceptual apparatus that could be used in the empirical research. As a result most anti-foundationalist work remains on the level of statement, metaphor, wordplay or puns. There is no clear answer to the question of how to overcome the methodological and conceptual arbitrariness of such a position. In the study of ethnic relations such a relativistic position can also have devastating policy outcomes, since in stating that every (ethnic) collective has its own regime of truth one denies the possibility of individual choice within an (ethnic) group. If held consistently, this position would have to allow for the persistence of the traditional practice of female genital mutilation among Somali girls living in European states on the grounds of non-interfering with the existing 'regime of truth' of the Somali community. The problem of cultural relativism is its insensitivity towards particularities within the particular. In other words, by assuming that a certain group of people (i.e., Italians, Aimara, Montenegrins) share the same 'regime of truth' one remains totalist on the level of the particular.

The second important problem in the anti-foundationalists' understanding of ethnicity is their overemphasis on the discursive construction of social relations. While they rightly focus on the study of cultural aspects of inter-group relations such as the genealogy or gramatology of particular ethnic group narratives, their obsession with the textual analysis leads them to attribute too much significance to culture at the expense of politics or economics. When ethnicity is analysed and interpreted as text only, one becomes completely removed from the harsh reality and profound materiality of everyday ethnic relations. In other words, anti-foundationalism, with its concentration on language and discourse analysis, often resembles a contemporary equivalent of medieval metaphysics which, with its idealism, had consciously removed itself from the material life of contemporary events. By contesting the concept of reality and looking at the social world in terms of a multiplicity of mutually confronted discourses, anti-foundationalism goes one step further than even symbolic interactionism towards an 'anything goes' logic of understanding (Feyerabend, 1975). However, unlike interactionism, where actors are given privileged positions, anti-foundationalists (with the possible exception of neo-Marxism[4]) treat individual and social actors as no more than carriers of action governed by dominant discourses. In the eyes of anti-foundationalists human subjectivity is always, in the last instance, created and articulated by omnipresent discursive practices. In this respect post-modernism and post-structuralism differ little from classical structuralism (Malešević, 2002b). This position is deeply problematic since, unlike symbolic interactionism, it operates with a hard and deterministic view of individual action. While being structurally and often systematically constrained, human actors are social beings precisely because they are able or are constantly engaged in attempts to create or recreate their own social reality. While ethnic group action is often dependent on a particular discursive articulation of group rights, interests or traditions, without the individual comprehension (regardless of how irrational it may seem) and tacit consent of the actors involved, ethnic group mobilization, and thus social action, is not possible.

Whereas feminism and psychoanalysis work with a softer understanding of discursive practices they too underestimate or misunderstand the strength and nature of human agency. Thus Žižek 's psychoanalytic analysis shifts too easily and too quickly from an individual/clinical to a collective level of analysis. The tools of psychoanalysis, developed to treat traumatic and psychotic individuals, cannot so easily be transposed on to the highly complex and dynamic world of collectivities. As Finlayson (1998: 157) rightly argues, this view anthropomorphizes ethnic groups as 'collective actors experiencing a trauma, a lack and able to engage in fantasy … [which] undercuts Žižek's critique since he bases the analysis on a collective subject, the existence of which he was initially problematising'. Similarly, feminist denunciation of the universalist narratives of modernity and reason as no more than hidden male-centred discourses, is not only premised upon a use of reason itself, but is highly deterministic in negating the possibility of individual (non-gender or ethnic-centred) action. A more nuanced analysis would be able to differenatiate between male-centric and gender-indeterminate individual social action. As they stand, and despite their commitment to reflexivity, many forms of feminism conflate these two levels of action, preventing a more comprehensive and nuanced analysis of ethnic relations.

Finally, and perhaps most damaging to the study of ethnic relations, is the anti-foundationalist obsession with the concept of 'identity' and its application to the analysis of cultural difference. This identarianism reduces ethnicity to being just one of many forms that groupness can take. While this is certainly true on the level of ontology, it is not only futile but is often counterproductive at the level of epistemology, leading to an extremely voluntaristic and hence largely unsociological view of ethnicity. Since identities (and among them ethnic identity) are seen, as Stuart Hall (1992, 1996b), puts it, as 'points of temporary attachment', any one of which one could identify with ethnic relations, then this becomes some form of cultural collage, a pastiche that one creates for oneself by picking and choosing from existing cultural artefacts. As consistently argued in this book, the process of self and group identification is often dependent on group categorization, and there is only limited space for voluntary action in having the possibility to switch ethnic group membership. The use of 'identity' allows for an extremely flexible understanding of the social which thus neglects these external constraints. However, the vague and un-analytical nature of this concept only prevents the development of proper analysis.

The concept of 'identity' was originally derived from mathematics and entered sociological discourse via psychology and psychiatry. As I have argued elsewhere (Malešević, 2002c), the dualistic mathematical understanding of identity as absolute zero difference and as relative non-zero difference as it was incorporated into sociological discourse was self-defeating from the very beginning, since, unlike the world of arithmetics the social world cannot operate with absolute concepts. A simple and crude assimilation of the concept which is, in many ways, alien to sociology has led to the contemporary situation where sociological analyses employing the concept of identity are 'profoundly weakened by an excessive and uncritical reliance on what has become a politicised, residual and undertheorised concept' (Bendle, 2002: 4). The current social science uses of 'identity' oscillate between rigid and inflexible conceptualizations that perceive identities in terms of group sameness or attribute such a condition to all forms of non-instrumental action on the one hand, and extremely loose understandings where identities are seen as contingent creations of group interaction or as detachable and fragmented forms of selfhood on the other (Brubaker and Cooper, 2000). Whereas the use of identity in a hard, fixed collectivist way leads to reification of group membership and provides yet another essentialist and flawed understanding of social reality, when used in a very soft and flexible way the concept disintegrates as a set of vague metaphors and looses its explanatory potential.

The use of the concept of identity often obscures and hinders a proper explanation, since 'identity' is often employed as an umbrella term to cover different events and forms of social action. For example, lumping all forms of non-instrumental action under the single idiom such as 'identity' prevents us from differentiating between emotional, habitual, traditional and value-rational sources of collective action (Weber, 1968). In other cases, when identity is articulated as a fluctuating and incoherent project of the self then the concept assumes such a degree of plasticity that it can accommodate any research design and any theoretical claim, which automatically renders it a futile analytical concept. Not only is the concept either too fuzzy and ambiguous or too inflexible for sociological research, but its pseudo-scientific acceptance has led to its popularity in political and activist discourse, where it continues to have devastating consequences when individuals and groups are incited to kill or die in the name of 'preserving one's identity'. The contemporary resurgence of so-called 'identity politics' is a good indicator of such an essentialist misuse of this concept, where 'one's hidden injury becomes the ground for a claim of valued identity'. Identity can be claimed … 'only to the extent that it can be represented as denied, repressed, injured or excluded by others' (Rose, 1999: 268). Thus, 'identity' suffers from acute conceptual weaknesses: it is either used in restricted and essentialist or in an all-embracing and vague way, which makes it dispensable and largely redundant as a categorical apparatus for sociological analysis.

Conclusion

Anti-foundationalism was born through the attempt to decentre and deconstruct the Cartesian concept of reason and modernity. As such it was articulated as an uncompromising attack on all 'conventional' sociological perspectives. In the eyes of anti-foundationalists the search for truth is ultimately a search for power, and instead of attempting to provide a coherent explanation one is to deconstruct the narratives of social reality. In their view ethnic relations, just as any other form of group relations, are to be analytically dissected to reveal the internal incoherence and inconsistencies and ambiguity rooted in any discursive practice. With its emphasis on fluidity, contingency and the historicity of particular ethnic discourses, this research strategy has proved very valuable. Moreover, its deconstruction of ethnic group narratives has demonstrated the inherent weakness and baselessness behind many essentialist claims to the primordiality of a particular ethnic group. Anti-foundationalism has also, extending the Weberian attempt, initiated development of much more open models of ethnicity, revealing that ethnicity is not a singular phenomenon but rather a concept that covers diverse forms of acting, thinking and categorizing selves and others. However, its radical relativism, which treats all truth claims as equal, its conceptual demeaning of human agency by attributing an omnipotent force to discourses, and its fixation with identity claims still prove insoluble obstacles. In other words, whereas anti-foundationalism is powerful at the level of social critique, it is for the most part futile if not counterproductive at the level of policy. When applied to the material world of ethnic group relations, the recognition of epistemological diversity and an 'anything goes' logic read as ethnic fundamentalism, despotism of cultural difference and inter-ethnic chaos. By privileging culture over politics in their studies, anti-foundationalists are prone to analytical blindness towards the everyday realities of inter-group relations, where any acknowledgement that all language games are equal and incommensurable can only be translated as a call to group-centred authoritarianism and the ascendancy of the strongest.

Notes

1 Omi and Winant's (1994) theory of 'racial formation' is very much in tune with Goldberg's Foucaldianism, providing a fine empirical analysis of the processes and discourses of 'racialisation' and 'racial formations' in the US in the last four decades.

2 As Žižek (1993) explains, enjoyment 'designates the paradoxical satisfaction procured by a painful encounter with a Thing that perturbs the equilibrium of the pleasure principle'. In other words, enjoyment is located 'beyond the pleasure principle'.

3   This concept directly refers to the Freudian Lost Thing which is not 'really' lost but is experienced as lost or stolen, invoking the promise of total fulfilment or completion.

4   Although post-Marxists such as Hall and Gilroy affirm the role of human agency, it is not entirely clear how this view is to be reconciled with their agreement that social reality is shaped through discourses.

Chapter Eleven

SOCIOLOGICAL THEORY AND ETHNIC RELATIONS: WHERE TO GO FROM HERE?

Who holds the master key?

Ethnicity is a multifaceted phenomenon. The analysis of eight leading sociological approaches reveals the extent of this complexity. The slippery nature of ethnic relations and the inherent ambiguity of the concept of ethnicity has engendered the proliferation of numerous very persuasive yet often mutually opposing, and occasionally profoundly incommensurable positions of analysis. As a result, ethnic relations are explained with reference to a set of very diverse factors, such as being a political resource of elites, genetic and memetic make up, class position, status privilege, economic utility and self-interest, functional necessity and group solidarity, actor's self-definition of the situation, theft of group enjoyment, discursive practices and so on. Building creatively and diversely on the heritage of classical sociological thought, contemporary approaches have developed powerful conceptual apparatuses for the study of ethnic relations. However, the palpable multiplicity of explanatory positions presents an immense difficulty when one attempts to engage with the everyday realities of culturally articulated inter-group animosities. Whereas theoretical diversity and conceptual sophistication are undoubtedly great assets in the endeavour to understand and comprehend all the subtleties of inter- and intra-group relations, it can also prove to be detrimental when opting for concrete policy requirements. In other words, such an epistemological plurality is likely to be problematic when having to choose between competing explanations for the very particular and concrete cases of social reality. For example, to comprehend analytically the 1994 genocide in Rwanda one could apply any of the eight theoretical positions analysed in this book.[1]

The neo-Marxist explanation would focus on the colonial strategy of *divide and rule* pursued by both German and Belgian colonizers, to amplify and articulate class differences masked as ethnic differences between the 'proletarian' Hutus and 'bourgeois' Tutsis. The roots of the conflict would also be found in the downfall of the Rwandan economy during the 1980s as a reflection of world-wide capitalist recession. It would also focus on the class dimension of recruiting Hutu militia (*interahamwe*) among the *lumpenproletariat* Hutus who were to become the main perpetuators of genocide over Tutsis and moderate Hutus.

Functionalist interpretations would emphasize the weakness or near non-existence of a common cultural system at the national level (i.e., Rwandan national identity), and the lack of differentiation and normative consensus in an environment of scant urbanization and industrialization with very low educational standards. Rwandan society would be described as an archetype of plural – that is, deeply divided – society with distinct modes of institutional incorporation. The Belgian institutionalization of ethnic group difference through the introduction of an identity card system in 1933, which categorizes every adult Rwandan as Tutsi, Hutu or Twa, and that granted a privileged status to some individuals on that basis (Tutsi), would be an ideal indicator of differential structures of group incorporation employed by the former colonizers.

Symbolic interactionists would point to divergent perceptions of inter-group reality between the two groups. The changing nature of the group position of Tutsis vis-à-vis Hutus, and especially the in-group and out-group perception of this change, affects their mutual relations. The fact that Belgian colonizers initially privileged the Tutsi aristocracy and later, when Tutsis became the leaders of the anti-colonial struggle for independence, they switched support to Hutus (which was reflected in the Hutus subordination of Tutsis at the national level), indicates the source of changing perceptions. The (historically) frequent changes of collective definitions of the group situation accelerated group animosities, which eventually led to genocide. The assassination of Rwandan president Habyarimana in April 1994 was a symbolic and spectacular event that delegitimized alternative definitions of the situation among Hutus (i.e., moderate and conciliatory views). Many Hutus came to perceive Tutsis as 'dangerous and bloodthirsty cockroaches'; a view that became crystallized as a genocidal *gestalt*.

The sociobiological view would emphasize that genocide at such a scale can only be explained by conceiving of ethnic groups as extended kinship networks. Deliberate targeting of Tutsi males for slaughter and Tutsi females for rape is in tune with the principle of inclusive fitness and kin selection, where one's in-group genes were to reproduce and multiply at the expense of those of the out-group. Relying on 'reliable' cultural and physical markers to separate in-group from out-group, such as height and the degree of skin colour (used and institutionalized by colonial policies), Hutu militia were able to quickly differentiate between tall, thin and light-skinned Tutsis and shorter, robust and darker Hutus. In fact, the entire history of Rwanda, with its persistent pattern of attempts at group domination along ethnic lines, invokes a sense of ethno-centric nepotism and the primordiality of ethnic groups defined by ethnic descent.

Rational choice sociologists would rather focus on individual self-interest behind those involved in the massacres. The Hutu supremacists were to provide material rewards to new militia recruits willing to take part in genocide. Not only did they supply the food, drink, alcohol and cigarettes, but they also provided cash payments and clothing and a promise of acquiring a house or land to tens of thousands of poor, unemployed, homeless and often hungry Hutu youths. Rational choice theorists would also highlight the belief formation based on incomplete information regarding the nature of the Tutsi threat. Although the mass media portrayed president Habyarimana's assassination as a Tutsi plot this was never proved, and it seems more likely that responsibility for his murder lies with Hutu extremists who saw the president as too soft towards Tutsis. Hence this killing created a chaotic and extreme situation where individuals were acting rationally in an 'imperfect market' and in Hobbesian conditions under constraints of possessing incomplete information.

Elite theory would concentrate more on the motives and behaviour of Hutu power holders. Rwanda was one of the most centralized states in the world and the orders for systematic killings came directly from the very top of government, in particular the minister of defence Theoneste Bagosora and the wife of assassinated president Habyarimana, Agathe Habyarimana, pointing to a decisive role played by elites. The elite theorists would stress that the entire process of ethnic group mobilization was conceived, initiated and organized at the top of the social pyramid, providing the means such as weapons, transport and technical support as well as the ideological support by broadcasting extreme propaganda messages of hatred through the government-controlled radio station. This radio station, which was the only media able to reach a majority of the population, was also decisive in encouraging Tutsi civilians to gather at stadiums, churches and schools, supposedly safe havens, were they were systematically exterminated with machine-guns and bombs.

The neo-Weberian approach would look at the role of geo-political factors in a macro-historical context. The sheer discrepancy of status position between Hutus and Tutsis has its historical roots in feudal arrangements between a Tutsi aristocracy and Hutu farmers, whereby Tutsi nobility would loan their cattle and land to Hutus in exchange for their unconditional services (a contract known as *ubuhake*), and this sets the historical terrain for inter-ethnic status struggle. The subjugation of Tutsis under the post-colonial regime of Habyarimina, when half a million were exiled, together with the geo-political prestige of Hutus in that period intensified inter-group animosities.[2] These enmities were to culminate in the development of the

Tutsi-controlled Rwandan Patriotic Front (RPF) in Uganda, which organized exiles into a powerful military force that was able to invade parts of Rwanda in 1992 and humiliate Habyarimina's forces. With this *de facto* military defeat and hence the loss of geo-political prestige of the Hutus, Habyarimina's regime lost its support base, and Hutu anger at status degradation was channelled by an extremist leadership into the mobilization of the masses for genocide against the Tutsis. Neo-Weberians would also explain this situation by referring to dominant patterns of monopolistic social closure of Tutsis over Hutus during the pre-colonial and most of the colonial period, as well as a reversal of the situation in the post-colonial period when Hutus used this mechanism to establish their control. This pattern is again evident after the genocide, when the RPF captured Kigali and the rest of the country in July 1994 and re-established hegemony of Tutsis over Hutus.

Finally, anti-foundationalists would focus on ambiguities in Hutu/Tutsi identities and how the meta-narratives of modernity and Enlightenment induced by European colonizers have created a situation where difference is structured, codified and institutionalized. It was European colonialism, with its discourses of progress and civilization, that introduced and articulated group diversities as ontological differences. As the historical record demonstrates, there was always ambiguity between Hutu/Tutsi identities. Not only do they all speak the same language of *kinyarwanda* and share many customs, but there were also never clear cut and definite identities, as poorer Tutsis would often become Hutus and vice versa. The European narratives of modernity were responsible for a rationalistic urge to transcend ambiguity, to centre, institutionalize and codify identities. Hence the Rwandan genocide has its roots in an attempt to impose order on difference (conceptualized as chaos). Just as in the case of the Nazi-driven Holocaust, this genocide was planned and executed from the centre of the modern state; it relied on the means of modernity such as mass media, weapons, delegation of tasks and so on. As a result 800,000 people were systematically exterminated in less than three months. The gender and psychoanalytical dimensions are also clearly visible, with patriarchal targeting of women for rape and men for extermination, as well as the projection of one's pain onto the Other. The anger with oneself and low self-esteem on the one hand, and lack of *jouissance* attributed to Tutsis on the other, on the part of the Hutu militia lead them to torture, humiliate and eventually annihilate the Other.

This short excursus in Rwandan ethnic relations only illustrates the difficulty in applying theoretical frameworks to concrete case studies. When confronted with this situation social researchers in most cases opt for one of the following three research strategies, which for the sake of simplicity I will call here relativism, rationalist fundamentalism, [3] and syntheticism. First, the mere existence of multiple frames of interpretation can lead to an ethically problematic but epistemologically legitimate position of 'anything goes'. As the Rwandan example shows, all eight theoretical positions find support for their arguments in the empirical data. Rational choice theory, just like symbolic interactionism, functionalism, sociobiology and the other leading sociological approaches, seems able to explain the roots of the Rwandan genocide. The fact that their interpretations of a particular social reality are so diverse and often mutually exclusive may lead to a relativist conclusion (ingrained partially in two of the approaches presented – symbolic interactionism and anti-foundationalism) that one should treat all interpretations of particular ethnic group conflict as epistemologically equivalent, and thus equally legitimate.

However, such radical relativism is unsustainable for a number of reasons. As already argued in the critique of anti-foundationalism (Chapter 10), radical relativism cuts the ground from under its own feet since the argument that all truth claims are relative is, in itself, an absolutist claim made from a particular standpoint. But more importantly from the point of view of policy, the position is very limited in its capacity to explain the phenomenon in question. This limitation comes from its absolutization of difference and contingency, that is, from an unsubstantiated view that conflates epistemological diversity with the equivalence of truth claims. In other words, the fact that all knowledge is partial, situational and historically contingent does not necessarily imply that all truth claims are equal (Bhaskar, 1979; Brown, 1994). That is, one can recognize the existence and validity of alternative regimes of truth and still be able to differentiate between more and less decisive forms of knowledge. From the policy point of view, such a nihilistic position leads directly to social and political paralysis. If all perceptions of reality are equally legitimate narratives that does not only imply that any social research is unnecessary or useless, but also that the Hutu militia interpretation of what happened in the spring and early summer of 1994 in Rwanda counts as much as the interpretations of those very few that survived the genocide. In other words, radical relativism is a profoundly problematic research strategy: it provides us with no adequate research tools for analysis, and it can make us accomplices in a crime.

The second research strategy is that of rationalist or epistemological fundamentalism. This position adopts a theoretically purist stance that holds the view that there is a single and universal truth. The belief is that, despite their diversity and uniqueness social events exhibit some universal features and display some common patterns which allow for law-like generalizations. Unlike the relativists, rationalist fundamentalism aims to maintain a strong distinction between a fact and a value, and upholds the principle of causality as a key methodological tool in uncovering the truth. Rationalist fundamentalists privilege the scientific method, that is, in Gellner's (1992: 80–4) words they 'absolutise some formal, one might say procedural, principles of knowledge'. Standing on positivist principles they see no major explanatory difference between the natural and social world, arguing that 'the laws to which this world is subject are symmetrical', and that everything inside nature is subject to its laws but the knowledge itself. In the study of ethnic relations this implies that only one of the eight approaches analysed here can rightfully claim to be the true one. The decision on which position can carry that title is to be determined on the basis of how well a particular theory corresponds to empirical reality. By empirical reality it is meant the measurement of only those actions and behaviour which can be directly observed or accessed.

This research strategy is, however, as problematic as the relativist one, since no observation in the world of humans is unbiased, completely detached or value free. On the contrary, all observations are theory laden since no one can entirely transcend his or her internalized values, knowledge and preconceptions. Even if one could do this and is able to start from a clean sheet, social reality is so rich with actors, events, unintended consequences of individual and social action, diverse perceptions of reality, historical contingencies and so on that no theory can make an uncontested claim of possessing such a privileged position. There is no external and universally accepted parameter or judge to assess whether, for example, the neo-Marxist account of what happened in Rwanda in 1994 is superior to neo-Weberian explanations of the same event. Thus rationalist fundamentalism remains a very constraining research strategy that ultimately may lead to dogmatism in insisting on a single, unreflexive theoretical and methodological framework.

Finally, the third popular research strategy is syntheticism. Being aware of the relativist and fundamentalist limitations, syntheticists aim towards the integration of distinctive theoretical positions. The most sophisticated synthetic attempts in general sociological theory are Giddens' structuration theory, Bourdieu's conceptualization of habitus conceived as a bridge between objectivism and subjectivism, Elias' figurational or processual sociology, and Archer's morphogenesis. Although very different, common to all these attempts is the intention of transcending analytical duality between structure and agency, between macro and micro levels of analysis, or between meaning and interest-centred explanations.[4]

Synthetic positions are conscious that any attribution of a privileged position to agents over structure, to values and meanings over interests and material motives or vice versa can only yield incomplete and reductionist explanations of social reality. However, unlike relativists, syntheticists argue that the solution is not in giving up the ambition of theory building, but, on the contrary, to provide a comprehensive explanation one has to integrate and reconcile alternative interpretative horizons. When applied to ethnicity this strategy involves bringing closer together all eight sociological explanatory frameworks in order to understand the social sources of the Rwandan genocide. This means that instead of claiming that the symbolic interactionist account of what happened in Rwanda is as good as the socio-biological account, as relativists would have it, or that only one of these interpretations is the right one, as fundamentalists would argue, syntheticists would hold the view that all eight (and possibly some other) approaches are able to explain a segment of the complex social phenomenon. Thus, the integration of all of these partial approaches is seen as the best way forward in providing a multidimensional account of ethnic relations.

However, despite its surface appeal, this research strategy is as problematic as the previous two. Since the point of explanation is the singling out of the key variables that make a particular situation, event or social action comprehensible, a mere mechanical synthesis of all the possible variables that can determine this is least likely to succeed. There is very little explanatory power in syntheticism. As Craib (1992: 10) rightly points out, 'New knowledge emerges from a range of activities; general synthetic theories close down the possibilities of investigation and explanation that are open to us. Theoretical work comes to be like putting together a jigsaw puzzle: before we start, we already know what the final picture will be like.' Most synthetic attempts are methodologically and research-wise futile, while in the theoretical sense they are often nothing but illusions. The complex and often fragmented nature of social reality cannot be fixed by tidy 'multifactored' integrationist attempts.

While all three research strategies are problematic if applied *in toto*, each offers valuable building blocks for a more comprehensive epistemology of ethnic relations. Thus relativism rightly indicates that any successful research has to account for the plurality and complexity of truth claims. What is worth preserving here is the emphasis on the partiality, contingency and epistemological diversity of truth claims without accepting relativist absolutism that holds all truth claims as equivalent. The fact that truth claims are not equal allows one to focus on detection, deconstruction and, in policy terms, on challenging these hegemonic meta-narratives. In the Rwandan case this means recognition that Hutu militia and Tutsi civilians operated with very different interpretations of Rwandan inter-ethnic group reality, which might well have roots in Enlightenment discourses of progress, modernity and sovereignty, should not prevent one from pinpointing the stark asymmetry between these two sets of truth claims. The political hegemony of the Hutu political elite, propped up by (albeit temporary) military might, has made their interpretation of social reality not only binding on most

Hutus but was also decisive as an ideological source of genocide over Tutsis. While Hutu and Tutsi narratives might be epistemologically equivalent, they were very clearly structurally and materially profoundly unequal.

Similarly rationalist fundamentalism's aim to provide coherent, generalizable explanations able to engage with very diverse forms of ethnic relations, with a view to deducing common denominators of social action, are commendable. The meaning and function of sociology is lost if the discipline is not capable of answering the basic policy requirements. To do so one has to highlight the conceptual and empirical advantages of the specific explanatory framework used. Epistemological fundamentalists are right in their loyalty to a particular paradigm and their commitment to look for the solutions within a given perspective. Excessive voluntarism or a pick and mix attitude that ignores the theoretical and historical background of particular perspectives, is more likely to prevent than to enable the development of consistent explanations of ethnic group relations. Nevertheless, working within a particular paradigm should not necessarily mean holding the stubborn view that there is a single, universal and omnipresent truth accessible only to those who develop the most sophisticated methodological and conceptual tools of inquiry. Nor does it mean stalling on the naïve perception of matching theory and praxis within the parameters of simple causality. Instead the superiority of a particular interpretative horizon is to be confirmed on the ground of how well it fits a particular historical and policy record. Although there is no commonly accepted measuring device to determine the success of neo-Weberian over neo-Marxist accounts of the Rwandan genocide, neo-Weberians could argue that, policy-wise, it would make more sense to address the status discrepancies institutionalized in mechanisms of monopolistic social closure between Hutus and Tutsis and the extant of geo-political imbalances, rather than attempt to overthrow the world-wide capitalist economy.

Syntheticism for its part offers a conceptual device for enhancing the particular interpretative horizon. While there is no great explanatory value in a simple and mechanical synthesis, such as in vague claims that structure is as important as agency, that values, meanings and ideas are as decisive as material and political interests, or that macro explanations are feeble without the understanding of micro foundations, careful and subtle syntheses of compatible approaches are likely to be constructive. Unlike 'catch them all' grand synthesis, the modest integration of positions with epistemologically complementary claims is possible and can be a productive strategy. This means that when attempting to interpret the Rwandan genocide it is barren to try to link such irreconcilable positions of analysis as sociobiology and symbolic interactionism, or functionalism and anti-foundationalism. There is no explanatory gain in artificial and forced integration. The elementary propositions of these theories are built on mutually exclusive assumptions. Seeing cultural differences between Hutus and Tutsis as rooted in the make up of their genetic pool is bound to contradict the interactionist argument about fluidity and fuzziness of all collective identities. Similarly, tying large-scale ethnic conflicts such as the ethnic cleansing of Tutsis to the levels of industrialization, urbanization and secularization of Rwandan society is pre-conditioned on the view that there is a singular progressive path to moder-nity – the exact opposite of anti-foundationalist claims. Hence, limited synthesis is possible and beneficial for explanatory purposes when the attempt is made to integrate like with like.

Epistemological integration makes sense only when it enhances explana-tion. As occasionally indicated throughout this study, it is my view that a subtle synthesis of neo-Weberianism and elite theory provides the most fruitful way of integrating two compatible paradigms. However, this is not to say that such an integrated theoretical position would provide a master key able to unlock all the secrets of ethnic relations. On the contrary, the aim is to operate with an open theoretical framework which would help us to point in which direction a fruitful sociological analysis of ethnicity could and should go.

Accepting the inevitable existence of epistemological plurality means that there is no master key for ethnic relations. All theoretical positions are incom-plete and that is in their 'nature'. But the very fact that they are incomplete enables them to engage analytically and attempt to explain social reality. The theory which can explain everything is not a theory but a mere registrar of events, actions, behaviours and beliefs. Nevertheless, this does not imply that 'anything goes' and that all positions carry the same weight. Some approaches, such as an integrated Weberian elite theory, have a greater explanatory poten-tial. To demonstrate this let us briefly explore the main epistemological points of dispute between leading sociological theories of ethnicity.

Sociological theories of ethnicity: main points of dispute

The eight sociological theories analysed in this study show a significant degree of difference in terms of their content, methodology, level of gener-alization and the historical tradition they are part of, as well as the empha-sis placed on a particular group of explanatory variables in attempting to provide a coherent interpretation of ethnic relations. However, in dealing with similar research questions these theoretical positions must occasionally also provide similar and overlapping explanations of social reality. To identify the intensity of similarity and difference between various positions of analysis one has to operate with an adequate parameter, one which is able to differentiate the main points of dispute. These 'points of dispute' are not only *differentia specifica* that point to what is distinctive about a particular sociological paradigm but, more importantly, they indicate the main 'explanatory elements' of which these theories are composed. In other words, the epistemological differences that often set these theoretical positions apart are not only indicators of their similarity or dissimilarity but are also the main building blocks on which these positions are constituted.

The following four[5] points of dispute are singled out as decisive for analytical comparison: individualism vs. holism, materialism vs. idealism, primordialism vs. situationism, objectivism vs. subjectivism. The fact that most sociological theories are too subtle, profound and complex to be fitted to such a fettering Procrustean bed denotes that any attempt at taxonomic dichotomization can only be provisional and incomplete. This Manichaean taxonomy is nothing more than such a provisional construction, the sole purpose of which is to make epistemological differences and similarities between leading sociological theories of ethnicity more transparent and perhaps more blatant. To do so one is forced to identify general categories of distinction, at least as far as this is possible. With the level of generalization becoming greater, the number of taxonomic categories is likely to become smaller and one is usually bound to operate with dichotomies. However as the poles of these dichotomies are no more than provisional ideal types, they allow for a great diversity of intensity. In other words, these dichotomies are rarely clear-cut opposites and, for the most part, they represent a continuum of characteristics with varying degrees of intensity.

Individualism vs. holism

The sociological interpretations of reality disagree over the question of whether this reality is for the most part socially or individually moulded. For methodological individualists no proper explanation is possible unless 'couched wholly in terms of facts about individuals' (Lukes, 1973: 110). As the leading proponent of this epistemological position, Jon Elster (1985) states that collective desires or collective beliefs do not exist. For the methodological individualist the analysis is valid if, and only if, it can be undertaken in reference to facts about tangible, material entities, that is, individual human beings. Although as Coleman (1990) points out, the job of sociologists is to study groups and social systems, these macro phenomena 'must be explained by factors internal to them, prototypically individuals'.

As its antipode, methodological holism starts from the Durkheimian idea that an individual behaviour can only be adequately understood when analysed through the prism of social networks. Not only are individuals fundamentally social beings but their action is unexplainable without comprehension of the structural features of the society of which they are an integral part. For holists 'all human societies are composed of an effectively infinite number of such networks, each of which is organised analytically by a structurally identical ordering principle, and is a microcosm of larger structures' (Filmer, 1998: 230).

Out of the eight sociological theories of ethnicity analysed here, five lean explicitly or implicitly towards individualism (rational choice theory, sociobiology, neo-Weberianism, elite theory and symbolic interactionism), and three towards methodological holism (neo-Marxism, functionalism and anti-foundationalism). The case of rational choice theory is obvious since actors, seen as rationally thinking creatures, are taken as the primary object of analysis, and collective action, such as in the group formation, is explained in terms of rational calculations for the purpose of individual benefit. Symbolic interactionism is also relatively straightforward, since it starts from the idea of self and builds on Mead's individualist philosophy of action. Although the concept of individual action is much more subtle and multilayered than that depicted in the rational choice position, symbolic interactionism views ethnic relations through the prism of individual self-perception of in-group and out-group definitions of the situation.

Elite theory, with its emphasis on intentionality behind elite manipulation of the masses, and with its perception of ethnic collectivities as interest groups comprised of diverse individuals, indicates the persistence of a methodologically strong individualist position. Sociobiology is a little bit more complicated, considering that inclusive fitness and nepotism are deduced from and for the species and not for the individual. However, the level of analysis adopted in sociobiological inquiry is profoundly individualistic since an individual is perceived as a unit of natural selection. Humans, just as other breeding creatures, compete primarily as individuals between themselves and then as group nepotists. More problematic are neo-Weberian accounts because while Weber clearly declared himself as a methodological individualist, Rex and Parkin mainly deal with the collectivist categories of class and status, and Collins and Mann focus on such macro phenomena as the State and geo-political factors. Although their focus of interest is often located on the macro group level, what is crucial is their individualist understanding of social action. For all four neo-Weberians discussed here, just like for Weber himself, ethnic groups are, like any other collective entity (i.e., class, status, estate), no more than quasi-groups, that is, situational and amorphous groupings of individuals. It is only through the social action of individuals that ethnic group formation becomes a possibility.

On the other side of this continuum are the three holistic approaches – neo-Marxism, functionalism and anti-foundationalism. Neo-Marxism explains ethnic relations on a very macro structural level, starting from capitalism and the modes of production as the general determinants of human action. People act and have interests primarily as members of larger collectivities such as a class, and their actions are in the last instance governed by laws of political economy and the patterns of historical necessity. Functionalism, in its structuralist as well as in its pluralist variants, is based on the same assumption that societies are above individuals. It is the social systems (or in the pluralist version, political units) that maintain the state of equilibrium and that provide for the systemic integration of particular ethnic groups into the framework of the nation-state (as in system theory), or different cultural-political units into a single state (as in plural society theory). For Parsons, voluntary action is possible, but 'what we normally perceive as free intentional activity must in fact involve the actor's application of an internal normative standard of judgement' (Alexander, 1978: 181). Anti-foundationalism is more tricky since it challenges all group identities including those of class and social system. No language game is to be privileged and all group-centred, as with the case of individual-centred, interpretations of reality are to be equally distrusted. However, with its strong emphasis on the discursive construction of human individuality, and reality mediated by meta-narratives, anti-foundationalist interpretations of ethnic relations are much closer to holistic than to individualistic research traditions. If dominant hegemonic ethnic discourses constitute individuals as members of particular groups, then their personal choices, motives and beliefs matter very little.

What is clear from this brief taxonomic exercise is that most sociological theories of ethnicity are closer to the individualist than to the collectivist pole of this continuum. And indeed, softer versions of individualism (such as those of neo-Weberians and elite theorists) provide a more compelling sociological framework of analysis. Holistic accounts of ethnic relations are much more likely to reify group categorizations by attributing to collectivities metaphorical or real features of individual human beings. Going back to our Rwandan example both neo-Marxism and functionalism operate with very hard collectivist notions of ethnic groups in seeing Hutus and Tutsis as real corporeal entities. In the neo-Marxist formulation the difference between the two real existing groups is premised on their economic position of inequality ('proletarian' Hutu vs. 'bourgeois' Tutsis), while functionalism conceives of the two groups as two (actual) competing value systems. While more sensitive towards the charge of reifying essentialism, anti-foundationalism still ascribes too much power to forces beyond human capacity. Such a perspective unjustifiably reduces human beings to mere passengers on the trains and boats which are constructed, directed, conducted and driven by others, that is, by systems in dispersion. The Rwandan tragedy is interpreted as something that was bound to happen since the colonial legacy cannot be erased. This view is as fatalistic as it is unhelpful in research terms.

At the other end of this continuum is the excessive hard individualism of sociobiology, rational choice theory and, in its own distinct way, symbolic interactionism. This view is seldom truly individualist since it reduces human beings to genes, drives of utility maximization or to the mental images they contain in their heads. Building on narrow and circular premises such a position can only provide *ex post facto* explanations that would see the Rwandan genocide as no more than another example of individual rationality in imperfect market conditions, as a capitalization on kin selection to bolster one's gene reproduction, or as changing and competing definitions of the situation. Unlike these extremes neo–Weberianism and elite theory offer more nuanced positions, which focus on social action as the key variable in creating groups as groups. To borrow from Bourdieu (1990), ethnicity is a category of practice. Individuals become social agents, that is group members, through social action, through participating in a particular collective practice. An ethnic group becomes a group through the dynamic process of active participation among its members. Individuals do not necessarily act as rational or utilitarian creatures – often they are governed by beliefs, habits, tradition and so on – but in the last instance group formation and collective action is dependent on individual action. This does not mean that there are no differences between the way an individual acts alone and as a member of a particular (ethnic) group. This only tells us something about the dynamics and plasticity of human beings and does not imply that collectives have a will of their own. Hence only when approached from this position, which looks at the collective action as it originates in the action of individual human beings, can the Rwandan genocide, just as any other case of ethnic relations, be adequately comprehended.

Materialism vs. idealism

The debate on whether social reality is predominantly intersubjective and created through meanings and values or whether it is for the most part material and constituted through the existence of the real and objective structures is as old as human thought. Whereas materialists explain the social world by focusing on economic or political determinants of human action, the idealists view the social world as being fashioned and maintained through value and norm-determined actions. Thus, while materialism searches for explanations in individual or group material interests and links those to institutions with real political, historical or economic foundations, 'which determine their nature and which produce the social activities that take place within them' (Walsh, 1998a: 207), idealism is geared towards the understanding of meanings, values and symbols that govern human action. While materialism states that human actions are mainly goal-oriented or determined by economic or political circumstances, idealism analyses humans as primarily norm-oriented, or following the idea that 'external social reality cannot exist independently of the everyday interactions and subjectivity of social actors' (Abercrombie et al., 1984: 150).

The materialist explanatory paradigm in the study of ethnicity is adopted in rational choice theory, neo-Marxism, elite theory and sociobiology, while the idealist position of analysis relates to functionalism, symbolic interactionism and most of the anti-foundationalist perspectives. Although the Weberian legacy is embedded in an amalgamation of the idealist and materialist positions, neo-Weberian theories of ethnicity are all distinctly materialist.

Viewing individuals as *homines economici* whose actions are always utility-oriented and where ethnic group membership only makes the achievement of individual goals more cost-effective, rational choice theory is, without doubt, a typical example of the materialist position of analysis. Similarly sociobiological explanations of ethnic relations build on the materialistic motivation of human actions. Although replacing economic with biological sources of individual motivation (gene reproduction through kin selection), just as in the rational choice position human beings are primarily governed by self-interests and not by culture. Elite theory shows more sensitivity towards symbolism and the role of culture in general, but by concentrating on elite self-interest and the use of symbolism for political purposes it demonstrates its profoundly materialist edge. Even though it shifts the emphasis from individual motivation on to structural sources of inequality, neo-Marxism remains staunchly materialist in its linking of capitalism to the ethnic division of labour, just as in its dissection of hegemonic practices of ethnic ideology.

Idealist interpretations of ethnic reality are most clearly expressed in functionalism and symbolic interactionism. The functionalist focus on the importance of 'shared value systems' and the explanation of social behaviour in terms of normatively guided action, where ethnic solidarity implies a sense of symbolic responsibility towards ancestors and descendants, strongly confirms the presence of idealist argumentation. For symbolic interactionism this idealism is not tied to the normative demands of ethnic collectivities but rather to actor's individual and group definitions of particular situations that are created in the process of interaction. Reality is what actors say it is. There is no objective world, there is only a world of different meanings and interpretations. What is important is not the objective position of an ethnic group, but their perception of this position.

Even though anti-foundationalism has firm roots in the materialist principles of Marxism, in the Nietzscheanism of Foucault and modernism, its fixation with discourses, meta-narratives and language games as structural generators of human subjectivity brings them much closer to the idealist than to the materialist camp. Despite Foucault's stress on the materiality of discourses and Hall's attempt to rescue agency, post-structuralist and post-Marxist deconstruction of ethnic discourses, as well as psychoanalytic and reflexive feminist dissection of ethnic relations remain occupied with profoundly idealist concerns such as language, meaning and culture. Finally neo-Weberian positions present us with a striking paradox – Weber's general theory was often viewed as an archetype of idealist sociology (Walsh, 1998a: 182), while contemporary neo-Weberian accounts of ethnicity are all deeply materialist. Whereas Parkin and Rex develop economic-centred materialist explanations of ethnicity that focus on monopolistic social closure, Collins and Mann, with their emphasis on the geo-political position of the State, provide a theory of ethnic relations that is grounded in principles of political materialism.

Just as in the individualism vs. holism debate, here more sociological theories of ethnicity have opted for materialist than for an idealist frame of reference. And here too it appears that despite all its deficiencies, materialism seems to be a more potent research position for explanatory and policy purposes. Idealist interpretations of ethnic relations such as those advocated by anti-foundationalists, interactionists and functionalists are more likely to lead towards radical relativism (in the case of former) or to cultural absolutism (in the case of latter).[6] While values, ideas, symbols and meanings are an integral part of human action, the understanding of which is a precondition of any serious attempt at comprehending ethnic relations, the absolutization of the values and ideas cannot help one explain the nature of ethnicity. In fact, instead of bringing one closer to explaining a particular case of ethnic conflict, idealist sociologies, with their focus on the relativity of individual and group perceptions and cultural uniqueness of experience, are much more likely to provide a powerful justifying tool which would obliterate the difference between a victim and a perpetrator of crime. There is a thin line between insisting that the Hutu militia and their predominantly Tutsi victims operated with profoundly different, even mutually opposing, perceptions of reality, and accepting these two interpretations of reality as equally legitimate. Similarly, the norm-centredness of functionalism which sees human beings as parts of a social system can tie individual behaviour too strongly to ethnic group features, and hence depict individual wrongdoing (of concrete members of the Hutu militia directly involved in genocide) as a form of collective responsibility (of all Hutus). Functionalist argument unreflexively chains individuals to their ethnic collectivities. Lastly idealist sociologies are the least likely to envisage and deal with dramatic social changes, typical of which is the Rwandan holocaust. Static concepts such as the functionalist stress on the normative equilibrium of systems, as well as extremely dynamic interactionist and anti-foundationalist notions of changing perceptions and fuzzy identities, are unable to account for a specific moment of seismic social change: while functionalism consciously ignores social change, interactionism and anti-foundationalism lose an analytical hold on this concept by invoking the presence of social change all the time, everywhere and in everyone.

This is not to say that the materialist angle of explanation is flawless. On the contrary, hard materialism, as present in the rational choice position, sociobiology and neo-Marxism, is insensitive towards the importance that social actors attribute to symbols and culture in general. Reducing culture to biology as in the sociobiological perspective, or to macro or micro economics (neo-Marxism and rational choice theory) does not only yield one-dimensional and forced explanations but is also ignorant of specific subtleties that constitute ethnic relations as such. Hard economic and biological materialism possesses very few research and conceptual tools for the fine tuning which is a precondition for any comprehensive understanding of ethnic relations. For these perspectives ethnicity is no more than an instrument, a second order reality, for achieving real goals – class unity, biological reproduction or personal benefit. A successful approach to the study of ethnic relations has to work with a much softer and wider, that is politically subtle, understanding of materialism. The roots of this position are present in much of elite theory and neo-Weberianism. While both aim to articulate a supple political interpretation of ethnicity with the emphasis on elite behaviour, geo-politics and ethnic-state relationships, there is also room for the role of values and beliefs such as status honour or ethnic symbolism. Although this cultural dimension of ethnic relations is well articulated in Weber it is scantily developed in neo-Weberian and elite approaches. To be explanatorily effective an integrated Weberian elite theory has to proceed in the direction of building on the heritage of classical Weberianism, which would allow for greater sensitivity to culture, without giving an equal weighting to material and ideal factors, as in unfruitful synthetic attempts.

Primordialism vs. situationism

The leading sociological theories of ethnicity differ most strikingly over the issue of persistence, intensity and nature of ethnic ties. While primordialist positions see ethnicity as a stable feature of individual and group life that is able to endure over historically long periods of time, situationism views ethnic relations in dynamic terms as fluid and changeable – not as a property of a group but as an aspect of relationships between groups, where ethnic boundaries do not necessarily correspond with cultural boundaries. The primordialist perspective treats ethnic identities as something that is broadly given. Ethnicity is for the most part equated with culture, and culture itself is viewed as a more or less constant, persistent, static, almost unchangeable feature that clearly demarcates groups one from another. Common cultural characteristics such as language, tradition, customs, regional attachments, rites, religion or ancestry are perceived as the core elements of one's ethnic identity, which are regularly internalized through the process of primary socialization in early childhood.[7] In this perspective ethnic identity is examined as 'an imperative status, as a more or less immutable aspect of the social person' (Eriksen, 1993: 55).

The situationalist perspective is the exact opposite of primordialism. It aims to explain ethnic group solidarity and the maintenance of intensive ethnic group bonds underlining historical, structural and cultural contingencies and circumstantial aspects in ethnic relations. The notions of interaction between culturally diverse groups and 'boundary maintenance' are the key terms in their analysis. Following Barth's idea (1969) that strong ethnic attachments are not the result of the social and territorial isolation of groups, but of their interaction with other groups, this approach highlights the dynamic quality of ethnicity. Ethnicity is not given, it is created in action and dependent on a variety of factors such as the impact of the social and political environment, actors' beliefs, individual self-interest, actors' perceptions and so on.

Sociobiology and functionalism are the only two perspectives that explicitly adopt a primordialist framework of explanation, while all other leading sociological theories of ethnicity operate with the situationist frame of analysis. Whereas both sociobiology and functionalism subscribe to a primordialist view of ethnic attachments, seeing them as something that is for the most part *a priori* given, objective and overpowering, they differ in their interpretation of primordiality. For sociobiologists ethnic bonds have their origin in biology, and are manifest in the form of permanent in-group favouritism: to preserve a genetic pool organisms, including human beings, will prefer kin over non-kin. The longevity and persistence of ethnic ties are explained by direct reference to these primordial, 'ineffable' sentiments.

The functionalist version of primordialism is more concerned to demonstrate that strong feelings of ethnic attachments are something atavistic and premodern.[8] Parsons' concept of de-differentiation is devised to interpret so-called ethnic revivals as regressive tendencies associated with the desocialization of cultural groups. Similarly, plural society theory operates with the unreflexive and hard notions of 'culture' and 'ethnicity', seeing them as predetermined and largely unchangeable obstacles preventing institutional incorporation. As McKay (1982: 398) points out: 'Rather than viewing ethnicity as a possible focus of identity it is seen as the cardinal orientation.' The major difference between these two positions is that sociobiology looks for the universal principles of human development in stating that human behaviour is motivated by basically the same stimuli, whereas functionalism attempts to show that there is a qualitative difference between the social life in traditional communities and modernized societies.

Although they share a common understanding of ethnicity as an active, effervescent and contingent force, situationist perspectives also exhibit a great variety in this understanding. Thus, rational choice theory depicts ethnic solidarity as no more than an instrument of individual selfishness, as a manoeuvre in the shaping of an individual's life chances, where ethnic group membership is viewed as highly voluntary. In elite theory this instrumentalism is associated more strongly with those who control political but also social and cultural institutions. In fact for authors such as Brass (1993) ethnicity has no autonomy, it is a pure creation of political elites. Neo-Marxism ties ethnic relations to the structural features of capitalist society where ethnic solidarity is explained as a reaction to economic exploitation (by the ruling classes, or in the case of internal colonialism, by the centre), and is a more fictive and instrumentalized phenomenon than a real form of group solidarity. Symbolic interactionism underlines the subjective dimension of ethnicity, where ethnic identity is analysed as one, not necessarily substantial, form of group identity. The emphasis is on the alteration of collective definitions and re-definitions of ethnic group membership, as well as on constant identity re-definition by individuals with multiple identities. Anti-foundationalism goes one step further: all identity claims are fragmented and provisional, composed of a melange of disparate and often competing narratives. Any declaration that particular group identity is given and essential is an attempt to establish hegemonic control.

Neo-Weberianism operates with a more restrained situationism. While it, too, clearly acknowledges (and even strongly emphasizes) the manipulative potential of ethnic markers such as in monopolistic social closure or in the State's mobilization of ethnic group action, it is well aware of the fact that ethnic attachments cannot be created *ex nihilo*. Ethnic groups are not tangible, real communities. They are, indeed meta- or quasi-communities. But they are also decisively dependent on the existence of belief in common descent.[9] As Weber clearly and rightly states, if there is no collective shared belief in common ethnic ancestry then there will be no ethnic collectivity. This is a crucial point in understanding the strength and intensity of ethnic ties. As historical and contemporary records demonstrate, it is evident that ethnicity in all its forms remains a more potent source of group action and solidarity than gender, class or any other form of sociability. This however has nothing to do with the essentialist claims of primordialism, which, as Eller and Coughlan (1993) rightly argue, for the most part work with profoundly unsociological notions of apriority, ineffability and simple affectivity. Stating that Hutus and Tutsis kill each other simply because of overpowering and ineffable ethnic attachments is not only morally repugnant but also shows a lack of elementary sociology. To paraphrase Cohen (1969: 199), people do not kill each other because their cultural habits are different, they kill each other because they associate these differences with real political or economic disparities. Instead of providing an explanation for the intensity of ethnic bonds, primordialism, with its non-analytical focus on primordial 'givens', only mystifies and obscures the social relations hidden behind these attachments. Rather than being obsessed with 'mystical appeal to natural primordial instincts' as sociobiology and functionalism are, one has to analyse the 'real ethnography of ethnic socialization – the practices that invent, modify, and perpetuate ethnic phenomena' (Eller and Coughlan, 1993: 198). This is not to say that ethnic attachments are fictitious, the sole creation of elites or self-benefiting rational individuals, linked exclusively to cycles of capitalist economy, or completely provisional and temporary. There is an obvious limit in how far any intentional or structural attempt at ethnic mobilization can go. Although ethnic group action determines the existence of ethnic groups as political actors this action is still dependent on real or symbolic individual and group shared belief in common descent. While this belief might be dormant and is only activated through social action, it nevertheless has to be there in some form. Thus, the Weberian understanding of situationism, which is sensitive, but not oversensitive like symbolic interactionism to the importance social actors attribute to their ethnic attachments, has more potential in providing convincing explanations of ethnic relations.

Subjectivism vs. objectivism

One of the key questions of polarization in sociology, and in the social sciences in general, is the one on how to study social phenomena – through the prism of objectivism, i.e., within a similar framework as that of the natural sciences, or through the lenses of subjectivism, i.e., with an assumption that human life involves persistent re-construction of meanings that can never be studied in the same way as a meaning-empty natural world. While objectivism is geared towards the study of the generality, causality and correlative nature of social events and actors, subjectivism emphasizes the unique character of individual and social phenomena attempting to penetrate into their roots to discover the specificity of these social actors and events. Bernstein (1991: 8) defines objectivism as a 'basic conviction that there is or must be some permanent, ahistorical matrix or framework to which we can ultimately appeal in determining the nature of rationality, knowledge, truth, reality, goodness, or rightness'. For objectivist sociologies society has an objective reality which is discernible in its existing institutionalized social relations, organizations and social rules. Objectivism takes the position that social action and events related to that action occur as relatively stable, regular and universally foreseeable patterns of behaviour that allow for prediction and generation of generalized principles. Subjectivism is its nemesis: the social world is nothing like the world of nature. Subjectivist sociologies view society as 'a subjective phenomenon in which the subject is the individual who is endowed with consciousness and acts in terms of his or her own ideas, values, interests and motives' (Walsh, 1998b: 298). Since social reality is composed of thinking creatures with different interpretations of that reality, involving also other thinking creatures who are part and parcel of that reality, any attempt to use research strategies and tools devised for the study of unthinking objects to analyse the world of human beings is doomed to failure. For subjectivists the social world can be comprehended only through the intersubjective understanding of actions and interactions of individual and social agents in a way they see these actions as meaningful.

The contemporary sociology of ethnic relations is dominated by objectivist approaches: rational choice theory, elite theory, neo-Marxism, sociobiology and functionalism. The subjectivist type of analysis is presented in symbolic interactionism and anti-foundationalism, while neo-Weberianism in some ways oscillates between the two.

Rational choice theory, elite theory and sociobiology follow the assumption that there is an 'explanatory matrix' that can be identified and then applied to ethnic relations in order to detect regularities in inter-group behaviour. For rational choice theory it is the notion of an actor's rationality that is the unquestionable principle of individual motivation and, consequently, social action. The degree of ethnic solidarity is seen as being likely to be proportional to one's individual gain. Sociobiology finds the same principle in the gene's permanent tendency to reproduce itself: there is nothing subjective in the process of ethnic kin selection via inclusive fitness; this principle applies to all living creatures. For elite theory it is the search for control and domination of the leaders and other influential groups that function as general principles which can explain human relations in general, and ethnic relations in particular. Regardless of the variety of forms it takes it is the fact that ethnicity is a universal and, as such, a potent political resource that sets it apart from other modes of sociability. Neo-Marxism and functionalism are based on a similar idea: that it is possible to generate objective historical 'laws' of human development, from primitive communities to classless society in the Marxist tradition, or from simple to complex modern societies in the evolutionist tradition of Parsons, Alexander and plural society theorists. For neo-Marxists these historical regularities are linked to class relations and the development of capitalism as a world process, where ethnic relations are predominately camouflaged class inequalities. For functionalists ethnicity is largely no more than an impediment, a regressive reaction to the inevitable process of modernization.

On the other side of the fence are symbolic interactionism and anti-foundationalism. Symbolic interactionism is the embodiment of a subjectivist approach that works within a framework of what Giddens (1977) has termed double hermeneutics, that is, the parallel existence of the 'nature of reality' and the nature of the understanding of this reality.[10] In this position ethnic relations are articulated as a question of individual and consequently collective definitions and re-interpretations of this reality. In the eyes of interactionists, despite the objective circumstances there are no objective and constant parameters that can determine why, when and how ethnic group-based hostilities will crop up. Anti-foundationalism is even more suspicious of any claims to scientific objectivity. In this perspective even the term science is a misnomer since it builds its legitimacy and acquires a sense of authority claiming to be value free, while the very fact that it is in a position to make such an uncontested claim makes it a hegemonic, power and control-driven project. Since science is perceived as just one among many meta-narratives, its account of particular ethnic group interactions is to be treated at the same level as the narratives constructed by those involved in those very interactions.

Finally there is a Weberian position which, as in the previous contesting dichotomies, represents a peculiar case. Classical Weberianism interprets human behaviour primarily in terms of conscious and meaning-oriented individual actions that cannot be examined as social facts in the Durkheimian sense. A multiplicity of meanings and subjective visions of other individuals and their actions are at the heart of an individual's perceptions that govern his or her behaviour. However, these very actions, either directly or through their unintended consequences, create structural constraints that limit the direction of individual action. Hence they can and do function as structural, objective determinants on the macro level. The contemporary Weberian accounts of ethnicity have for the most part focused on this structural, macro level in aiming to establish a certain objectivist regularity of behavioural patterns. However, even here there is an inherent appreciation of human subjectivity where no collectivity is seen as permanent or fixed. For Mann ethnicity refers to 'socially constructed aggregates' of individuals, for Collins ethnic groups are meta-communities structured through social action, whereas Rex (1986a: 3) explains ethnic relations fully through social action, arguing 'that which appears to constrain us from outside is in fact the product of human action and can be changed by human action'.

This version of softer, reflexive objectivism seems most plausible in addressing the complexity of ethnic relations. On the one hand it stands against hard and (for an understanding of the human world) inappropriate positivism as exemplified in sociobiology, functionalism, rational choice theory and to a lesser extent in neo-Marxism and elite theory,[11] and on the other hand it rejects radical interpretativism that paralyses both social research and social policy, as epitomized by anti-foundationalism and symbolic interactionism. In other words, the study of ethnic relations in terms of generalizations is possible and necessary but these generalizations are only analytically relevant when the meanings that human beings attribute to their actions and the actions of others are taken fully into account. What this means when applied to the Rwandan case is that although all the actors involved in the conflict had their own unique perception of reality of what took place in the late spring of 1994, taking into account the collective definition of historical grievances of the Hutu majority under the rule of the Tutsi minority, there is a possibility to establish a relatively objective sociological account of the roots of this massacre. To explain this event one would have to look at the macro history and changing geo-politics of the region, the failure in the process of post-colonial state formation, the historical patterns of the monopolistic social closure between the two meta-communities, as well as the direct role of political elites in intensifying ethnic mass mobilization through demonized media portrayals of the Other. Such an analysis would never lose sight of the fact that it deals with the action of conscious and thinking individuals prone to alterations in the articulation and definition of their ever-changing social reality. This soft objectivism would simultaneously allow for the analysis of what was unique and specific about this tragic event, and could also point towards some generalizable patterns of social action that can shed light on other extreme cases of ethnic conflict elsewhere in the world.

Conclusion: towards Weberian elite theory of ethnicity?

The aim of this final chapter was not to formulate an alternative theory of ethnic relations. As repeatedly argued in this book, there is no master code to crack which would reveal all the secrets of ethnic relations or which would help us end inter-group antagonisms based on ethnicity. Ethnic group relations, just as any other aspect of social reality, are too vast, too complex and too vibrant to allow for the employment of neat conceptual apparatuses which would generate instant explanations and quick solutions. However, this is not to say that as sociologists we can do little more than just observe and describe ethnic phenomena in all their diversity. On the contrary, as evident from this study, sociology has created potent theoretical and empirical research tools able to engage with the most convoluted cases of inter-ethnic relations. The problem is not that we have no adequate research tools and prescriptions – the problem is that we have too many. When faced with concrete policy requirements one has to opt between recommendations with very diverse and often mutually opposing diagnoses of the social event and the actors involved in that event. To prevent, or at least to minimize the excesses of any future ethnic cleansing should one aim towards value integration of a particular nation-state, as recommended by functionalists, or should one opt for the exact opposite and stimulate and foster group difference to crush any attempt to create a hegemonic meta-discourse which might be decisive for the emergence of ethnic group hostility, as recommended by anti-foundationalism?

There are no easy answers. In some cases either one of the two options can work, in other cases neither of these or any other recommended sociological alternative would be operational. There is very little certainty in the social world. Nevertheless, what seems to give the least assurance are attempts towards simple, 'pick and mix' syntheses. Both epistemologically and policy-wise this is, as a rule, if not directly harmful then at least not a particularly helpful strategy. Although often crisp and with a certain surface appeal, the attempts of creating grand syntheses are for the most part no more than a self-serving exercise in theory and concept juggling. In epistemological terms, such a super synthesis does not present us with an explanatory design any more. As Craib (1992: 108) rightly points out, such a 'theory offers an ontology of social life; it tells us, if you like, what sort of things are out there in the world, not what is happening to or between them; it does not give us anything to test or to find out'. In policy terms it offers us no concrete and consistent advice. If one recognizes that everything is of equal importance – people are both equally individuals and collective beings, material factors are as important as values and meanings, ethnic identities are evenly primordial and situational, and so on – then no meaningful explanation is possible. If the aim is to explain a particular social event or the actions of actors involved in that event, then one has to identify the exact axial points and to make generalizations on the basis of these. Proper explanation is located in the accentuation of some variables at the expense of others.

From the policy point of view, a coherent and relatively certain answer is indispensable. Superficial mix and match advice is unlikely to work in the long run. Since policy requirements largely depend on the value of the explanatory logic employed, the most rational strategy is to attempt to maintain epistemological consistency and coherence.

The view expressed here is that an intrinsic compatibility between Weberian and elite theory permits the development of such a theoretically coherent and empirically viable option. While as is clear from this study, these two perspectives are far from being impeccable, they provide a sound basis for the understanding of ethnic relations in all their forms. The integrated Weberian elite position would be articulated as a reflexive, actor-centred, politically materialist, sensitive situationist and soft objectivist theoretical framework, able to engage directly with empirical reality. By focusing primarily on the role of elites in instigating or enhancing inter-ethnic animosities, by linking culture with politics, by emphasizing a multiplicity of ethnic forms, and by explaining ethnic relations through social action, this position seems broad enough to accommodate diverse types of ethnic group relations and yet tight enough to prevent epistemological relativism and naïve syntheticism. Although powerful explanatory models in their own right, neo-Weberianism and elite theory alone lack a strong connection between culture and politics in their interpretation of ethnicity. In addition to their common disregard for the cultural dimension in ethnic relations, neo-Weberianism and elite theory also suffer from more specific shortcomings, such as the fragmentary nature of the theory, the lack of plausible political interpretation of ethnic group mobilization (neo-Weberian approaches), and the thin theoretical foundations and profound underestimation of mass behaviour (elite theory). This link between culture and politics is only attainable by integrating these two positions with the key tenets of classical Weberianism. Indicating the direction in which more promising theoretical and empirical developments could, and should go clearly re-affirms the belief that generalization is the cornerstone of any comprehensive sociological account of ethnic relations. Even though ethnicity is a concept, a group label, which we have created to make sense of diverse forms of cultural difference, since ethnic relations are part and parcel of social relations one can never understand and explain a particular case of ethnic relations without clear reference to some wider, universalist, generalizing sociological theory of ethnicity. My belief is that the development of an integrated Weberian elite theory would help us to understand and explain ethnic relations through a sound universalist framework which would, at the same time, be equally sensitive to the uniqueness and specificity of every individual instance of politicized forms of cultural difference.

Notes

1   Detailed historical information on Rwandan ethnic relations is available in M. Mamdani (2001), F. Keane (1996), C. C. Taylor (1999), L. Melvern (2000) and P. Gourevitch (2000).

2   One should also emphasize the fact that Habyarmina come to power in a coup in 1973 and held power for 20 years.

3   I use this label in clear reference to Gellner (1992), who described himself as an Enlightenment rationalist fundamentalist.

4   Since the focus of this book is ethnic relations and not the philosophy or sociology of knowledge, I will restrict myself here to a brief and very summary glance at these very profound debates in sociological theory.

5   This is not to say that with these four points the list is complete, but only that they are the most visible and epistemologically most important differences. Elsewhere (Malešević, 1998) I have elaborated a six-point taxonomy.

6   Idealist arguments have been extensively scrutinized and refuted by philosophers such as Bertrand Russell and G. E. Moore, who point out that the idealist notion of *esse est percipi* makes no distinction between a 'subject's act of perceiving and the perceptual object of this act', which is referred to as 'sense datum'.

7   Geertz's definition of primordial bonds is often taken as the epitome of this position:

> By primordial attachment it is meant one that stems from the 'givens' – or, more precisely, as culture is inevitably involved in such matters, the assumed 'givens' – of social existence: immediate continguity and kin connection mainly, but beyond them the givenness that stems from being born into a particular religious community, speaking a particular language, or even a dialect of a language, and following particular social practices. These congruities of blood, speech, custom and so on, are seen to have an ineffable, and at times overpowering coerciveness in and of themselves. (1973: 259)

8   However, it is important to note that both van den Berghe (1981) and Parsons (1951) view ethnicity as a form of extended kinship, whereas Alexander (1980) defines ethnicity in terms of 'primordial qualities'.

9   Van den Berghe (1986: 256) is right when he argues that 'it is impossible to constitute an *ethnie* on a basis other than a credible concept of common descent'. However, he is wrong when he links this concept to biology only.

10 Giddens' concept of double hermeneutics refers to the notion that human beings are constantly involved in the process of self-interpretation, and this process of an actor's self-interpretation is then subjected to the second layer of interpretation by the sociologist.

11 While Marx's epistemology fuses positivism with dialectics (Walsh, 1998b), the Gramscian tradition in the study of ethnicity is more open to individual action and self-reflection. It is similar to the more positivist Gurr and Brass and the less positivist, but still firmly objectivist, Cohen and van Dijk.

REFERENCES

Abercrombie, N., Hill S. and Turner, B. S. (1984) *Dictionary of Sociology*. London: Penguin.

Alexander, J. (1980) 'Core solidarity, ethnic outgroup, and social differentiation: a multidimensional model of inclusion in modern societies', in J. Dofney and A. Akiwowo (eds), *National and Ethnic Movements*. London: Sage.

Alexander, J. (ed.) (1985) *Neofunctionalism*. London: Sage.

Alexander, J. (1998) *Neofunctionalism and After*. London: Blackwell.

Alexander, J. and Colomy, P. (eds) (1990) *Differentiation Theory and Social Change*. New York: Columbia University Press.

Alexander, J. C. (1978) 'Formal and substantive voluntarism in the work of Talcott Parsons: a theoretical and ideological reinterpretation', *American Sociological Review*, 43: 177–98.

Althusser, L. (1994) 'Ideology and ideological state apparatuses (notes towards an investigation)', in S. Žižek (ed.), *Mapping Ideology*. London: Verso.

Anderson, B. (1991) *Imagined Communities: Reflections on the Origins and Spread of Nationalism*. London: Verso.

Anthias, F. and Yuval-Davis, N. (1983) 'Contextualizing feminism: gender, ethnic and class divisions', *Feminist Review*, 15: 62–75.

Archer, M. (2000) *Being Human: The Problem of Agency*. Cambridge: Cambridge University Press.

Avineri, S. (1964) 'Marx and Jewish emancipation', *Journal of the History of Ideas*, 25 (3): 445–50.

Bacova, V. and Ellis, P. (1996) 'Cultural-political differences in perception of ethnic concepts in Central-Eastern and Western Europe', in G. M. Breakwell and E. Lyons (eds), *Changing European Identities*. Oxford: Butterworth-Heinemann.

Baert, P. (1998) *Social Theory in the Twentieth Century*. Cambridge: Polity Press.

Banton, M. (1980) 'Ethnic groups and the theory of rational choice', in *Sociological Theories: Race and Colonialism*. Paris: Unesco.

Banton, M. (1983) *Racial and Ethnic Competition*. Cambridge: Cambridge University Press.

Banton, M. (1987) *Racial Theories*. Cambridge: Cambridge University Press.

Banton, M. (1994) 'Modelling ethnic and national relations', *Ethnic and Racial Studies*, 17 (1): 2–10.

Banton, M. (2000) 'Ethnic conflict', *Sociology*, 34 (3): 481–98.

Barth, F. (1969) 'Introduction', in F. Barth (ed.), *Ethnic Groups and Boundaries*. Bergen: Universitetsforlaget.

Barthes, R. (1993) *Mythologies*. London: Vintage.

Bartlett, R. (2001) 'Medieval and modern concepts of race and ethnicity', *Journal of Medieval and Early Modern Studies*, 31 (1): 39–55.

Bauman, Z. (1987) *Legislators and Interpreters*. Cambridge: Polity Press.

Bauman, Z. (1989) *Modernity and the Holocaust*. Cambridge: Polity Press.

Bauman, Z. (1991) *Modernity and Ambivalence*. Cambridge: Polity Press.

Bauman, Z. (1993) *Postmodern Ethics*. Cambridge: Polity Press.

Beck, U. (1991) *Risk Society*. Cambridge: Polity Press.

Becker, G. (1976) *The Economic Approach to Human Behavior*. Chicago: Chicago University Press.

Bendle, M. F. (2002) 'The crisis of "identity" in high modernity', *British Journal of Sociology*, 53 (1): 1–18.

Ben-Tovim, G., Gabriel, J., Law, I. and Stredder, K. (1986) 'A political analysis of local struggles for racial equality', in J. Rex and D. Mason (eds), *Theories of Race and Ethnic Relations*. Cambridge: Cambridge University Press.

Berlin, I. (1992) *The Crooked Timber of Humanity*. New York: Vintage.

Bernstein, R. J. (1991) *Beyond Objectivism and Relativism: Science, Hermeneutics and Praxis*. Philadelphia: University of Pennsylvania Press.

Berting, J. (1980) 'An appraisal of functionalist theories in relation to race and colonial societies', in *Sociological Theories: Race and Colonialism*. Paris: Unesco.

Bhabha, H. (1990) 'DissemiNation: time, narrative and the margins of the modern nation', in H. Bhabha (ed.), *Nation and Narration*. London: Routledge.

Bhabha, H. (1994) *The Location of Culture*. London: Routledge.

Bhaskar, R. (1979) *The Possibility of Naturalism: A Critique of the Contemporary Human Science*. Brighton: Harvester Press.

Billig, M. (1995) *Banal Nationalism*. London: Sage.

Billig, M. (2002) 'Ideology, language and discursive psychology', in S. Malešević and I. Mackenzie (eds), *Ideology after Poststructuralism*. London: Pluto.

Blackmore, S. (1999) *The Meme Machine*. Oxford: Oxford University Press.

Blumer, H. (1958) 'Race prejudice as a sense of group position', *Pacific Sociological Review*, 1: 3–8.

Blumer, H. (1969) *Symbolic Interactionism: Perspective and Method*. Englewood Cliffs, NJ: Prentice Hall.

Blumer, H. and Duster, T. (1980) 'Theories of race and social action', in *Sociological Theories: Race and Colonialism*. Paris: Unesco.

Bonacich, E. (1972) 'A theory of ethnic antagonism: the split labor market', *American Sociological Review*, 37: 547–59.

Bonacich, E. (1976) 'Advanced capitalism and Black/White relations in the United States: a split labor market interpretation', *American Sociological Review*, 41: 34–51.

Boudon, R. (1987) 'The individualistic tradition in sociology', in J. Alexander, B. Giesen, R. Munch and N. Smelser (eds), *The Micro–Macro Link*. Berkeley: University of California Press.

Boudon, R. (1989) *The Analysis of Ideology*. Cambridge: Polity Press.

Bourdieu, P. (1990) *The Logic of Practice*. Cambridge: Polity Press.

Brass, P. (1979) 'Elite groups, symbol manipulation and ethnic identity among the Muslims of South Asia', in D. Taylor and M. Yapp (eds), *Political Identity in South Asia*. Dublin: Curzon Press.

Brass, P. (1991) *Ethnicity and Nationalism: Theory and Comparison*. London: Sage.

Brass, P. (1993) 'Elite competition and the origins of ethnic nationalism', in J. G. Beramendi, R. Maiz and X. Nunez (eds), *Nationalism in Europe: Past and Present*. Santiago de Compostela: University of Santiago de Compostela.

Brass, P. (1997) *Theft of an Idol: Text and Context in the Representation of Collective Violence*. Princeton, NJ: Princeton University Press.

Breuilly, J. (2001) 'The State and nationalism', in M. Guibernau and J. Hutchinson (eds), *Understanding Nationalism*. Cambridge: Polity Press.

Brown, R.H. (1994) 'Reconstructing social theory after the postmodern critique', in H. Simons and M. Billig (eds), *After Postmodernism*. London: Sage.

Brubaker, R. (1996) *Nationalism Reframed: Nationhood and the National Question in the New Europe*. Cambridge: Cambridge University Press.

Brubaker, R. (1998) 'Myths and misconceptions in the study of nationalism', in J. A. Hall (ed.), *The State of the Nation: Ernest Gellner and the Theory of Nationalism*. Cambridge: Cambridge University Press.

Brubaker, R. and Cooper, F. (2000) 'Beyond "Identity"', *Theory and Society*, 29 (1): 1–37.

Burawoy, M. (1981) 'The Capitalist State in South Africa: Marxist and sociological perspectives on race and class', *Political Power and Social Theory*, 2: 279–335.

Burke, E. (1968[1790]) *Reflections on the Revolution in France*. Harmondsworth: Penguin.

Carter, B. (1997) 'Rejecting truthful identities: Foucault, "Race" and politics', in M. Loyd and A. Thacker (eds), *The Impact of Michel Foucault on the Social Sciences and Humanities*. London: Macmillan.

Cavalli-Sforza, L. L., Menozzi, P. and Piazza, A. (1996) *The History and Geography of Human Genes*. Princeton, NJ: Princeton University Press.

Chivers, T.S. (1985) 'Introduction', *Ethnic and Racial Studies*, 8 (4): 465–70.

Claeys, G. (2000) 'The "survival of the fittest" and the origins of Social Darwinism', *Journal of the History of Ideas*, 61 (2): 223–40.

Cohen, A. (1969) *Custom and Politics in Urban Africa*. Berkeley: University of California Press.

Cohen, A. (1974a) *Two-Dimensional Man: An Essay on the Anthropology of Power and Symbolism in Complex Society*. London: Routledge and Kegan Paul.

Cohen, A. (1974b) 'Introduction: the lesson of ethnicity', in A. Cohen (ed.), *Urban Ethnicity*. London: Tavistock.

Cohen, A. (1977) 'Symbolic action and the structure of the self', in I. M. Lewis (ed.), *Symbols and Sentiments*. London: Academic Press.

Cohen, A. (1979) 'Political symbolism', *Annual Review of Anthropology*, 8: 87–113.

Cohen, A. (1981) *The Politics of Elite Culture*. Berkeley: University of California Press.

Cole, J. W. and Wolf, E. R. (1974) *The Hidden Frontier: Ecology and Ethnicity in an Alpine Valley*. New York: Academic Press.

Coleman, J. (1990) *Foundations of Social Theory*. Cambridge, MA: Belknap Press.

Coleman, J. and Fararo, T. (eds) (1992) *Rational Choice Theory: Advocacy and Critique*. London: Sage.

Collins, R. (1981) 'On the microfoundations of macrosociology', *American Journal of Sociology*, 86 (2): 984–1014.

Collins, R. (1986) *Weberian Sociological Theory*. Cambridge: Cambridge University Press.

Collins, R. (1999) *Macrohistory: Essays in Sociology of the Long Run*. Stanford, CA: Stanford University Press.

Connor, W. (1978) 'A nation is a nation, is a state, is an ethnic group is a … ', *Ethnic and Racial Studies*, 1 (4): 377–400.

Connor, W. (1994) *Ethnonationalism: The Quest for Understanding*. Princeton, NJ: Princeton University Press.

Cooley, C. H. (1964[1902]) *Human Nature and the Social Order*. New York: Schocken.

Cox, O. (1945) 'Race and caste: a distinction', *American Journal of Sociology*, 50 (5): 360–8.

Cox, O. (1948) *Caste, Class and Race*. New York: Monthly Review.

Craib, I. (1992) *Anthony Giddens*. London: Routledge.

Dawkins, R. (1986) *The Blind Watchmaker*. New York: Norton.

Dawkins, R. (1989) *The Selfish Gene*. Oxford: Oxford University Press.

Derrida, J. (1976) *Of Grammatology*. Baltimore: Johns Hopkins University Press.

Despres, L. A. (1968) 'Anthropological theory, cultural pluralism, and the study of complex societies', *Current Anthropology*, 9 (1): 3–26.

Dex, S. (1985) 'The use of economists' models in sociology', *Ethnic and Racial Studies*, 8 (4): 516–33.

Duijzings, G. (1992) 'The Egyptians in Kosovo and Macedonia', *Amsterdams Sociologisch Tijdschrift*, 18 (4): 24–38.

Durkheim, E. (1986) *Durkheim on Politics and the State*, edited by A. Giddens. Cambridge: Polity Press.

Durkheim, E. (1995) *The Elementary Forms of Religious Life*. New York: Free Press.

Durkheim, E. (1996) *Suicide: A Study in Sociology*. London: Routledge.

Durkheim, E. (1997) *The Division of Labor in Society*. New York: The Free Press.

Eibl Eibesfeldt, I. and Salter, F. K. (eds) (2001) *Ethnic Conflict and Indoctrination*. Oxford: Berghan.

Eisenstadt, S. N. (2002) 'The construction of collective identities and the continual reconstruction of primordiality', in S. Malešević and M. Haugaard (eds), *Making Sense of Collectivity: Ethnicity, Nationalism and Globalisation*. London: Pluto.

Eller, J. and R. Coughlan (1993) 'The poverty of primordialism: the demystification of ethnic attachments', *Ethnic and Racial Studies*, 16 (2): 183–202.

Elster, J. (1985) *Making Sense of Marx*. Cambridge: Cambridge University Press.

Elster, J. (ed.) (1986) *Rational Choice*. Oxford: Basil Blackwell.

Elster, J. (1990) *Nuts and Bolts for the Social Sciences*. Cambridge: Cambridge University Press.

Eriksen, T. H. (1993) *Ethnicity and Nationalism: Anthropological Perspectives*. London: Pluto.

Fanon, F. (1967) *Black Skin, White Masks*. New York: Grove Press.

Femia, J. V. (1998) *The Machiavellian Legacy: Essays in Italian Political Thought*. New York: St. Martin's Press.

Fenton, S. (1980) 'Race, class and politics in the works of Emile Durkheim', in *Sociological Theories: Race and Colonialism*. Paris: Unesco.

Fenton, S. (1999) *Ethnicity: Racism, Class and Culture*. London: Macmillan.

Feyerabend, P. (1975) *Against Method*. London: New Left Books.

Field, G. L. and Higley, J. (1980) *Elitism*. Boston, MA: Routledge and Kegan Paul.

Filmer, P. (1998) 'Theory/Practice', in C. Jenks (ed.), *Core Sociological Dichotomies*. London: Sage.

Finlayson, A. (1998) 'Psychology, psychoanalysis and theories of nationalism', *Nations and Nationalism*, 4 (2): 145–62.

Foucault, M. (1980) 'Truth and power', in C. Gordon (ed.), *Michael Foucault, Power/Knowledge*. Brighton: Harvester Press.

Frisby, D. (1984) *Georg Simmel*. London: Tavistock.

Furnivall, J.S. (1948) *Colonial Policy and Practice*. Cambridge: Cambridge University Press.

Gabriel, J. and Ben-Tovim, G. (1979) 'The conceptualization of race relations in sociological theory', *Ethnic and Racial Studies*, 2 (2): 190–212.

Geertz, C. (1973) *The Interpretation of Cultures*. London: Fontana.

Gellner, E. (1983) *Nations and Nationalism*. Oxford: Basil Blackwell.

Gellner, E. (1992) *Postmodernism, Reason and Religion*. London: Routledge.

Giddens, A. (1977) *Studies in Social and Political Theory*. New York: Basic Books.

Giddens, A. (1984) *The Constitution of Society: An Outline of the Theory of Structuration*. Cambridge: Polity Press.

Giddens, A. (1985) *The Nation-State and Violence*. Cambridge: Polity Press.

Gilroy, P. (1982) 'Steppin' out of Babylon – race, class and autonomy', in Centre for Contemporary Cultural Studies, *The Empire Strikes Back: Race and Racism in 70s Britain*. London: Hutchinson.

Gilroy, P. (1987) *There ain't no Black in the Union Jack*. London: Hutchinson.

Gilroy, P. (1990) 'The end of anti-racism', *New Community*, 17 (1): 71–83.

Gilroy, P. (1992) 'Cultural studies and ethnic absolutism', in L. Grossberg, C. Nelson and P. Treichler (eds), *Cultural Studies*. London: Routledge.

Gilroy, P. (2000a) 'The dialectics of diaspora identification', in L. Back and J. Solomos (eds), *Theories of Race and Racism: A Reader*. London: Routledge.

Gilroy, P. (2000b) *Against Race: Imagining Political Culture Beyond the Color Line*. Cambridge, MA: Harvard University Press.

Glazer, N. and Moynihan, D. (eds) (1975) *Ethnicity: Theory and Experience*. Cambridge, MA: Harvard University Press.

Goffman, E. (1961) *Asylums: Essays on the Social Situation of Mental Patients and Other Inmates*. New York: Doubleday Anchor.

Goffman, E. (1963) *Stigma: Notes on the Management of Spoiled Identity*. Englewood Cliffs, NJ: Prentice Hall.

Goldberg, D. (1993) *Racist Culture: Philosophy and the Politics of Meaning*. Oxford: Blackwell.

Gouldner, A. (1970) *The Coming Crisis of Western Sociology*. New York: Basic Books.

Gourevitch, P. (2000) *We Wish to Inform You that Tomorrow We Will be Killed with Our Families: Stories from Rwanda*. London: Picador.

Gramsci, A. (1971) *Selections from the Prison Notebooks*. London: Lawrence and Wishart.

Gramsci, A. (1978) *Selections from the Political Writings (1921–1926)*. London: Lawrence and Wishart.

Guibernau, M. (1996) *Nationalisms: The Nation-State and Nationalism in the Twentieth Century*. Cambridge: Polity Press.

Guillaumin, C. (1995) *Racism, Sexism, Power and Ideology*. London: Routledge.

Gurr, T. R. (1986) 'The political origins of state violence and terror: a theoretical analysis', in M. Stohl and G. A. Lopez (eds), *Government Violence and Repression: An Agenda for Research*. New York: Greenwood Press.

Gurr, T. R. (1993) *Minorities and Risk: A Global View of Ethnopolitical Conflicts*. Washington, DC: US Institute of Peace Press.

Gurr, T. R. (2000a) *Peoples versus States: Minorities at Risk in the New Century*. Washington, DC: US Institute of Peace Press.

Gurr, T. R. (2000b) 'Ethnic warfare on the wane', *Foreign Affairs*, 79 (3) May/June: 52–64.

Gurr, T. and B. Harff (1994) *Ethnic Conflict in World Politics*. Boulder, CO: Westview Press.

Habermas, J. (1987) *The Philosophical Discourse of Modernity*. Cambridge: Polity Press.

Hall, J. A. (1985) *Powers and Liberties*. London: Blackwell.

Hall, J. A. (1993) 'Nationalisms: classified and explained', *Daedalus*, 122 (3): 1–28.

Hall, J. A. and Ikenberry, G. (1989) *The State*. London: Open University Press.

Hall, S. (1980) 'Race, articulation and societies structured in dominance', in *Sociological Theories: Race and Colonialism*. Paris: Unesco.

Hall, S. (1986) 'Gramsci's relevance for the study of race and ethnicity', *Journal of Communication Inquiry*, 10 (2): 5–27.

Hall, S. (1991) 'Old and new ethnicities', in A. D. King (ed.), *Culture, Globalization and the World System*. London: Macmillan.

Hall, S. (1992) 'The question of cultural identity', in S. Hall, D. Held and T. McGrew (eds), *Modernity and Its Features*. London: Open University Press.

Hall, S. (1996a) 'On postmodernism and articulation: an interview with Stuart Hall', in D. Morley, and C. Kuan-Hsing (eds), *Stuart Hall: Critical Dialogues*. London: Routledge.

Hall, S. (1996b) 'Who needs identity?', in S. Hall and P. du Gay (eds), *Questions of Cultural Identity*. London: Sage.

Hamilton, W. D. (1964) 'The genetical evolution of social behaviour II', in G. C. Williams (ed.), *Group Selection*. Chicago: Aldine Atherton.

Hechter, M. (1974) 'The political economy of ethnic change', *American Journal of Sociology*, 79 (5): 1151–78.

Hechter, M. (1975) *Internal Colonialism: The Celtic Fringe in British National Development, 1536–1966*. Berkeley: University of California Press.

Hechter, M. (1976a) 'Ethnicity and industrialization: on the proliferation of the cultural division of labor', *Ethnicity*, 3: 214–24.

Hechter, M. (1976b) 'Response to Cohen: Max Weber on ethnicity and ethnic change', *American Journal of Sociology*, 81: 1162–8.

Hechter, M. (1978) 'Group formation and the cultural division of labor', *American Journal of Sociology*, 84: 293–318.

Hechter, M. (1986) 'Rational Choice Theory and the study of race and ethnic relations', in J. Rex and D. Mason (eds), *Theories of Race and Ethnic Relations*. Cambridge: Cambridge University Press.

Hechter, M. (1995) 'Explaining nationalist violence', *Nations and Nationalism*, 1 (1): 53–68.

Hechter, M. (1997) 'Religion and Rational Choice Theory', in L. Young (ed.), *Rational Choice Theory and Religion*. London: Routledge.

Hechter, M. (2000) *Containing Nationalism*. Oxford: Oxford University Press.

Hechter, M. and Levi, M. (1985) 'The rise and decline of ethnoregionalist political parties: Scotland, Wales, and Brittany', in H. Vermeulen and J. Boissevain (eds), *Ethnic Challenge: The Politics of Ethnicity in Europe*. Gottingen: Edition Herodot.

Higley, J. and Burton, M.G. (1987) 'Elite settlements', *American Sociological Review*, 52: 295–307.

Higley, J. and Burton, M. G. (1989) 'The elite variable in democratic transitions and breakdowns', *American Sociological Review*, 54: 17–32.

Hindess, B. (1988) *Choice, Rationality and Social Theory*. London: Unwin Hyman.

Hobsbawm, E. (1990) *Nations and Nationalism since 1780*. Cambridge: Cambridge University Press.

Hodson, R., Sekulić, D. and Massey, G. (1994) 'National tolerance in the former Yugoslavia', *American Journal of Sociology*, 99 (6): 1534–58.

hooks, b. (2000) 'Racism and feminism', in L. Back and J. Solomos (eds), *Theories of Race and Racism: A Reader*. London: Routledge.

International Encyclopaedia of the Social Sciences (1972) Edited by D. L. Shills. London: Macmillan.

Isajiw, W. W. (2000) 'Approaches to ethnic conflict resolution: paradigms and principles', *International Journal of Intercultural Relations*, 24 (1): 105–24.

Jackson, M. (1982/83) 'An analysis of Max Weber's theory of ethnicity', *Humboldt Journal of Social Relations*, 1 (10): 4–18.

Jenkins, R. (1986) 'Social anthropological models of inter-ethnic relations', in J. Rex and D. Mason (eds), *Theories of Race and Ethnic Relations*. Cambridge: Cambridge University Press.

Jenkins, R. (1994) 'Rethinking ethnicity: identity, categorization and power', *Ethnic and Racial Studies*, 17 (2): 197–221.

Jenkins, R. (1996) *Social Identity*. London: Routledge.

Jenkins, R. (1997) *Rethinking Ethnicity*. London: Sage.

Jenkins, R. (2002a) *Foundations of Sociology: Towards a Better Understanding of the Human World*. London: Palgrave.

Jenkins, R. (2002b) 'Different societies? Different cultures? What are human collectivities?', in S. Malešević and M. Haugaard (eds), *Making Sense of Collectivity: Ethnicity, Nationalism and Globalisation*. London: Pluto.

Joas, H. (1999) 'The modernity of war', *International Sociology*, 14 (4): 457–72.

Katunarić, V. (1991) 'Uoči novih etno-političkih raskola – Hrvatska i Bosna i Hercegovina', *Sociologija*, 33 (3): 373–85.

Keane, F. (1996) *Season of Blood: A Rwandan Journey*. Harmondsworth: Penguin.

Kedourie, E. (1960) *Nationalism*. London: Hutchinson.

Kellas, J. G. (1991) *The Politics of Nationalism and Ethnicity*. London: Macmillan.

Kellner, D. (1995) *Media Culture*. London: Routledge.

Kristeva, J. (1984) *Revolution in Poetic Language*. London: Methuen.

Kuper, L. (1971) 'Plural societies, perspectives and problems', in L. Kuper and M.G. Smith (eds), *Pluralism in Africa*. Berkeley: University of California Press.

Kuper, L. (1974) *Race, Class, and Power: Ideology and Revolutionary Change in Plural Societies*. Chicago: Aldine.

Kuper, L. (1980) 'The theory of plural society, race and conquest', in *Sociological Theories: Race and Colonialism*. Paris: Unesco.

Laclau, E. and Mouffe, C. (1985) *Hegemony and Socialist Strategy*. London: Verso.

Lal, B. B. (1986) 'The "Chicago School" of American sociology, symbolic interactionism, and race relations theory', in J. Rex and D. Mason (eds), *Theories of Race and Ethnic Relations*. Cambridge: Cambridge University Press.

Lal, B. B. (1993) 'The celebration of ethnicity as a critique of American life: opposition to Robert E. Park's view of cultural pluralism and democracy', in R. Gubert and L. Thomasi (eds), *Robert E. Park and the 'Melting Pot' Theory*. Trento: Reverdito Edizioni.

Lal, B. B. (1995) 'Symbolic interaction theories', *American Behavioral Scientist*, 38 (3): 421–41.

Lecourt, D. (1980) 'On Marxism as a critique of sociological theories', in *Sociological Theories: Race and Colonialism*. Paris: Unesco.

Lendvai, P. (1971) *Anti-Semitism without Jews*. Garden City, NY: Doubleday.

Levi-Strauss, C. (1989) *The Savage Mind*. London: Weidenfeld & Nicolson.

Lukes, S. (1973) *Individualism*. Oxford: Basil Blackwell.

Lukes, S. (1992) *Èmile Durkheim*. London: Penguin.

Lumsden, C. J. and Wilson, E. O. (1981) *Genes, Mind and Culture: The Coevolutionary Process*. Cambridge, MA: Harvard University Press.

Lyman, S. M. and Douglass, W. A. (1973) 'Ethnicity: strategies of collective and individual impression management', *Social Research*, 40 (2): 344–65.

Lyotard, F. (1984) *The Postmodern Condition: A Report on Knowledge*. Manchester: Manchester University Press.

MacDonald, K. (2000) 'An integrative evolutionary perspective on ethnicity', paper presented at the Meetings of the Association of Politics and the Life Sciences, Washington, DC, 3 September.

Machiavelli, N. (1997) *The Prince*. Ware, Hertfordshire: Wordsworth.

McKay, J. (1982) 'An explanatory synthesis of primordial and mobilizationist approaches to ethnic phenomena', *Ethnic and Racial Studies*, 5 (4): 395–420.

Malešević, S. (1998) 'Ethnic relations in contemporary sociological theory: one taxonomy', *Europa Ethnica*, 55 (3–4): 105–21.

Malešević, S. (2000) 'Ethnicity and federalism in communist Yugoslavia and its successor States', in Y. Ghai (ed.), *Autonomy and Ethnicity: Negotiating Competing Claims in Multiethnic States*. Cambridge: Cambridge University Press.

Malešević, S. (2002a) *Ideology, Legitimacy and the New State: Yugoslavia, Serbia and Croatia*. London: Frank Cass.

Malešević, S. (2002b) 'Rehabilitating ideology after poststructuralism', in S. Malešević and I. MacKenzie (eds), *Ideology after Poststructuralism*. London: Pluto Press.

Malešević, S. (2002c) 'Identity: conceptual, operational and historical critique', in S. Malešević and M. Haugaard (eds), *Making Sense of Collectivity: Ethnicity, Nationalism and Globalisation*. London: Pluto Press.

Malešević, S. (2002d) 'From organic legislators to organicistic interpreters: intellectuals in Yugoslavia and post-Yugoslav states', *Government and Opposition*, 37 (1): 55–75.

Mamdani, M. (2001) *When Victims Become Killers: Colonialism, Nativism and the Genocide in Rwanda*. Princeton, NJ: Princeton University Press.

Mann, M. (1988) *States, War, and Capitalism: Studies in Political Sociology*. Oxford: Blackwell.

Mann, M. (1995) 'A political theory of nationalism and its excesses', in S. Periwal (ed.), *Notions of Nationalism*. Budapest: CEU Press.

Mann, M. (1999) 'The dark side of democracy: the modern tradition of ethnic and political cleansing', *New Left Review*, 235, May–June: 18–45.

Mann, M. (2001) 'Explaining murderous ethnic cleansing: the macro-level', in M. Guibernau and J. Hutchinson (eds), *Understanding Nationalism*. Cambridge: Polity Press.

Marx, K. (1985) *Early Writings*. London: Penguin.

Marx, K. and Engels, F. (1977) *Collected Works*. London: Lawrence and Wishart.

Marx, K. and Engels, F. (1982a) *The German Ideology*. London: Lawrence and Wishart.

Marx, K. and Engels, F. (1982b) *Selected Correspondence*. Moscow: Progress.

Mead, G. H. (1962[1934]) *Mind, Self and Society from the Standpoint of a Social Behaviorist*. Chicago: Chicago University Press.

Melvern, L. (2000) *A People Betrayed: The Role of the West in Rwanda's Genocide*. London: Zed Books.

Michels, R. (1962) *Political Parties*. New York: Free Press.

Midgley, M. (1980) 'Gene-juggling', in A. Montagu (ed.), *Sociobiology Examined*. Oxford: Oxford University Press.

Miles, R. (1982) *Racism and Migrant Labour*. London: Routledge.

Miles, R. (1984) 'Marxism versus the sociology of "race relations"', *Ethnic and Racial Studies*, 7 (2): 217–37.

Miles, R. (1988) 'Racism, Marxism and British politics', *Economy and Society*, 17 (2): 428–60.

Miles, R. (1989) *Racism*. London: Routledge.

Mosca, G. (1939) *The Ruling Class*. New York: McGraw Hill.

Nair, T. (1977) *The Break-up of Britain*. London: New Left Books.

Nash, K. (2000) *Contemporary Political Sociology*. Oxford: Blackwell.

Nimni, E. (1991) *Marxism and Nationalism: Theoretical Origins of a Political Crisis*. London: Pluto Press.

Olzak, S. (1983) 'Contemporary ethnic mobilization', *Annual Review of Sociology*, 9: 355–74.

Olzak, S. and Nigel, J. (eds) (1986) *Competitive Ethnic Relations*. Orlando, FL: Academic Press.

Omi, M. and Winant, H. (1994) *Racial Formation in the United States: From the 1960s to the 1990s*. London: Routledge.

Pareto, V. (1963) *The Mind and Society: A Treatise on General Sociology*. New York: Dover Publications.

Pareto, V. (1966) *Sociological Writings*. Oxford: Basil Blackwell.

Park, R. E. (1950) *Race and Culture: Essays in the Sociology of Contemporary Man*. Glencoe, IL: The Free Press.

Park, R. E. and Burgess, E. W. (1969[1921]) *An Introduction to the Science of Sociology*. Chicago: Chicago University Press.

Parkin, F. (1979) *Marxism and Class Theory: A Bourgeois Critique*. London: Tavistock.

Parsons, T. (1951) *Social System*. New York: The Free Press.

Parsons, T. (1966) *Societies: Evolutionary and Comparative Perspectives*. Englewood Cliffs, NJ: Prentice Hall.

Parsons, T. (1971) *The System of Modern Societies*. Englewood Cliffs, NJ: Prentice Hall.

Parsons, T. (1975) 'Some theoretical considerations on the nature and trends of change of ethnicity', in N. Glazer and D. P. Moynihan (eds), *Ethnicity: Theory and Experience*. Cambridge, MA: Harvard University Press.

Pešić, V. (1995) 'Društveni i državni aspekt multikulturalnosti u Bosni i Hercegovni', in B. Jakšić (ed.), *Interkulturalnost*. Belgrade: IFDT.

Philpott, T. L. (1978) *The Slum and the Ghetto: Neighborhood Deterioration and Middle-Class Reform: Chicago, 1880–1930*. New York: Oxford University Press.

Phizacklea, A. (1999) 'Gender and transnational labour migration', in R. Barot, H. Bradley and S. Fenton (eds), *Ethnicity, Gender and Social Change*. London: Macmillan.

Poggi, G. (2000) *Durkheim*. Oxford: Oxford University Press.

Rattansi, A. (1999) 'Racism, "postmodernism", and reflexive multiculturalism', in S. May (ed.), *Critical Multiculturalism: Rethinking Multicultural and Antiracist Education*. London: The Falmer Press.

Rex, J. (1980) 'The theory of race relations: a Weberian approach', in *Sociological Theories: Race and Colonialism*. Paris: Unesco.

Rex, J. (1986a) *Race and Ethnicity*. London: Open University Press.

Rex, J. (1986b) 'The role of class analysis in the study of race relations: a Weberian perspective', in J. Rex and D. Mason (eds), *Theories of Race and Ethnic Relations*. Cambridge: Cambridge University Press.

Rex, J. (1996) *Ethnic Minorities and the Modern Nation State*. London: Macmillan.

Rex, J. (2002) 'The fundamentals of the theory of ethnicity', in S. Malešević and M. Haugaard (eds), *Making Sense of Collectivity: Ethnicity, Nationalism and Globalisation*. London: Pluto.

Rose, N. (1999) *Governing the Soul*. London: Free Association Books.

Rushton, J. P. (1999) 'Genetic similarity theory and the nature of ethnocentrism', in K. Thienpont and R. Cliquet (eds), *In-Group/Out-Group Behaviour in Modern Societies: An Evolutionary Perspective*. Brussels: NIDI CBGS Publications.

Schermerhorn, R. A. (1970) *Comparative Ethnic Relations: A Framework for Theory*. New York: Random House.

Schumpeter, J. A. (1942) *Capitalism, Socialism and Democracy*. New York: Harper & Row.

Sherman, P. (1977) 'Nepotism and the evolution of alarm calls', *Science*, 197: 1246–53.

Shils, E. (1957) 'Primordial, personal, sacred and civil ties', *British Journal of Sociology*, 8 (2): 130–45.

Simmel, G. (1950) *The Sociology of Georg Simmel*. New York: The Free Press.

Simmel, G. (1955) *Conflict and the Web of Group Affiliations*. New York: The Free Press.

Simmel, G. (1971) *On Individuality and Social Forms*. Chicago: Chicago University Press.

Simmel, G. (1978) *The Philosophy of Money*. London: Routledge.

Simmel, G. (1996) 'The Stranger' and 'The Web of Group Affiliations', in W. Sollors (ed.), *Theories of Ethnicity: A Classical Reader*. London: Macmillan.

Simpson, J. C. (1995) 'Pluralism: the evolution of a nebulous concept', *American Behavioral Scientist*, 38 (3): 459–77.

Smelser, N. (1992) 'The rational choice perspective: a theoretical assessment', *Rationality and Society*, 4 (3): 381–410.

Smith, A. (1981) *The Ethnic Revival in the Modern World*. Cambridge: Cambridge University Press.

Smith, A. (1983) *Theories of Nationalism*. London: Duckworth.

Smith, A. (1991) *National Identity*. Harmondsworth: Penguin.

Smith, A. (1998) *Nationalism and Modernism*. London: Routledge.

Smith, M. G. (1965) *The Plural Society in the British West Indies*. Berkeley: University of California Press.

Smith, M. G. (1971) 'Some developments in the analytic framework of pluralism', in L. Kuper and M. G. Smith (eds), *Pluralism in Africa*. Berkeley: University of California Press.

Smith, M. G. (1986) 'Pluralism, race and ethnicity in selected African countries', in J. Rex and D. Mason (eds), *Theories of Race and Ethnic Relations*. Cambridge: Cambridge University Press.

Solomos, J. (1986) 'Varieties of Marxist conceptions of "race", class and the state: a critical analysis', in J. Rex and D. Mason (eds), *Theories of Race and Ethnic Relations*. Cambridge: Cambridge University Press.

Solomos, J. (1995) 'Marxism, racism and ethnicity', *American Behavioral Scientist*, 38 (3): 407–20.

Sparks, A. (1995) *South Africa: An Interim Report*. Ottawa: CSIS.

Steen, R. G. (1996) *DNA and Destiny: Nature and Nurture in Human Behavior*. New York: Plenum Press.

Stone, J. (ed.) (1977) *Race, Ethnicity and Social Change*. Belmont, CA: Wadsworth.

Stone, J. (1995) 'Race, ethnicity, and the Weberian legacy', *American Behavioral Scientist*, 38 (3): 391–406.

Tajfel, H. (1978) 'Social categorization, social identity and social comparison', in H. Tajfel (ed.), *Differentiation between Social Groups: Studies in the Social Psychology of Intergroup Relations*. London: Academic Press.

Taylor, C. (1984) 'Foucault on freedom and truth', *Political Theory*, 12 (2): 152–83.

Taylor, C. C. (1999) *Sacrifice as Terror: The Rwandan Genocide of 1994*. Oxford: Berg.

Thomas, W. I. (1969[1923]) *The Unadjusted Girl: With Cases and Standpoint for Behavior Analysis*. Criminal Science Monograph No. 4. Boston: Little, Brown and Company.

Uzelac, G. (1999) 'Perceptions of the nation: the example of Croatian students', *Canadian Review of Studies in Nationalism*, 26 (1): 123–33.

Uzelac, G. (2002) 'When is the nation?: constituent elements and processes', *Geopolitics*, 7 (2): 33–52.

van den Berghe, P. L. (1971) 'Social and cultural pluralism', in C. F. Andrain (ed.), *Political Life and Social Change*. Belmont, CA: Wadsworth.

van den Berghe, P. L. (1978) 'Race and ethnicity: a sociobiological perspective', *Ethnic and Racial Studies*, 1 (4): 401–11.

van den Berghe, P. L. (1981) *The Ethnic Phenomenon*. New York: Elsevier.

van den Berghe, P. L. (1983) 'Class, race and ethnicity in Africa', *Ethnic and Racial Studies*, 6 (4): 221–36.

van den Berghe, P. L. (1986) 'Ethnicity and the sociobiology debate' in J. Rex and D. Mason (eds), *Theories of Race and Ethnic Relations*. Cambridge: Cambridge University Press.

van den Berghe, P. L. (1990) 'Why most sociologists don't (and won't) think evolutionarily?', *Sociological Forum*, 5 (2): 173–85.

van den Berghe, P. L. (1995) 'Does race matter?', *Nations and Nationalism*, 1 (3): 357–68.

van den Berghe, P. L. (1999) 'Racism, ethnocentrism and xenophobia: in our genes or in our memes?', in K. Thienpont and R. Cliquet (eds), *In-Group/Out-Group Behaviour in Modern Societies: An Evolutionary Perspective*. Brussels: NIDI CBGS Publications.

van der Dennen, J. (1991) 'Studies of conflict', in M. Maxwell (ed.), *The Sociobiological Imagination*. Albany, NY: The State University of New York Press.

van der Dennen, J. (1999) 'Of badges, bonds and boundaries: in-group/out-group differentiation and ethnocentrism revisited', in K. Thienpont and R. Cliquet (eds), *In-Group/Out-Group Behaviour in Modern Societies: An Evolutionary Perspective*. Brussels: NIDI CBGS Publications.

van Dijk, T. A. (1991) *Racism and the Press*. London: Routledge.

van Dijk, T. A. (1993) *Elite Discourse and Racism*. London: Sage.

Vanhanen, T. (1999) *Ethnic Conflict Explained by Ethnic Nepotism*. Stamford, CT: JAI Press.

Walsh, D. F. (1998a) 'Idealism/materialism', in C. Jenks (ed.), *Core Sociological Dichotomies*. London: Sage.

Walsh, D. F. (1998b) 'Subject/object', in C. Jenks (ed.), *Core Sociological Dichotomies*. London: Sage.

Weber, M. (1948) *From Max Weber: Essays in Sociology*. Edited by H. Gerth and C. W. Mills. London: Routledge and Kegan Paul.

Weber, M. (1958) *The Protestant Ethnic and the Spirit of Capitalism*. New York: Scribners.

Weber, M. (1961) *General Economic History*. New York: Collier Books.

Weber, M. (1967) *Ancient Judaism*. New York: The Free Press.

Weber, M. (1968) *Economy and Society*. Berkeley: University of California Press.

Weber, M. (1992) *Religion of India*. Ottawa: Laurier Books.

Wilson, E. O. (1975) *Sociobiology: The New Synthesis*. Cambridge, MA: Harvard University Press.

Wilson, E. O. (1998) *Consilience: The Unity of Knowledge*. Boston: Little, Brown and Company.

Winthrop, R. H. (1991) *Dictionary of Concepts in Cultural Anthropology*. New York: Greenwich Press.

Wirth, L. (1945) 'Human ecology', *American Journal of Sociology*, 50 (6): 483–8.

Yuval-Davis, N. (1993) 'Gender and nation', *Ethnic and Racial Studies*, 16 (4): 621–32.

Yuval-Davis, N. (1997) *Gender and Nation*. London: Sage.

Yuval-Davis, N. and Anthias, F. (1989) *Women, Nation, State*. London: Macmillan.

Žižek, S. (1989) *The Sublime Object of Ideology*. London: Verso.

Žižek, S. (1993) *Tarrying with the Negative*. Durham, NC: Duke University Press.

Zubaida, S. (1978) 'Theories of nationalism', in G. Littlejohn, B. Smart, J. Wakeford and N. Yuval-Davis (eds), *Power and the State*. London: Croom Helm.

Županov, J. (1977) *Sociologija i samoupravljanje*. Zagreb: Školska knjiga.

Županov, J. (1985) *Samoupravljanje i društvena moć*. Zagreb: Globus.

NAME INDEX

SUBJECT INDEX